The Ambrosial Hour

The Ambrosial Hour

talks by

Baba Sawan Singh Ji
Sant Kirpal Singh Ji
Sant Ajaib Singh Ji

and others

Sant Bani Ashram
Sanbornton, New Hampshire

Photo Credits

Many thanks to the following photographers, whose work appears as follows: front & back cover paintings, Jonas Gerard; p. xii, Pat Brown; p. 2, Charlie Boynton; p. 32, Jonas Gerard; p. 38, courtesy of Jonas Gerard; p. 46, Charlie Boynton; p. 54, Pat Brown; p. 96, courtesy of Jonas Gerard; p. 107, Gurmel Singh; pp. 110, 122, 144, Charlie Boynton; p. 148, Jonas Gerard; p. 152, Sant Bani archives; p. 166, Jonas Gerard; p. 170, Charlie Boynton; p. 180, Pat Brown; p. 194, Neil Wolf; p. 204, Charlie Boynton; p. 212, Terry Barnum; pp. 216, 220, Charlie Boynton; p. 228, Pat Brown; p. 236, Dick Shannon; p. 239, Pat Brown; p. 242, Bobbe Baker; pp. 256, 288, Neil Wolf; p. 296, Pat Brown; p. 304, John Pianowski; p. 361, Pat Brown; pp. 364, 370, Charlie Boynton; p. 374, Neil Wolf; p. 380, Jonas Gerard; pp. 384, 390, Charlie Boynton; p. 394, Sant Bani archives; p. 400, Jonas Gerard; p. 410, Bobbe Baker; p. 414, Neil Wolf; p. 426, Charlie Boynton; pp. 442, 448, Bobbe Baker.

International Standard Book Number: 0-89142-048-7
Library of Congress Catalog Card Number: 96-85751
Printed at The Sant Bani Press, Tilton, NH
First printing, 1996, 2000 copies

Acknowledgments

The inspiration and behind-the-scenes direction and grace came from Sant Ajaib Singh Ji, and many people contributed to the task of getting this book published. Daryl Rubin, over a period of years, selected and compiled the talks in manuscript form; his comments can be found in the Introduction. Pappu (Raaj Kumar Bagga), did a wonderful job of translating during Sant Ji's talks; other people transcribed the Masters' talks, either from notes taken at the time an early talk was given, or in recent years, transcribing from tape recordings. The people who lugged around tape recorders to record these talks deserve our thanks for providing the raw material. Early talks in this book depend on work done by Russell Perkins. *Sat Sandesh* was published for six years by Sant Bani Ashram and edited by Russell, later *Sant Bani Magazine* was created to present talks by the Masters. From 1976 until late 1987 Russell continued the work of editing *Sant Bani*, assisted by his wife Judith (who also co-ordinates group travel to many of the retreats). Sant Ji refers to each of them in some of these talks. Later talks were typed, organized and edited by the present magazine staff.

For this volume, older talks were scanned by optical character reading (OCR), a computer process which eliminates the need for hours of typing; it occasionally introduces new spelling errors. All talks were re-edited in the hope of making style and usage consistent throughout. If any errors escaped our notice we apologize.

During the last few frantic weeks the project was given a tremendous boost from the following people: John Campbell, Mary Fewel Tulin, Daryl Rubin, Bethany Stephenson, Susan Shannon, and Cab Vinton.

Finally, many people worked long hours at the printing company; without Carol Corson, Joe Gelbard, Chris Gilb, Joe Sereni, and Leah Storey we would never have finished this project.

To everyone who helped with this book, we thank you.

Richard Shannon

Table of Contents

PART III

Meditation on the Naam of the Lord

PART IV

Meditation: Questions & Answers

PART V

The Glory of the Company of Saints

Foreword

Maulana Rumi, the great Sufi Master, has said that twenty minutes in the company of a Saint has more spiritual value than a hundred years of meditation. The very essential writings gathered in this book give us the instruction we need to make the best use of that twenty minutes, but underlying both Maulana Rumi's statement and these writings is the unfathomable love of the Master, which is the expression of the forgiveness and grace of God.

Sant Ajaib Singh has said that the Master comes down in order to love; and that love makes everything possible. Sant Kirpal Singh used to say that it is He Who first loved us; our love is only reciprocal. His love, the love of God, calls to the love which is the essence of our soul and awakens it; and when that love is awakened, what can we not do? His love is the key to the mysteries of the universe, and it is incarnated in the person of the Living Master. Swami Ji has said that the Satguru is an incarnation eternally existent upon the earth. That is the promise and the reality.

Russell Perkins

Introduction

This book is a collection of talks given by very great Saints of our time. They speak of the Love of The Almighty Lord, of the Saints whom He sends into this world to distribute that Love, and how They work to awaken that Love in the hearts of those who come into Their company.

First of all, I wish to express my deepest thanks and gratitude to the Masters, for Their gracious granting of the opportunity to live this life in Their devotion and protection; and for the privilege of collecting and organizing Their true and sacred words.

This book presents more than eighty talks by three great Saints* Who have incarnated in a land called India, and Whose Lives have been a perfect and immaculate example of their Masters teachings. All three, Baba Sawan Singh Ji, Maharaj Kirpal Singh Ji, and the present Master, Sant Ajaib Singh Ji (Sant Ji), have graciously allowed Their Western disciples to visit Them in India and take much advantage of the aura and presence of a Living Saint. Presently, the visits happen in the form of group trips which occur regularly to a retreat place in some Indian city or village, and an intensive meditation and Satsang schedule is followed by the guests under the direct personal guidance of the Master.

Over the years, many groups have made these trips, and there have been many requests for information on how to best prepare for such a sacred pilgrimage, and how to make the best use of this rare opportunity. So with kind permission and loving guidance from Sant Ajaib Singh Ji, these talks of the Masters have been compiled. The book can also be useful reading before seeing the Master on any of His tours, during the retreats, and also for the many retreats held around the world in His remembrance

* A hymn of Soami Ji Maharaj and of Guru Arjan Dev are also included.

where He may not be physically present.

The book is entitled The Ambrosial Hour — as the many references herein will make clear, this human life is an ambrosial hour, the Holy Initiation is an ambrosial hour, and the daily meditation on Naam, which the Masters teach, is also an Ambrosial Hour. When anyone follows the words of such a Master, at any time, and in any degree, the benefit he receives is also an Ambrosial Hour in his life.

These talks have been organized, in five parts, around the sequence of events that unfold on this holy pilgrimage of Spirituality. First is a group of talks on how one may prepare at home for being in the Master's presence and on gaining some receptivity before going to see Him. Next are some of Their words on how to conduct oneself at a retreat place, the value of seclusion, and how to sit in the presence of the Master.

The third part of the book is a collection of meditation talks. Meditation is the main purpose for which these programs are held. As Sant Ji has said, "Meditation is the only means of receiving the grace of the Masters," which They want to give Their disciples in great abundance. He said that at these programs much emphasis and importance should be given to meditation, and for whoever will follow this, it will definitely prove to be very beneficial. He said too that, "If you are receptive, these days can change your life and can become the most remarkable days of your life."

In response to a question, Sant Ji once said that Master Kirpal Singh Ji also placed great importance on meditation, and that Master Kirpal, in His unique and gentle way, always believed that whenever anyone would become aware of his failings and shortcomings, and would sincerely wish to rise above them, that person would undertake doing meditation himself. In the same reply, Sant Ji also mentioned that Master Kirpal knew, and took delight in the knowledge, that the One Who would work in His place was going to be very strict about this, and would make the dear ones who came to Him work very hard at their meditation practices.

The fourth part contains the Master's replies to questions asked about meditation.

In the fifth part of the book are talks which were given at the end of these group programs, either underground room talks in Rajasthan,** or farewell talks after the city programs. Sant Ji talks a lot about the meditation He has done in His Life, and what He got by doing it. He tells us to take inspiration from that blessed place and to utilize the sacred gift of Naam to bring the real peace and happiness to our own soul. He also speaks about how to maintain, preserve, and increase the grace and benefit that one has received by making this holy trip to be in the presence of the Master, and He gives encouragement to work hard in our meditation and gain progress towards our spiritual upliftment and purification.

In the end is a brief hymn of a great Master in the line of the ten Sikh Gurus, Guru Arjan Dev Ji, on the glory of the company of a Saint. Anyone who has been blessed to be in the company of these great Saints can only bow down at the truth of His words.

The original idea for this book was to be a collection of meditation talks and a retreat information book. As the material was being gathered it became clear there was much more than was first planned, and if the book were expanded to include more talks, it would be useful in other ways also. Sant Ji was asked if He would like the book to be done in this larger and expanded version, and He approved of the idea, adding this comment, "This book will be very valuable and helpful to many dear ones. For those who are initiated and striving to practice the path, and for the dear ones who have just received or who are waiting for the Initiation, and who will be starting their life on the Path, this book will be very helpful. And there will be many people who are searching for Spiritual Truth and who will be interested to know what Sant Mat is, what this Path of the Masters teaches, and how these teachings compare to other paths, and for those dear ones, this book will also be very helpful."

Daryl Rubin, June 1996

** The "underground room" refers to the blessed place at Sant Ji's ashram in Rajasthan, where He did continuous meditation at the instruction of Sant Kirpal Singh Ji.

PART I

Preparing to be with the Master: Gaining Receptivity

By meditating on the Naam of God all the pain vanishes.
Nanak says, this is the state of Sahaj.

GURU ARJAN DEV

Very lovingly the Master explains to us about the glory of Naam. He tells us that we cannot get Naam unless we go in the Company of a perfect Master, and that unless we go and sit in the Satsang we cannot become aware of our faults. Whenever a soul is sitting in the meditation of Shabd Naam and whenever he is doing even a little bit of Simran, his attendance is marked in the Court of the Lord.

SANT JI

1

Come to Your Senses

Sant Ajaib Singh Ji

dictated by Sant Ji and first read out to the sangat in Rajasthan, on April 29, 1994

My Great Satguru Supreme Father Kirpal's created and adorned Sadh Sangat:

May Hazur Sawan and Kirpal's grace be with you always, and may Their sweet remembrance always remain fresh in your hearts. Supreme Father Kirpal used to explain that time and tide wait for no one. Time is going out of our hands uncontrolled, and we all are coming closer to that moment, or that event, which we call death. Every Master has warned us about it in His own way and in His own words, but we the jivas are such that it doesn't affect us.

According to the orders of my Great Master, in the Satsangs, darshans, and through the letters to the dear ones, I have always talked about this reality, that we do not know when we may have to leave this body whom we understand as our companion. So we should do that work, or collect that wealth, which goes with us, and which is useful to us in the other world. And that work is the meditation of Shabd Naam, remembrance of the Master, love for the Master, and to have the fear of Him becoming displeased. Even though this is very important and the most personal work of ours, still we do not pay any attention to it, and we are wasting our precious time in the deep slumber of ignorance.

These are the words of Gurbani: "Awake, awake, O Sleeping Ones, the traveler has left." At another place Guru Sahib has written: "Awake, O Traveler, why have you taken so long?" It means, O Traveler, wake up. Come to your senses, and walk towards your goal.

Dear Children, up until now no one has ever become, and no one shall ever be successful in the Path of Spirituality without doing meditation, without doing the Simran, and without sacrificing. This is our very own work, and this is the only thing which helps us in the moment of crisis. But it is a pity that we are not aware of it.

Even though Kabir Sahib was All-Owner and the first Saint to incarnate and He said, "O Kabir, I know the secret of the Real Home and I have brought the Divine Word," still, He spent many nights in search of the Lord, and made us understand that without sacrifice we cannot achieve Him. Kabir Sahib said, "The whole world is happy as they eat and sleep. Servant Kabir is unhappy, as He remains awake and weeps in the separation from God."

In His search for God, Guru Nanak made a bed of stones for eleven years. You know that Baba Jaimal Singh bore thirst and hunger, and used to tie His hair to a nail for meditation. Baba Sawan Singh used to meditate for many nights continuously, and would stand and meditate if sleep would bother Him. Supreme Father Kirpal used to stand in the icy water of the River Ravi and meditate like that.

Dear Children, do not remain in any illusion or misunderstanding. You won't get any place in the Court of the Lord if you do not meditate and if you do not have the meditation and sacrifice with you. So it is my request, my wish, that from today, from right now, start devoting time in meditation regularly. First of all, in the beginning, your mind won't like it, because it is not easy. But it is not at all impossible. It is the work of the beggar to sit at the door and beg. If we will sit at the door of the Lord and, forgetting the worldly business and attachments, will beg and cry for His help, then surely He Who is within us and is watching our every single action, will listen to our pleas and will reward our efforts.

This work cannot be done by talking, or by celebrating

bhandaras or organizing conferences or by worldly materials or arrangements. The work of cleaning the soul can be done only by sitting in seclusion with humility and faith in front of the Master, and begging Him for His grace. In making such efforts we will definitely have His grace and mercy.

So Dear Children, understand my words, appreciate my feelings, and come to your senses, and walk on the Path shown by Hazur Sawan and Kirpal from this very day. The work which we have been given by our Beloved Lords — do it. Definitely do it. If you will do this, it will help my health and also it will help me in my work.

One thing which I want to put a lot of emphasis on is that from now onwards, no dear one should ever write me about their family problems, or their personal or physical problems. If people will write me about their physical problems, I will not reply. You know that I have spent all my life in the remembrance and the search of Lord Almighty. I went to many places, I did so many things to realize God Almighty. I got kicked and knocked at many places. I went to many masters and teachers, and I visited many holy places. When I met Baba Bishan Das, his company and the time which I spent in his company — you know that he used to rebuke me, he used to slap me — and all the grace which he showered upon me was one of the things which I experienced while I was searching for Him. He was the one who laid the stepping-stone of my spiritual life, and when he gave me the Initiation into the first two words, with his grace and with his help only, sitting underground I meditated for eighteen years, and with his grace I got the experience and I became practically successful in that. After that, when I was able to meet Beloved Lord Sawan, His innocent and divine Form caught hold of my soul in such a way that I could not do anything else, and still I cannot forget the love which I received from Hazur Sawan and the Form which I saw of Him. That Form of Beloved Sawan is dwelling in my heart in such a way that I cannot forget Him.

It was all due to the grace and the blessing of the Almighty Lord Sawan that the Form of Sawan, Lord Kirpal Himself came to my home after traveling for five hundred kilometers, and when I told Him, "Beloved Lord, I do not know what I should ask You, what question should I put to You," He replied, "I have come here only after seeing the empty place."

So the Husband, the Beloved Lord for Whom I was searching ever since my childhood, I got Him; and the desire which I had since my childhood, Lord Kirpal fulfilled that desire, and He married me. He gave me a ring.

So Dear Children, if we will prepare the bed of our heart, He will definitely come and sit on that bed.

You know that this ashram, which I have bought myself, I do the farming here, and I maintain myself. Whatever is left over, I give that to the langar, and selflessly I am doing the service of the Sadh Sangat. Gurmel and Balwant also work very hard, and they also help me in the langar. Sardar Rattan Singh, Baba Bagh Singh, Paras Ram, and the *chaudri* who sits at the gate, they also own a lot of property in land, and they also do the selfless seva of the dear ones. As I have always said, this langar is of Lord Supreme Father Kirpal, and He is always providing us with whatever we need. And it was only due to His orders that in the beginning I had asked Mr. Oberoi to make the announcement that no one needs to do any seva here, because my Beloved Lord has promised that He will take care of everything, and up until now He has been fulfilling His promise.

My Dear Children, once again I would like you to know about my fervent wish. This is my desire, that all of you, along with doing your worldly work, should do your meditation right from today, because this is the Path of doing, and not of talking.

Even now, if you will believe me and will obey my words, and even today, if you will start the journey back to your Home, I am sure that with His grace, surely you will reach your goal, you will reach your destination. My best wishes and help are always with you.

Ajaib Singh,
the one who wipes the feet
and the shoes of the sangat.

2

The Tradition of the Path of Love

Sant Ajaib Singh Ji

a talk given by Sant Ji in Jaipur, in March 1992,
in answer to a question about His illness

Whenever I have fallen sick, the dear ones have asked many questions about my health. Many times I have answered those questions, and those answers have been published in the magazines. Still I will answer your question.

Dear Ones, whenever the Master Power manifests Himself within anyone, He brings along with Him all riches: no shortage is left there. Grace, peace, and sympathy reign there. The account of karmas is finished much earlier, when one attains such a position. He within whom the Master is manifested does not even spit at kingdoms. For Him poverty and wealth are alike. Poverty does not make Him sad, nor does wealth make Him happy. For Him friends and enemies are equal. In fact, He does not have any enemy, as He sees only God within all. Whether one is black or white, American or Indian, all are equal in His eyes. He prays for the welfare of everyone. Every single cell of His body sings the glory of His Master. He considers Himself the shoe-wiper of the Sangat. Those who come in His company also become intoxicated with the Master's love, and devote themselves to the Master's remembrance.

Now the question is: how is such a condition achieved? Does it come by itself, or by studying or learning, or can it be bought with money? Or can it be snatched with force and power? No, Dear Ones, these are not the means of attaining such a position. Supreme Father Kirpal used to say that Spirituality is the Path of sacrifice and love and meditation. Whosoever does it can have it. If someone's own does it, he can have it; if some alien does it, he takes it. Beloved Lord also used to say emphatically that the Inner Power doesn't spare anyone.

Dear Ones, such a devotee of Master within whom the Master is manifested is a living example of sacrifice and meditation. He has obeyed every single word of the Master. He has suffered thirst and hunger in the separation of the Master, giving up worldly pleasures, name and fame. He has sacrificed Himself completely on His Master. He does have a physical body like us; He eats, drinks, sleeps, and does other things like us; but within He is very different from us. He is connected with God; in fact, He has become the Form of God. When He opens His eyes He is in this world; when He closes His eyes He is in Sach Khand. It is very difficult to understand Him outwardly. When we go to Him, He takes us in His loving embrace by His beautiful smile and loving words, and we build faith and trust in Him. But our greatest enemy, our mind, who is sitting within us, creates illusions and breaks our faith and devotion. Until we go within by meditating, we cannot develop unshakable faith in the Master, and we cannot see His true glory within.

Only such a devotee of the Master is called a Sadhu, Saint, or perfect disciple, and only to such an ascended soul, does the perfect Master give His work of awakening the souls and connecting them to God Almighty before He leaves the physical body.

You know that when Hazur Baba Sawan Singh Ji Maharaj entrusted this duty to Supreme Father Kirpal, He said, "Kirpal Singh, make sure this perfect science does not disappear, because there will be many who can explain the theory, but not having meditated, they will not have the true knowledge and will mislead the souls."

The same thing was said to me by True Lord Kirpal when He ordered me to give the message of Truth. He said, "Nowadays propaganda and preaching are at their highest, and educated people, with the support of parties, will become gurus. They will make true false and false true. They themselves will be in illusion because of not meditating, and will lead others into the ditch of ignorance. To deceive someone's soul is the greatest sin." Emphatically He said, "The Path of Truth must continue, so that the needs of those souls who have real desire for God may be fulfilled."

Dear Ones, it is very difficult to discharge this duty. When the Master gives this order to the one who has to do this work, hearing the words of his Master, his soul trembles. He cries and weeps and begs at the Feet of his Master that his Master may please continue to be in the physical body so that the Sangat may keep getting the benefit of His darshan. He desires to, and makes every possible effort to, prevent the Master from giving him this job. Even the smallest thought of Master's leaving is not less than his own death. He wants that his Master may always remain over his head even on the physical plane.

The duty given to such a devotee is not to make big ashrams or *deras* or to collect material things for the ashrams. Instead He is a lover of simplicity. He lives a very simple life, and He tells those who come to Him to minimize their needs and live a simple life. He never has any desire to increase the number of the Sangat. His true duty is to connect the souls with Truth, so that following the True Path they may return to their True Home.

Do you know that a perfect living Master is a living representative of God Almighty on this plane? It is His duty to connect those souls who yearn for God Almighty with Naam, after contacting them physically, no matter in which corner of this earth that soul may be. Either He Himself goes where the soul is, or He makes the arrangements for that soul to come to Him for Naam Initiation.

Also there are numerous souls who do not have the good fortune of coming to the Path of Naam, nor do they necessarily believe in God Almighty; but when they are in pain they cry out, "O God, wherever You are, please have pity on us, save us, protect us!" In such circumstances the perfect living Master, as one aspect of His duty, reaches out and provides reasonable help to those suffering souls. The perfect living Masters not only take upon Themselves the karmic burden of Their initiates, but They also take on the load of those suffering souls who call for God's help. Also those who lovingly remember the Master, and even those who have only once greeted Him with respect and love — Master takes the sufferings of such souls on His body.

Master Sawan Singh Ji used to say that Masters not only help Their initiates, but They also extend Their protection to the relatives and pets of Their initiates. This naturally casts a massive burden on Their health.

Master Sawan Singh Ji also used to say that all the karmas done must be paid off, either by the disciple or by the Master. He used to say that the Negative Power doesn't spare even one karma. Also, it is up to the Negative Power to decide how he wants the karmas to be paid. The Masters cannot deny the Negative Power, even if he asks for a part of the body of the Master as part of the payment of the karmas of the disciples. Masters never hesitate. They happily pay off the karmas of Their disciples.

Now the question is: how do the Saints take upon Themselves the karmic burden of the jivas, and how do They pay for it?

You know that this question is related to one's soul and is far beyond the mind and intellect. We cannot see this with our eyes. Only after going within, with the grace of the Master, can we understand this matter. Once a very renowned surgeon who had performed many operations told Baba Sawan Singh that he had never seen any plane or Brahmand within the human body, although he had done so many operations on the human body. Master Sawan Singh Ji replied, "These planes are astral and causal, and so we cannot see them with our physical eyes; we can only see them when we operate through the astral and causal bodies." In the same way we cannot understand this matter unless we go to the plane where this takes place. Until then, we cannot get even the slightest idea of how this happens and how the Masters pay off the karmas of other jivas, and how They take upon Themselves the burden of karmas.

Dear Ones, such a devotee of Master Who has become the Form of the Master after meeting Him, doesn't have any karmas of His own to pay off, as I said earlier. Being controlled by the love and devotion of the dear ones, He takes upon Himself their karmas. He burns Himself in the fire of others; He suffers for others' sufferings; and while doing so, He doesn't even complain, nor does He mention that He is doing this for others. Many times it so happens that the dear one whose karmas He is paying off is having bad thoughts and loses faith when he sees the Master suffering so much. Master always extends feasible help; but sometimes He is drenched so much in the love that He takes up the karmas much beyond the limits, far in excess of the human capacity to bear them, and that proves to be very detrimental to the health of the Master. But still the Master remains happy in the Will of God. He never shows off or claims that He has helped, because He knows that everything is in the Will of God Almighty, His Master.

During the last days of Master Sawan on this plane, His health was not very good. The sangat used to implore Him to cure Himself and to pray to Master Baba Jaimal Singh to keep Him in this world for the sake of the sangat. Master Sawan Singh used to say that He could not make this request as this would affect His discipleship. Master Kirpal Singh used to beg Master Sawan Singh, "We cannot bear the sufferings You have to suffer. Kindly shower grace on us and cure Yourself so that the blessings of Your physical presence may always remain on our heads." One day Master Sawan Singh called Master Kirpal Singh and said, "You always ask me to cure myself and remain on this plane. Today this decision is going to be made in Sach Khand. Close your eyes and see for yourself what happens." Master Kirpal Singh saw that all the perfect Masters — Guru Nanak, Kabir, Tulsi Sahib, Swami Ji Maharaj, Paltu Sahib and others — were present. All the Masters agreed that Master Sawan Singh could remain on this plane for some more time.

But Baba Jaimal Singh said, "No, Baba Sawan Singh has already taken so much burden on Himself; no more burden should be put on Him, and He should be brought back." When Master Kirpal Singh saw this He couldn't say even a word. He just kept looking into the love-filled eyes of Beloved Sawan which gave Him so much intoxication that, as Master Kirpal used to say Himself, "That intoxication cannot be described in words."

In the same way once when Beloved Lord Kirpal was very sick, one dear one asked Him if He would not cure Himself. He replied, "You see, if your dearest friend sends you any gift, would you not accept it? Would you return it?" Then He said, "This physical pain has come in the Will of my Master. It is a gift sent by Him. How can I not accept it? It is my duty to welcome and embrace this gift of my Beloved."

So Dear Ones, this is the tradition of the Path of Love; this is the ritual of this Path Divine. How can I go against it even in thought? It is my duty to accept the gift given by my Master, remain in His Will, and always be grateful to Him for His grace.

I know that all of you want my health to be better. I appreciate all of your sympathy and concern for my health. If you really want to help me, there are certain things you can do to ease the burden. There are certain sacrifices you can do easily.

Increase the time and your efforts in meditation. If you will make efforts, I assure you that the Inner Power will help you manifold. By meditating, you will be accomplishing two things: one, you will be earning the pleasure of the Master Power; and two, you will be doing your own work.

Resolve all the disputes you may have with your friends, relatives, satsangis, etc., lovingly. We have come in contact with each other only because of our past karmas. Square up these karmas lovingly, as it is very important for us to finish off all our karmas in this very birth. Rarely do I receive any letter about meditation. Usually the letters I receive are full of disputes. And then dear ones expect me to say, "You are right and he is wrong." Is this the principle of Sant Mat? Dear Ones, in the Court of the Saints there is only forgiveness. So be wise and avoid disputes. Forgive and forget the faults of others. Clear yourself up within and you will see how the love of the Master manifests there.

Abstain from criticism. Don't deceive others with your sweet words. Love all. If you will do all these, you will progress in meditation by leaps and bounds.

Those dear ones who have been given seva should do it with love and humility. They should make an environment of love by respecting other fellow sevadars. Do the Simran while doing seva. This will help you to feel the grace of the Master, and also it will help you to see very clearly that Master is the doer, we are just His instruments.

There is one more thing I would like to say, and that is: whenever under the instruction of the Master we get together in His remembrance to do His devotion, the Negative Power is also very eager to disturb that atmosphere by one method or another. Master Kirpal used to say that when a soul goes to a perfect Master, then Kal and Maya beat their breasts thinking that one more soul has gone out of their clutches. He also used to say that Kal has numerous ways of deluding the souls. He may create disunity among the sevadars and make them fight with each other; he makes the dear ones lose faith in the Master. From within those who do the Satsang he makes them believe that whatever they say or however they explain the teachings is understood by the dear ones much better and easier. So they start talking more and reading the words of the Master or playing the tape of the Master less. Gradually they play the tape of the Master only for a few minutes, and the rest of the time they talk on the level of the mind and intellect, which does not leave any impression on the souls of the dear ones. It only entertains their minds and satisfies their intellects.

Dear Ones, Saints have risen above the mind and intellect, and whatever They say is full of Their experience. Their words are full of Their grace and carry the radiance of Their meditation. Their words may be simple, but since they come out of a pure within they touch our soul. There is no room for explanation of the Master's words. This does not mean that important things should not be explained. They should be explained; but don't get carried away too far, and do not replace the Master's words with your own talks.

Dear ones come to the ashram or go to the programs after spending so much money and time. So don't waste it in gossip. Utilize it for the purpose for which you have come here. Remain in His sweet remembrance, and meditate as much as you can.

So if the dear ones will remember all this and will do all that I have said, it will help me very much and I will be able to serve you better for a longer time. I hope all of you will stand on your own feet and will become less of a burden for the Master Power.

3
Factors Necessary for Progress

Sant Kirpal Singh Ji

a talk given on October 12, 1972, in New York City, during Master Kirpal's Third World Tour

During these days here we have had four or five talks on the different aspects of Spirituality. Our purpose is to progress on the way. To progress on the way, there are certain things which are very essential. If they are not there, progress won't be there.

First of all is regularity. As you take food daily for your body, twice or three times a day, similarly you are here for the main purpose of giving food to the soul. Bread of Life, Water of Life, the capital of which each one of you have had. So the first thing is regularity. Regularity will only give you better food if you maintain the diary for self-introspection accurately.

Generally we don't care about the maintenance of the diary with respect to self-introspection. The result is not good progress on the Path: sometimes we progress, sometimes we recede. For that, you know, I have prescribed in the diary to have no ill will for anybody, even in thought, word, and deed. Thoughts are very potent. You say, "Somebody will say something against me, what should I do?" Blood cannot be washed away by blood, the Water of Life is required to wash it away. If anybody thinks ill of you, just for a while consider calmly whether what he thinks — is there any truth in it? Examine your own self. If there is anything, be thankful for it. You see either an enemy will tell you something which is not right in you, or sometimes a close friend will tell you, as a matter of counsel and advice, because you have full love with that particular friend. If that is not so, then — "Father, forgive them for they know not what they do." — pray for them. That's the only way, otherwise this thought is rankling in your mind throughout. You'll have no rest. Whenever you sit that thing will creep up.

The second is truthfulness. You know? No acting, posing — your heart, your speech, your brain should be in unison. Only that is true, when these three things agree. Sometimes we say something for outer show, while the heart is thinking something else, and the brain is thinking something else. These are the things to be watched very carefully. Nobody can watch you properly, as you can yourself; you know better. If we do anything [untrue], first we deceive our own selves. Not only do we deceive our own selves, but the God in us. He is there watching our every action. He knows even the very tendencies of our going. So this is further counsel.

Then comes the chastity of life. Chastity is life, sexuality is death. The more chaste you become, the better. That will pay. You will have blessedness in you. When there is anything wrong — lies, or we have been acting and posing to show something which we are not — the result is you'll feel a big wall between you and the God within you. That curtain thickens. So always be true to your own self. Don't spare yourself. If we want to progress on the spiritual way these things are most necessary.

Further still this thing comes up: we are all of the same essence as that of God. We are drops in the Ocean of All Consciousness; we are all brothers and sisters in God. No high, no low. According to the reaction of the past, we have our own positions in life; some have difficulties in life, that's another thing. All the same, God has given us equal privileges, as physical body, as soul, as worshippers of the same Power which controls all Creation and which controls us in the body.

So man is one who lives for others. If our hearts are true — truth is above all, and true living is still above truth. If there is light in the bulb, and the bulb is besmeared with black dots, how much light will be there? Light is within you: *Take heed that the Light within you is not darkness.* This you have to watch. Nobody else can watch it for you. And if anything might come to somebody's notice and they point it out to you, out of enmity to defame you, or out of hearty love for Him, *so that your brother may not be misled.* So these are the things most necessary. *When money is lost, nothing is lost. If health is lost, something is lost. And if character is lost, everything is lost.* As I told you, regularity first, but these are the helping factors to have success in the spiritual way.

These are no new things which I am putting before you. If you are one-eyed you will know better. If you have to give a talk, I think you will speak more creditably, more vehemently, with bombastic words, and with all the force at your command. But the only thing is, we should be true to our own self.

If a man has a lamp in his hand, and falls in the pit — what to do? So we want progress. That Power is within you; God is watching your every action. **Be true to Him, that's all.** That's the only farewell talk I can give to you. It should stand forever. If you take one step that way, a hundred steps you'll come up. Otherwise, our failures in life — after how long will you consider them? If you'll not consider the ones in you, you see, He put's a thick curtain between you and Him. So that is why this prayer has come: "O God, we are thankful to You that you have kept this secret from the worldly wise, and given it to the babes." What does it mean? To the innocent. Innocent men. The innocent man has none of these failures in his life.

So I wish you all progress, you see. That God Power, Christ Power, Guru Power is within you. It sometimes speaks through the human pole to guide you. Because we do not listen to the dictates given by Him inside — He gives once, twice, thrice — if you don't listen, He will stop. That you might call the Voice of Conscience. If you are true to your own self, you are not to be afraid of even God, I would say. You are true to your God within you. God does not reside in the heavens. He is permeating all creation, controlling all creation, and controlling you in the body. He is nearer to you than your hands and feet. **Keep your diary, strictly. Don't spare yourself. If anything comes to eliminate, weed out please.**

Otherwise, suppose you have a pain in your stomach, how

far will you be acting and posing? If you have caught on fire, how far will you keep quiet and act and pose? You will cry. This is the most necessary factor which will go to help your progress on the way. God within you is watching every action. He is watching the very tendency that our mind is going.

So in few words, perhaps you know, each of you, better than what I have told to you. These are no new things which I am telling you. But the only thing is: *we are not true to our own self,* that's all.

Mouth should speak what is in our heart. Brain should think what we have got in our heart. We have progressed in head, I would say, not with the heart. That's the whole trouble. Brain thinks, you see, and becomes selfish. Haughty. Narrow-minded. It becomes the boss, wants to control everybody. He would even like to surpass everybody, at the sacrifice of all others. This is a fact you will find in all the troubles going on in the world today. They have no heart with them, you see. If your brain thinks, and your heart — does it agree with you? I don't think so. If you think to kill somebody, would your heart say, "Yes. Do it"? No!

So heart is the seat of the soul of God within you. Progress by head, but let the heart be with you, then you will be saved from many things. All atrocities, all these things coming before you in the world today, they will be re-ranked. All these things have come up, why? because we have progressed only in head, not by head and heart. If those two had gone together, do you think the shooting would go on?

So whenever you are true to your own self, you see, remain where you are; these are schools of thought. The basic teachings of all are the same. God has created you with equal privileges. You have got body, soul and controlling Power. All are equal. So we have joined different schools of thought just to realize that unity which already exists. We are stuck to the [boundary]. This was meant to give us development, progress. You have not come up to understand the principles for which God made man, and also for which all these schools of thought came into being. Then there's conflict. There's cleverness, so many things.

So that Power is with you always, watching your every action. If you are true to Him, you are true to God. Be regular. This is the Bread of Life, the Water of Life. If your soul becomes strong — if a horse is strong, it will be able to carry the broken carriage. The difficulty is the body has become intellectually strong and spiritually weak. It is very feeble, very frail.

This is all I can place before you. To the best as it has come to me now; I have not thought over this before talking. But this is what we need. **Be regular in your meditations.** That is the Bread of Life. You should develop all around: physically, intellectually, and we should also develop spiritually. Twice blessed is man. Remain in contact, physically too. Through correspondence and that will be when you send your diaries — true diaries. What do I mean to say by "true diaries"? That which truly interprets what you are thinking in mind, word, and deed. "What have I been thinking in my head?" In thought, word, and deed. Sometimes, the diaries are almost blank, and the result is given: "I am putting in two hours," such and such, "and no progress." What should I believe? You can deceive outside people but not the One within you Who is always watching you. If your diary is all right and you put in regular time, accurately, there is no reason why you should not progress. The Master Power works. That is the Holy Ghost; it works from time to time to guide you back. Listen to His voice. And remain in contact, that's all.

We've been having a meditation hour, and I hope that each one of you must have gotten better. If you go on like that, with due respect to your self-introspection and weeding out all failures, under these heads that I have put before you, which you already have in your diaries, God will help you more from day to day.

So as I told you, in my talks, every Saint has His past and every sinner a future. There's hope for everybody. Don't be disheartened. You have some Power to help you, over your head, those who have been initiated on the way especially. You are not all alone. Listen to His words within you and, so long as you are not in conscious contact with that Power, remain in contact outside physically. I think what I am telling you, must be appealing to each one of you. I am just talking from the level of man, as a man to man.

So simple life and high thinking is what we want. A loving heart. No high, no low. He is most beautiful who has got the Light of God refulgent within him. That house looks very beautiful in which electric bulbs are giving light. If there are no bulbs there, even the most magnificent house looks all dark. So this is what is required. I think you should take these things to heart and live up to them. And God will help you.

My wishes will always be with you, here, there, anywhere. Because the actual form of the Master is with you always. As I told you, until you contact Him consciously face to face, within you, guidance from outside from that human pole is necessary. I think this is the gist of all these directions.

So the minimum time is given as two hours: this is binding. If you can do more, you will earn His pleasure. In 1912 I knew a Mohammedan professor. You see, men of the same views will love. He would meet me; I also used to meet him. This was in 1912, sixty years back. He had put a sign: "No Admission without Permission" on his house. I was free to go to him. Sometimes I went and he was saying prayers in his own Mohammedan way. In their prayers, five times they sit, bow down, and then stand. That is the general rule. When I went there, he used to say prayers for hours. One hour, two hours, three. I was simply watching. I once asked him, "Well, dear friend, prayers have only five sittings, and you go on for hours?" He said, "Five sittings are binding to a Mohammedan, and this I do to earn His will and pleasure." You see? So to put in two hours, that is a tithe; this is binding on each one of you. And if you do more, it will earn His pleasure.

This is your work; you have to do it. And then less is bad, of course. Suppose a man is a thief. He wants any chance to grab money, day or night. You are really after your spiritual progress.

Snatch away time, any time you can. The pity is — where there is a will there is a way — we have no will. That is why we are not able to give full justice to the work. Manbody is the highest in all creation, and this is the golden opportunity we have got. If we can't do this, nobody else will do it for you. And even you have to go.

Last night I was telling people, how in lectures, in this and that thing, I have been talking to you on death alone. The five talks main purpose was — this is a golden opportunity — make the best use of it. What is meditation? What is spirituality? What is a Master? . . . You see? Where is God? How can we find Him? All these things went on, from the commencement to the end, we were talking on the word death, the name of which we do not like to hear. But with all that we have to pass through it. Death is no bugbear; we have to leave the body. And generally you'll find anyone, they don't give a talk on that.

So my best wishes are with you. That's all I can say. That Power is within you, watching you, your every tendency, every thought. And It is extending all feasible help and protection without asking for it. So it is a great blessing to have somebody living on earth like us to guide [us]. You are all dear to me. Why? Because you have been put on the Path, as such we are all brothers and sisters, real relatives, this is such a relation which cannot be broken after death. How fortunate you are! If you do care, [pause] so that's all right. This is the sum total of all teachings in these few words. If you will live by them, you will progress even more than me. I pray that you all become ambassadors. But we should be sincere in word, thought and deed.

Now I am going today [to the next stop on the Tour]. All of you who have come from outside, you should have your own way back. Those who would like to go further, if they can well afford it, their circumstance they know, I have no objection. But perhaps you will have to make your own arrangements. Whatever possible those people also will do, but don't go totally dependent on them.

You follow my point now? Be regular in your meditations.

No ill will for anybody. Be truthful, be chaste in thought, and love for all. You are not born to live for your own selves. You are man: *man is one who lives for others, not for his own self only.* And be regular in devoting your time to come in contact with All-Consciousness within you, which is controlling all creation, and permeating all creation. Remain in any social body you like, that makes no difference. The purpose of all that is to reach God. The purpose of marriage is also to have a companion to help each other to know God. That will give you permanent joy and peace. With these words I think we should end. This is the best of the meditations, you see. Consider these points which I have placed before you. Five minutes, ten minutes. Take it to heart, and live up to them. Your faces will be shining gloriously if you live up to them. Your eyes will be open, bright.

4

The Eternal Song

Sant Kirpal Singh Ji

In the beginning was the Word, and the Word was with God, and the Word was God. . . .

All things were made by Him; and without Him was not anything made that was made.

In Him was life; and the life was the light of men.

And the light shineth in darkness; and the darkness comprehendeth it not.

And the Word was made flesh, and dwelt among us, and we beheld His glory, (the glory as of the only begotten of the Father), full of grace and truth.

JOHN 1:1, 3-5, 14

The Kingdom of God is at hand. . . .

MARK 1:15

July 10, 1961

Dear Children of Light,

I convey my love to you all and speak to you from the core of my heart on the auspicious birth anniversary of my Master Sawan Singh Ji Maharaj.

Blessed indeed is the hour when the Timeless comes into Time, the Formless assumes a Form and the Wordless becomes the Word, and the Word puts on the mantle of flesh to dwell amongst us. Verily, ye are, essentially and potentially, the Timeless, the Formless, and the Wordless. The Word is in you and you live in and by the Word, though you may for the time being be living on the plane of the senses and unaware of your real identity.

A tree is known by the fruit it bears. Lectures, messages, statements and discourses of any kind, spiritual or otherwise, imparted through utterances or writings, are just idle talk when not acted upon or lived up to.

Live up to the Divine Word which is the Word of words, the manifestation of Truth. This Word is harkened by the Soul. It is the Eternal Song which was sung ages ago; and that Song produced the phenomena called the universe.

When that Song is heard, you will have some glimpses of the Lord and the True Master. Some will have a little, some more, and some still more. Souls embedded in the Master Power will be lighted. The more receptive the souls to the Master Power; the more Light they will emit.

If you wish to love God truly in the most practical way, it is to love our fellow-beings; feel for others in the same way as we feel for our dear ones. Instead of seeing faults in others, we look within ourselves; suffer in the suffering of others and feel happy in the happiness of others; endure all that comes, cheerfully accepting it as His Will; and do not hurt or harm any of His beings. To love God, we must live for God and die for God.

I would like to sow the seed of love in your hearts, so that the feelings of love are brought about among all the nations, creeds, sects and castes of the world. All Saints preached the same. Love and all things shall be added unto you.

Without love there is no peace here or hereafter.

KABIR

Those who do not know love cannot know God.

CHRIST

Hear ye all, I tell you the Truth,
God cannot be approached without Love.

GURU GOBIND SINGH

The main purpose of my Master was to awaken mankind to the Truth taught and preached by all Saints who came in the past. His job was to awaken the Divinity in every heart and guide each to his or her goal of life.

Like the Great Masters of the past, He drew people of all castes and colors by living example. He awakened humanity to the fundamental inviolable unity of all life. All mankind is one. The True Brotherhood will arise by awakening to the unity already existing in man. Man is an ensouled body. Soul is a conscious entity — a drop of the Ocean of All-Consciousness. Man is the oldest of all. Social bodies were made by man for the attainment of God. My Master did not come to establish a new religion. The religion He taught is the knowledge of the Self and the One behind the many, which can be achieved by tapping inside by inversion — by reading the great book of one's self, where God is revealed — the book of all books, the Bible of all Bibles, which holds the key to the mystery of life. The way to Truth is simple: the way is to know oneself so as to know God. When one is awakened to Self-consciousness, his or her outer attachments are shaken off and God floods his or her soul.

The only rules that He gave at all, if any, were meditation, pure ethical life and selfless service. He did not say for you to cease to be a Christian, a Hindu, a Sikh, a Mohammedan, or a Zoroastrian, but to be a true follower of Christ, Lord Krishna, Guru Nanak, Prophet Mohammed, or Zoroaster — that is, to do what They said. He did not ask the skeptical man or woman of today to accept any dogma, but in the spirit of humility to obey the God reverberating in the heart of all. He advised us to look at each other from the level of the soul and not through the garbs of various religions we are wearing, and to love all. He did not advocate change of forms, but to look within oneself where all are one. He did say that whatever religion one has, it should transform our life. We should lead an ethical life. He did not bring Eastern or Western thoughts for us to act upon, but helped us to act upon the basic Truth that we already have in our religions. He revived the forgotten Truth that is Eternal.

Example is better than precept. The Teacher that the age wants is a living example of what all may become; the only Teacher that we can accept is One who has experienced God.

He must be One who has consciously bridged the gulf between Time and Eternity and can show others how to do likewise. He enables us to discover our Selves. We get through Him a change of heart, and He has the power to transmit grace, kindle love, and bestow contact with the Light of God. He is overflowing with the love of God and of all creation, and those who come in contact with Him are enkindled with that love; and the God-Power working through Him awakens God in others.

Books cannot replace teachers. Unless one meets the teacher in the flesh, one cannot unravel the Mystery of Self. What a man has done another can do, of course with proper guidance and help. You have been put on the Path — the Path that leads you to the Divine in you. You have been blessed with a conscious contact with the holy Light and Harmony, the life and soul of all that is, and you can develop your initial experience of the living contact to any length you may. It all depends on you. Where there is a will there is a way. Strive for it ceaselessly. It is the essence of life and the greatest gift on earth. Rear it up with tender care and loving devotion lest you may again lose hold of the lifelines in the stormy sea of life.

"Awake, arise, and stop not till the Goal is reached!" is the time-honored message coming down as it does from eternity, and I repeat it today with all the emphasis at my command. Make hay while the sun shines. The Kingdom of God verily is at hand, and the Power of God unmistakably beckons you to it. Avail yourself of the golden opportunity that God has given you, for human birth is a rare privilege and thrice blessed is man. Make the most of it while there is yet time. Let not dissensions creep into your thoughts and corrode your progress in any way. You are one of the fortunate children of Invincible Light. Live up to that sacred Truth. Master Power is always with you and will be extending you all love and grace.

If we live up to the teachings, it is a panacea for all ills and evils.

With fondest love to you all,

KIRPAL SINGH

5

Learn to be Receptive

Sant Kirpal Singh Ji

reprinted from Spiritual Elixir

Regular attendance at the Satsang meetings is very useful and helpful. It keeps the mind on the spiritual track. Avoidance of undesirable society is still another necessary factor, and all of these are extremely important in the beginning. A sapling needs water and nourishment. These factors go to nourish it, until it grows into a big tree which mighty elephants cannot shake. The outgoing faculties are to be inverted and the mind stilled. For this the remedy has already been given to you. Consider how great a blessing of God you have received. You can develop it while living in the world. Be brave. You cannot run away. That is the work of a coward. But there is one important thing to note. Try to surrender completely to the Master and under the cover of His power, protection and grace, you will wade through the waters of life unscathed. The loving Father will protect you like a baby, in the might of His strong arms, and pass you scot-free from the fires of life without a burn. Everyone errs. Through these errors you have to grow into a pure and lustrous soul. Weed out the shortcomings, one by one. The diary is a necessity and must be used for this purpose. It helps you to keep an eye on your ethical side of life, for this must be developed along with the spiritual growth. Remember that the Father wants to embrace His child. If the child's clothing is soiled with dirt or mud, He will not forsake him, but cleanse the child and take him or her into His lap. He is always with His children whom He loves, a hundred times more than the proverbial love of a mother.

I am glad you felt the Master walking with you . . . to shake off your great load of anxiety and paralyzing nervous reactions of the wrongs done to you by others, and that it toned your spirits. As long as you live in the world, you must be up and doing. You must work with ambition and whole-heartedly, and therein lies all beauty. All of creation is beautiful. You love God. As He is immanent in every form, you must love all His creation. But be not attached. Just as you go to a garden, you enjoy the beauty of the flowers and the verdure of the bushes, but you do not pluck the flowers or uproot the plants, otherwise the gardener would take you to task. You cannot have the results according to your desires or expectations. So always do your best and leave the results to the Master overhead and whatever the results are, take them with good cheer. They are always beneficial to the initiated, because the Master-Power working overhead knows what is best for His ailing child.

Married life is no bar to spirituality, provided it is led in accordance with the scriptural injunctions. You may seek a companion for your earthly sojourn, one who is of your way of thinking, and anxious to seek a higher worldly life. It would be helpful to both of you. My best wishes are always with you. You may go where you like, live anywhere, and do anything that may serve to help your inner progress. Anything that may retard your inner progress will not be in your interest.

Should you get a chance to come to India on any assignment and are able to be near me, I will be glad to see you. The effect of personal aura and personal environments cannot be underrated. But while it is so, the Master is not limited by time or space. He is always with you even though He be thousands of miles away.

Please learn to be receptive to His grace and feel His kindly presence riding with you on the buses, chatting with you in the street, sitting with you in the park, by your office desk, accompanying you every morning to the office, slowing down by the lily pond to check the new flowers and walking with you in the evening all the way back by the new moon.

Master is always with the disciple and never leaves him or her until the end of the world. The Father will never disown His children.

6

To Get Mastery Over Our Mind

Baba Sawan Singh Ji

from a letter, dated August 1, 1912

My Dear Daughter: I was very much pleased to receive your letter full of love and faith and to know that you are making good progress in the exercises though it was marred by your shifting to a new house. Now that by the grace of the Holy Father you have got a comfortable house and other worldly anxieties are over, you should apply yourself, heart and soul, to the service of the Father and give as much time to the exercises as you can easily take from your business. But, mind you, your business must not suffer in the least. All the luxuries of this world and the world itself — the sun, moon, stars — in short, everything that we see here, is liable to destruction. Only the soul is immortal. So try to live this short span of life in a manner which best pleases God, that your wanderings in this world may cease and you may find your Eternal Home, where it is all bliss — unalloyed.

Regarding exercises, you say you cannot remain in the exact position for a long time, so there is no harm in using a pillow as you do. Or you can ask Sasmas to get a *beragan* made for you. It is a sort of flat piece of wood attached to a short stick in the shape [of a T]. The piece of wood is a foot and a half in length and two inches in breadth. The stick is placed in the middle of the wood which supports our two elbows while [doing bhajan]. . .

One word about general behavior. The biggest part of our time is devoted towards worldly ends, and by sitting in contemplation for a few hours, our soul cannot properly enjoy the Holy Sound. Again and again, the mind goes out and remains thinking of worldly matters. So keep a sharp eye over its working during the whole of the day and take care that it may not carry you away. Try to resist its mean cravings and check their outward manifestation through senses. Always remain one-pointed and never allow your mind to engage in foolish fancies. This is possible only by keeping your mind engaged in the Holy Names. At all times, whether walking, eating, drinking, or doing any other work which does not require much attention, try to concentrate your attention on the Holy Names and never allow your senses to wander away. Be always on your guard; this is the only way to get mastery over our mind.

Secondly, whatever good or bad happens to you, through whatever person or object, directly proceeds from our loving Father. All persons and objects are but tools in His hand. If an evil befalls you, think it as His greatest mercy. We have to suffer for our past actions sooner or later. Our Master, by taking us through these sufferings speedily and by hastening the approach of those which were to come later, intends to relieve us of our burden earlier. And by this early payment of debt — because debt it is — the amount of the suffering is very much lessened. If we had to pay one ton at first, now we are released by paying one pound only. So never be disheartened if you are to pay some severe debt. It is all for your good. Suppose a man ill treats you without any fault on your part, you should see in this ill treatment the Hand of the Master working. He wants to find out, and to make known to you, whether your self-reverence has died out or not, and how deep has meekness and love taken root in you. Again, suppose a man loses his son. It is to test the decrease in love for earthly relatives. Father wants to loosen these heavy chains which bind us down to this earth. More love towards earthly relatives means less with the Master. So all events which appear to be misfortunes are not really so. They come to chasten us and add to our power of resistance and leave us better men in the end. Be always resigned to His

Will. What Father does, He does for the best. In this world, those persons who are engaged in upward march have constantly to face the inroads of two powerful enemies — the Mind and the Matter. They try to put many obstacles in our way. If an untoward event happens, we need not be disheartened. Rather, we should rise with redoubled love and final victory is ours.

Our Father is Love and we are small drops from that Ocean of Love. This huge machinery of universe is working on the eternal principle of love. So try to bring yourself in harmony with this principle of love. The deeper the love of the Master will take root in you, the fainter the love of "earth" will remain in you. His love will displace the love of earthly things. Spirit will uproot the flesh. The curtains will rise before you one by one. The dark mysteries of the universe will become revealed to you and you will find yourself in the loving lap of the Holy Father — one with Him.

He out of His mercy has bestowed upon you such a noble gift that all the treasures of this world stand in no comparison with it. But it will not improve your condition if you will not use it. A hungry man is never satisfied simply by counting the names of various dishes that lie before him. Though the teachings you have got are invaluable, yet they cannot be of any good unless you act up to them and daily engage in the exercises for as long a time as you can spare from your worldly engagements.

To sum up, you must be careful about the following:

1. Control of mind
2. Check on senses
3. Resignation to His Will
4. Love for Him, and
5. Punctuality in exercises.

You can keep these letters for your guidance and need not destroy them.

Yours affectionately,
SAWAN SINGH

7

Make Each Breath an Offering

Sant Kirpal Singh Ji

from an evening talk given February 20, 1971, at Master's house on Rajpur Road, Dehra Dun, India

Always live in the living present — in the living moment. Did you read my circular on that point? If you care for the living moment, you can care for eternity. Read the circulars and go into them deeply. If you care for the pennies, pounds will be saved, is it not so? If you keep your mind occupied every moment, then nothing can go wrong. It is given very briefly in the circulars. Brevity is the soul of all creation. The Master's sayings are very brief, but to the point.

If you watch your present moment, then everything is all right. If you don't care, sometimes for hours you're oblivious and in those vacant hours there's so much trouble that comes up which affects your meditations. So when you sit for meditation, forget the past, forget the future; live in the living present. This is the one thing that will give you success in your meditations. But the vacant hours in which you've not kept the mind occupied with some constructive thought affect your meditation.

So that is the remedy that accounts for all these things: If you would pass your every hour in peace, with no ill will against anybody and no attachment to anybody, if you can pass each hour like that for one day, then continuously for some days, no such ramifications of mind will come up to affect your meditations. We are frittering away our moments of life in suchlike pursuits. Kabir says, "Make each breath you take the offering to your Master." Do you follow what I have said?

Every breath you take, make it an offering to your Master. This is very valuable, Kabir says, and we fritter away a fortune. If a dying man wishes to stay for a few minutes longer, he cannot.

How frivolously we kill our time. Every moment of life is very valuable. Make the best use of it. When death overtakes us, that is the time you say, "Oh, had some time been given to me, I would have done this and that thing." Is it not so? But you cannot get time then which you have frittered away so ruthlessly, so cruelly. Kabir says, "In one breath he crossed three planes: physical, astral, causal." One breath is very valuable.

. . . One Saint says, "If you can pass three days and nights in sweet, constant remembrance of God, you go to His Feet." Three days — can we? It's not much. Let no other thought other than God strike your mind. Why not start with one day? Start from today. All right, from now on till tomorrow evening, no thought — constant remembrance, even when you eat, don't forget Him. Try one day. That will give you good training. We don't care for the trifling things, but that is where the substantial thing comes from. One day is not much. You have been here how many days? So many days. And if you had passed even one day and night in constant remembrance, you would have changed very much.

an excerpt from chapter 58 of The Light of Kirpal

8
The Cage of the Soul
Sant Kirpal Singh Ji

from a letter

Man has got himself so enmeshed in mind and the outgoing faculties that his release from them can only be brought about by struggle and perseverance. His plight is, in a way, similar to that of a bird that has been kept in a cage for so many years. Even if you should open the door of the cage, the bird will be loathe to fly out. Instead, it will fly from one side of the cage to the other, clinging with its talons to the wire mesh, but it does not wish to be free and fly out through the open door of the cage.

Similarly, the soul has become so attached to the body and the outgoing faculties that it clings to outside things and does not wish to let go of them. It does not wish to fly through the door that has been opened by the Master at the time of Holy Initiation, at the threshold of which the Radiant Form of the Master is patiently waiting to receive the child disciple. True discipleship does not start until one has risen above body consciousness.

It is from this point that the disciple will feel not only comfort, but will begin to experience the joy and bliss that awaits him in the Beyond. He will have as his companion the charming Radiant Form of the Master, Who is ever at hand to impart the guidance that is so necessary in order to avoid the pitfalls on the way. Until this point is reached, the disciple is, as it were, on probation, but such probation that cannot be severed. It is during this probationary period that the soul will feel some discomfort. It has become so besmeared with the dirt of the senses that it has lost its original purity of heart and is not fit to be raised up out of the prison house of the body.

Even though the door has been opened, it is so attached to the things of the outside world that it does not wish to be free. It is only when the soul begins to regain its original purity of heart and mind that it can at last want to be free of the desires of the flesh and outward attachments. The loving Master tries to avoid all possible discomfort to the child disciple by explaining what are the vices to be avoided and the virtues to be developed in order to regain this purity.

Unfortunately, more often than not, the words of the Master do not sink in and little or no action is taken by the disciple to amend his ways. Therefore, the Master Power must take firmer measures to bring home to the disciple the importance of the truths that have been explained in words. Hence the discomfort that is sometimes felt by the dear ones in their day-to-day living. If implicit obedience would be given to the commandments of the Master, all difficulties and discomforts would vanish. If a child gets itself so dirty that the only way the mother can wash it clean is by using a scrubbing brush, can it be said that the child will feel comfortable during the scrubbing process? It will only feel comfortable after the scrubbing has ceased and it is shining clean and pure.

Help and protection is always extended by the Master to His followers. He looks after their comforts in every way, both outer and inner. Even the effects of the reactions of the past -— from the gallows to an ordinary pin prick — so much concession is given. As the mother sacrifices everything for the sake of her child, even so does the Master sacrifice everything for the sake of His children. The follower in fact does not dream of what the Master does for him. He fills his followers with His own thought, with His own life impulses. When we remember Him, He remembers us with all His heart and soul. He is not the body. He is the Word personified, the Word made flesh. To get the full benefit of the Master Power, the disciple must develop receptivity. It is impossible to develop receptivity until implicit obedience is given to the commandments of the Master. When you pay heed to the Master's commandments, then that is a sign that you are growing in love for Him and the more you grow in love for Him, the more receptivity you will develop.

When you begin to develop this receptivity, all discomfort will vanish and you will truly begin to tread the Path in the firm assurance that you are on the right way, together with the loving companionship of One who will demonstrate more and more His greatness and His power on each step of the way until you find that it is the very God Himself who is your Guide and Mentor, who will never leave you until He has safely escorted you back to the true home of the Father.

While on the way, one of the main functions of the Master is to wind up the back karmas of the disciple. It is through conscious contact with the Sound Current only that the karmas of back lives can be burnt away. This process is started at the time of Holy Initiation, at which time the disciple is given a contact with the Light and Sound Principle, or God-into-Expression Power. To avoid opening a new account of bad deeds, the disciple is enjoined to lead a clean life and weed out all imperfections in him by self-introspection from day to day. This is the sublime principle behind keeping the diary, which the disciple is asked to maintain in order to become aware of the shortcomings which stand in his way to God.

Ego is the self-assertive principle in man that makes him feel that "I do this" or "I do that." When one rises above body consciousness and knows himself and he becomes a conscious co-worker of the Divine Plan, he sees that he is not the "doer" but is a mere puppet in the hands of God, he will cease to be responsible for his actions and will become *jivan mukta,* or a free soul. The ego in man is part of the grand delusion that he is laboring under. It will cease to act, or will be nullified, only when a great degree of purity has been attained by the disciple, in which all of his actions will reflect the Master in him. Like Christ, he will proclaim, "I and my Father are One."

9
On Judging Others

Sant Kirpal Singh Ji

notes of the Satsang of January 28, 1967,
reprinted from the June 1970, Sat Sandesh

If we realize that death is certain, then there will be a change in our life. You must remain attentive in meditation. If not, the mind will think of others and judge their actions, criticizing, etc. Instead of the good actions of others, we take their bad actions to be our guiding factor. If you see the bad qualities of others, you will become those bad qualities. *As you think, so you become.*

God has said, "He is my loveliest child who sees me in others." Thoughts are very potent. You should see the good qualities of others rather than their bad qualities. You must have a sweet tongue; it should not injure the feelings of others. You want to love God, yet you curse others in whom God resides. Injuring the feelings of others is a great sin; it is a sin of the highest degree. If you have to face a person with such bad qualities, get on to one side rather than face him. Analyze yourself and see your own shortcomings instead of seeing the shortcomings of others. Who are you to take out the shortcomings of others? It is easy to seek God, but very difficult to mend yourself. If you realize that God resides in others, would you want to hurt them? One by one, you should give up your shortcomings. This is why I insist on all initiates keeping a diary.

If a man won't give up his evil ways of hurting others, why should you depart from your sweet ways of helping others? If you must observe others, then observe their virtuous qualities.

There are shortcomings in all, but also good qualities.

Swami Ji says, "I will give you a tip: If you want to see shortcomings, then look into your own self; if you want to see virtues, then see them in others." Listen to what I say, and take heed; if not, you will be sorry and then it will be too late in the day. I have selected the best piece of advice for you. Now it is up to you to follow it. God has given us this tongue to remember Him and not to hurt the feelings of others.

10

Content In the Will of God

Sant Ajaib Singh Ji

an excerpt from a Satsang given at Sant Bani Ashram, Village 16 PS, Rajasthan, India, March 29, 1986

. . . So lovingly He says, "You need not do any outer rite or ritual, you just need to do the meditation of Shabd Naam." That Naam is not written in Hindi, nor in Punjabi, not even in Sanskrit, nor any other language. That is the Naam of the Lord which is unwritten law and unspoken language, and God Almighty always sends His beloved children into this world to give us the knowledge of that Naam. Naam is that power with the support of which the Khands and Brahmands — the divisions and grand divisions of this creation — are surviving and being sustained. That Naam is within us; and the perfect Masters who come in this world in the will of God who are sent by God, give us the knowledge of that Naam.

It is a pity that even though the Masters of the highest degree came in this world, few were those souls who could take advantage of, and benefit from, the coming of those Masters. Once somebody asked Master Sawan Singh about outer signs of the perfect Master. Master Sawan Singh said that the perfect Masters do not hang a board on their neck, they do not have any sign on their forehead, saying "He is a hypocrite," or "He is a perfect one." If you want to realize the perfectness of the Master, you have to go within.

We know about the goodness of a tree only by eating its fruit. In the same way if we mold our life according to the teachings of the Master, if we sincerely do the things which the Master has told us to do, only then can we realize the perfectness and the competence of the Master. Because the Masters do not tell us things from hearsay, they tell us only those things which they have actually done in Their own lives.

There is an instance in the history of the King of Rum. When he was talking once to the people in his court, a question came up about patience and contentment. That King asked his people, "What does it mean to be patient, to be content?" He had so many people in his court who were very wise and learned, and they all tried to answer that question according to their own intelligence; but the King was not convinced. So he called his Prime Minister and asked him about it; "Tell me, what is the meaning of 'patience'?" The Prime Minister tried to explain to him about patience and contentment but the King was not satisfied. He asked him, "Who can give the answer to this question?" Then he himself told the Prime Minister, "I have heard that in the country of India there is a very mighty emperor whose name is Aurangzeb; he is a very wise and learned emperor, and he has many good people in his court. It is possible that if you go there and ask him about this, he would be able to give you the answer. But you should come back only when you are convinced, and only when you feel that you can convince me. In case they cannot answer this question, you should try to find a Fakir who lives in India, whose name is Sarmad; I have heard that he is a Fakir of the highest degree, and he will be able to answer this question. So you go to India and find out the answer and tell me what is the meaning of 'being patient,' and what it means to 'be content.' " So the Prime Minister went to India and met with Aurangzeb, and asked him the question about patience and contentment. Aurangzeb was very learned and he tried to explain to him, but he could not give the exact answer which the Prime Minister was looking for to take back to his King. Then he talked with the other people there but he was not convinced by them either, even though everybody tried their best to explain patience and contentment to the Prime Minister.

So then he asked the people about the whereabouts of the

Fakir Sarmad; but they told him, "Aurangzeb is a very strict religious-minded person, and he has not allowed any Fakir or Saint to live outside; he has put them all in jail, and it is very difficult to find out exactly where he is; but wherever he is, he's in bad condition. He doesn't have any clothes to wear, he doesn't get good food to eat, he gets only one cup of water to drink a day, and he gets only a few bad chapaties to eat every day. But it will be difficult to find him."

Since the Prime Minister had the job of finding the Fakir Sarmad and getting the answer to his King's question, he went on trying to find him; and you know that when you are devoted to something and work hard for it, you definitely achieve success. So he finally found Sarmad in a very dark cell. He was naked and, as the people had told him, He was in very poor condition. Before he could talk to Him, he saw a person who had been sent by the Emperor who, without giving any alarm or explanation, suddenly started beating Sarmad; he whipped him, but Sarmad did not sigh or complain, He just patiently suffered whatever was going on there. Then the Prime Minister saw that somebody brought a cup of water and a dry chapati which was not of good quality. Sarmad accepted that in the Will of God, and with a lot of contentment he ate the chapati. Then the Prime Minister of Rum asked Sarmad his question: "Tell me, what is the meaning of 'patience' and what is the meaning of 'being content?' Sarmad said, "I will reply to this tomorrow. When you come tomorrow bring a big sheet and a leather bag full of water. Then I will answer your question."

So the next day the Prime Minister of Rum took a lot of water and a big sheet of cloth to Sarmad, who, with His gracious sight, opened the door of that prison and allowed the Prime Minister to come into His cell. Sarmad took a bath with the water which the Prime Minister had brought, and after that He covered Himself with that sheet of cloth which the Prime Minister had brought for Him, and then He sat in meditation. He also made that Prime Minister sit in meditation, and with His grace He took the soul of the Prime Minister up into the

Court of the Lord. There the Prime Minister saw that Sarmad was with the other souls who had reached the home of the Lord and all those great souls were asking Sarmad, "If you tell us we can destroy Aurangzeb and his kingdom because he is giving you a hard time." But Sarmad the fakir was folding His hands to all those great souls and saying, "No, don't do any harm to Aurangzeb or to his people; just forgive him, because he does not know what he is doing." The Prime Minister of Rum was very surprised to see that even though Sarmad was almighty, and had all the powers of God, still He had so much patience in the Will of God that He did not want anyone to do any harm to Aurangzeb even though Aurangzeb was giving Him a lot of suffering. When the Prime Minister of Rum saw the real glory and the real position of Sarmad the fakir there, he was very moved, and when Sarmad brought him down, He told him, "Now you have the answer to your question. If you have all things given to you by Almighty God but you do not use your power, that means being content in the Will of God; and, even though you are able to do everything, if you do not do anything to harm others, that means to be patient in the Will of God."

Sheikh Farid also says, "The perfect Masters are the beloveds of God. They have so much patience and they remain content in the Will of God. Even though they live near God, still they do not tell people that they are one with God." Just as Sarmad took the Prime Minister up and showed him that whatever was happening was in the Will of God, so we should be patient and content in His Will; and just as Sarmad showed the Prime Minister the truth, in the same way, towards the end of His life when Baba Sawan Singh was suffering a great deal, and His beloved son Maharaj Kirpal Singh Ji could not bear to see that suffering, every day He requested Master Sawan to remove His suffering Himself and stay in this world for a few more years. Once it so happened that Master Sawan Singh called Master Kirpal Singh and told Him to sit by His bed, because every day Master Kirpal was making that request to Master Sawan Singh, Master Sawan Singh was passing it on to

His Master. So when Master Sawan had called Master Kirpal to come and sit by His bed, He told Him, "Sit and close your eyes: today in the Court of the Lord the decision is going to be made, and you will see with your own eyes what it is going to be."

Master Kirpal Singh told me Himself that He saw the Court of the Lord in Sach Khand, and all the Mahatmas who had reached Sach Khand were there; it was like a council of all the Masters. Everyone wanted Master Sawan Singh to live in this world for a few more years; everyone except Baba Jaimal Singh. He said, "No. Right now the conditions in the world are not so good and I will not let Sawan Singh stay in this world for any more time. Now is the time for Him to come back, because He has already had enough suffering." When Master Sawan Singh brought Master Kirpal down, he said, "Kirpal Singh, have you seen this? Did you hear the decision with your own ears? This is the Will of God, and whatever is going to happen will happen in the Will of God."

So Guru Ramdas Ji Maharaj says that liberation is in Naam, and one gets the Naam from the Master. If you want to cross this ocean of life you should do the meditation of Shabd Naam.

11

Sant Ji's First Message

Sant Ajaib Singh Ji

a message sent to western disciples of Sant Kirpal Singh Ji, in May 1976

Dear Satsangis, Brothers and Sisters:

Master Kirpal has not left us. He is always with us and protecting us in every aspect of our life. Master never disappears from this world. He never dies; He is eternal. His soul is deathless; He leaves only His physical body but His presence is still to be felt. And we should love each other in order to carry out the teachings of our Master.

Meditation will bring peace to our soul; and if our soul is at rest and at peace, then only will we love each other. All satsangis are related to one another by the ties of brotherhood and sisterhood; so we should respect and love each other. Hazur Babaji (Master Kirpal) has left a message of love for us. It is our duty to take care of His message and follow His teaching.

If we criticize or talk ill of anybody, it is our great loss. Our Master used to say that if we criticize others, all their sins become ours; and all our good deeds become theirs. The one who finds fault with others always loses; so we should never do it. Guru Nanak also says that by criticizing others we make our tongue, mouth and mind dirty; by finding fault with others we are making our way to hell.

Baba Sawan Singh also told me the same thing: that there is no taste in speaking ill of others. He said that there is taste or pleasure in sense enjoyments, but where is the pleasure in finding fault?

So, Dear Brothers and Sisters, I request you not to criticize any Satsangi or any other person because when anyone is initiated by a Master, the Master takes His seat within the disciple. So if you criticize or abuse any disciple, then it is the same as if we were abusing our Master. So I request you not to find fault with anybody, to put in more time in meditation, and Bhajan and Simran will be very good for your life.

Our Master told us to *leave a hundred urgent works to attend Satsang and a thousand urgent works for meditation.* I request you to put in more time for meditation, to attend Satsang, and not to criticize anybody because criticism will not help your meditation. It is the ones who are not meditating who are abusing others. So you are to be careful that you are not criticizing or speaking ill or abusing, and are putting in more time for meditation.

I hope you have followed what I have said.

Dass Ajaib Singh

12

The Test of a Gurumukh

Swami Ji Maharaj

reprinted from the book The Two Ways

Out of mercy, the Satguru always takes care of the jiva (embodied or bound soul) and is desirous that all His disciples should have great love and faith in His feet, but the mind does not like that the jiva should attain this state. It therefore tries to draw him towards the enjoyment of sensual pleasures and wants the jiva to obey its dictates. The jivas should, therefore, continue their devotion at the feet of the Satguru, beware of the ambush of the mind and see that they do not fall into its trap.

A brief account of the ways of a Gurumukh* and the ways of a manmukh is given here to enable the jiva to test and regulate his conduct. The jiva should go on applying this test to himself.

1. The dealings of the Gurumukh are always true and straight with everybody. He shuns evil and does not deceive anyone. Whatever he does, he does for the Satguru, and relies upon His mercy.

A manmukh is sly and insincere in his dealings, and will deceive others to secure his own interests. He depends upon his own cleverness and intelligence, and wishes to proclaim himself.

* Gurumukh — "One through whom the Guru speaks," that is, one who has risen above his ego, individual mind, desires, etc., so that his higher Self which is identical with the Guru is actively manifest. Manmukh — "One through whom the mind speaks," that is, one who has not become a Gurumukh and is still living in the fallen state which keeps him away and separate from his higher Self, Guru or God.

2. A Gurumukh controls his mind and senses and is humble in spirit. He puts up with taunting words, lends a willing ear to advice and does not seek to be honored.

A manmukh does not like his mind to be curbed. He does not like to submit to anyone or obey anybody, and is jealous of the greatness of others.

3. A Gurumukh does not oppress anybody. He is always willing and ready to serve and please and wishes to do good to others. He seeks not his own fame or honor, but keeps happy and absorbed in the thoughts of the Satguru and in His Holy Feet.

A manmukh dominates others and makes them serve him. He seeks honor and does not care for others except for his own selfish interests. He enjoys being honored and made much of, and does not remain absorbed in the Holy Feet of the Satguru.

4. A Gurumukh never gives up his humility and gentleness. He does not resent it if he is slandered or slighted or shown disrespect. He regards all this as conducive to his own good.

A manmukh fears slander and dishonor, does not willingly put up with disrespect, and solicits praise.

5. A Gurumukh works hard and never remains idle.

A manmukh seeks bodily ease and comfort, and is lazy.

6. A Gurumukh leads a simple and humble life, and is ready to live contentedly on whatever falls to his lot, be it dry and un-buttered (bread), or rough and coarse (clothing).

A manmukh always loves and craves dainty dishes. He does not like to have dry and un-buttered bread and things of low value.

7. A Gurumukh is not engrossed by earthly goods and the meshes of the world, and feels no pain or pleasure in losing them or getting them. He is not upset by unbecoming remarks

made against him. He keeps an eye on the salvation of his soul and on pleasing his Satguru.

A manmukh thinks too much of the world and its goods. He feels pain if he loses them and pleasure if he gets them. If one talks harshly to him, he immediately flies into anger, forgets the grace and power of the Satguru, and does not rely on Him.

8. A Gurumukh is frank and sincere in all matters. He is liberal-minded, helps others and wishes them well. He is contented with little, and does not desire to take from others.

A manmukh is greedy. He is always ready to take things from others, but does not want to give. He always thinks of his own interest in everything and does not care for others. He goes on multiplying his desires and is not straight in his dealings.

9. A Gurumukh is not attached to worldly people. He does not crave or care for pleasures or enjoyments, nor does he long for sight-seeing and amusements. His only desire is to be at the Feet of Satguru, and he remains absorbed in that bliss.

A manmukh loves worldly people and things, desires enjoyments and pleasures, and feels happy in sight-seeing and amusements.

10. Whatever a Gurumukh does, he does to please his Satguru, and craves for grace and mercy from Him. He praises only the Satguru, wishes to see only Him honored, and has no worldly desires.

A manmukh has some self-interest or pleasure in whatever he does, for he cannot undertake anything which does not contribute to his self-interest. He wishes to be praised and honored, and the worldly desires predominate in him.

11. A Gurumukh is not antagonistic towards anyone; rather, he loves even those who are antagonistic to him. He is not proud of his family, caste, position, or the friendship of great men, and loves devoted and spiritually-minded people. He

always keeps alive his love and devotion in the Feet of the Satguru, and always wishes to gain more and more the mercy and grace of the Satguru.

A manmukh is anxious to have a big family and friends, courts rich and influential people and is proud of the friendship of such persons and of his own caste. He always wishes to do things for show and cares little for the approval of the Satguru.

12. A Gurumukh is not distressed by poverty and want, but bears with fortitude any calamity that may befall him, always trusts in the mercy of the Satguru, and is grateful to Him.

A manmukh is quickly distressed by adversity and calls aloud for help. He feels pain and grumbles if he is poor.

13. A Gurumukh leaves everything to the Divine Will, and whether it turns out well or ill, he never brings in his own ego. He does not try to prove his own point nor does he try to prove the hollowness of others. He will not permit himself to be entangled in controversial acts. Always watching the Will of the Satguru, he passes his days singing the Satguru's praises.

A manmukh asserts himself in everything; for his own delight and gain, he undertakes things involving strife and dispute. He gets angry and is even ready to quarrel to maintain his own side.

14. A Gurumukh does not run after new and novel things, for he sees that they have their root in the material world. He conceals his own virtues from the world, and does not like to be praised. From whatever he sees or hears, he selects that point which is calculated to contribute to his love and devotion for the Satguru, and goes on singing the praises of the Satguru who is the treasure of all good.

A manmukh is always anxious to see and hear novel things. He is eager to pry into the secrets of others and to know their private affairs. He wishes to add to his intelligence and cleverness by gathering points from here and there, with a view to display his great intelligence and secure praise; and is highly pleased when he is praised.

15. A Gurumukh is steady in the performance of spiritual practices; always relies upon the grace and mercy of the Satguru and has unshaken faith in His Holy Feet.

A manmukh is hasty in everything and wishes to finish things hurriedly. In his haste, over and over again he forgets his trust in the grace and mercy of the Satguru and in His words.

16. All that has been said about the conduct of a Gurumukh will be acquired solely by the grace of the Satguru. Only he to whom He is merciful will receive this gift. Those who love His Holy Feet and have faith in Him will surely receive this gift one day. Love for the Holy Feet of the Satguru is the source of all virtues. All virtues will automatically come to him who receives the gift of Love; then all the manmukh characteristics will disappear in a minute.

SAR BACHAN 2:262

13

When the Yearning is Created

Sant Ajaib Singh Ji

a talk given during a bhajan session, October 9, 1992, in Ahmedabad, India

Who can separate us from the Master? No distance can keep us away from the Master; The Master is already within us. We just need to develop the yearning for Him. As far as He is concerned He does not have any shortcomings, He does not have any dearth, He always is ready to shower His grace upon us. But all the lackings, all the shortcomings, are on our part. We do not have that much yearning. We do not have that much love for Him, we do not have that much remembrance for Him. But if we create such a yearning as is described in this bhajan, if we maintain the remembrance, if we love Him, then He is there, and He comes into the courtyard of our Heart.

We receive a lot of teachings, a lot of wisdom, from reading the writings of the perfect Masters, because whatever They had in Their hearts only that came from Their mouth. In Their writings the Masters have expressed Their love and devotion for Their Masters, and when we read those writings, we also get to know how much love and yearning They had for Their Masters.

When the yearning is created within the disciple, such a disciple always finds a way to convey his yearning to the Master in the direction where the ashram or the residence of the Master is. If the wind is blowing towards that direction, the disciple says, "O Wind, take my message to my beloved Lord, to my beloved Master." If any animal, any being, if anyone is going towards the ashram or the place where the Master lives, that dear one with a yearning for the Master always tells that person or that animal to convey his yearning, to convey his message, to his beloved Master. When the disciple gets such a condition, such yearning, for the Master, the tears start rolling down his cheeks and in his heart he has only love for his Master. The condition of such a disciple becomes such which cannot be described in words; only a person who has such yearning knows about his condition. And the Master for whom he has been yearning knows about his condition. So when the disciple has such a yearning, such a love for the Master, the Master, Who is All-knowing, Who is full of grace, He also cannot resist, He comes down, He comes into the courtyard of the disciple who has such yearning for Him.

It has been a long time since the program in Ahmedabad was announced and all of you have been looking forward to this program, preparing for it, and creating the yearning to be here, to be in this program. In fact, it is Master Kirpal, Lord Kirpal Himself, Who has created this yearning within you, Who has made this program, Who has made the desire, Who has made all the arrangements here. So now all of us should come together and take advantage of this precious opportunity which our beloved Lord has given to us. Whatever minute or second we have got we should spend that in His remembrance and, whether we are asleep or awake, we should always be remembering Him, we should always be doing His Simran. We should utilize every single moment, which He has graciously given to us, in His remembrance.

I am very happy to come here and to be able to spend time with you. I am always very happy to sit in meditation with you. Do you know Who will be happy to share the time with other dear ones, Who will be very happy to sit in the meditation with the other dear ones? Only He within whom the Master is sitting.

14
The Steps from Sach Khand
Sant Ajaib Singh Ji

This talk was given October 2, 1986, from the balcony at Sant Bani Ashram, Village 16 PS, Rajasthan. Sant Ji had been ill, and this was given as Sant Ji's illness was abating.

Many days have passed during which of you have shown a lot of patience and done your Bhajan and Simran. I have a lot of respect and appreciation for all of you in my heart. I respect this Bhajan and Simran very much. If there is anything which a perfect Saint or Master expects from His disciples, it is the gift of Bhajan and Simran. My Gurudev, Who is the owner of my soul, the Oversoul of my soul, came into this world assuming this human body; and He used to say that the heart of a satsangi should be made of iron, because iron is a very strong metal and a satsangi's heart should be as strong as iron.

In the *Anurag Sagar* [*The Ocean of Love*] you would have read the names of the three famous deities, Shiva, Brahma and Vishnu. Shiva is the one who is responsible for destruction, Vishnu is the one who is responsible for nourishing, and Brahma is the one who in the Will of God makes our bodies; according to the orders given to him he makes bodies for the people.

Out of these three famous deities, Lord Shiva was very innocent and very beautiful, even though nowadays the pictures you see of him are different, because people in different parts of the world have made pictures according to their own imagination. The pictures which the people in Bombay have made are not exactly the same as the ones which people in Rajasthan make, because people use their own imaginations to make pictures of deities. So that is why in the pictures he may look different. But in fact he was very beautiful, he was very innocent, he was very devoted to his father and he always used to do the devotion of his father.

Parvati was a princess and she wanted to marry Lord Shiva. She thought, "It is worth waiting for many births to marry a person like Lord Shiva because many people believe in him." So she did her devotion for many births. She performed the austerities only to get this boon — that she would marry Lord Shiva. Many people tried to tell her, "You are a princess and Lord Shiva eats poison and lives among ashes and he is not fit for you"; but she did not believe in them and she continued with her austerities.

You know that the habit or work of the mind is to make a person waver, even a person who has reached the top. It is the job of the mind to bring him down. Even Narada, who is often referred to as the mind of God, came to Parvati and told her, "What are you doing? You are crazy. Why are you wasting your energy waiting for Lord Shiva? Why do you want to marry him? He eats poison and he is always living in ashes! You are a princess, and it is not good for you to wait for such a person who doesn't suit you." But Parvati replied, "Even if I have to wait for millions of births, even if I have to do austerities for billions of births, I will wait, and I will marry only Lord Shiva. Otherwise I will not get married." She had such determination that she did not want to bow down in front of anyone. In the same way, a satsangi should have so much faith and determination in the words of the Master that he should not bow down to anyone. Even if the minister of God or God Himself comes to test him, still he should not bow down. He should always have faith in the Master and he should rely only on the Master.

I have often talked about the condition of my childhood. I used to have this longing within me: "May I meet a Master who has risen above the mind and the organs of senses. May I meet

Someone who has lived His life very purely like the Masters I have read about." I always had this longing, and I always used to make this prayer, that I should meet only such a Master Who had risen above the mind and the organs of senses and Who always kept His life pure. I did not want to meet anyone who had lived a dirty life and who had always indulged the mind and the organs of senses. I did not want to meet anyone's master who slept with his disciples.

So I always used to make this prayer and have this yearning. I always used to think that maybe I would be able to meet someone as the Master, and I am very grateful that my beloved Master Kirpal Singh Ji was exactly the same as I was yearning for and looking for. Even though I had met His perfect Master, Baba Sawan Singh Ji also, Who was equally pure as Master Kirpal Singh still, whatever I was looking for in my Master, my beloved Master Kirpal Singh was like that. He had risen above the mind and the organs of senses. He had lived His life very purely and He was perfect in all His natures and was exactly what I was looking for. And I am very grateful that with the grace of Baba Bishan Das and Baba Sawan Singh I was able to make myself one who would be looking for such a real Master. They made me receptive to the purity of the Master, and I am very grateful that my Master was exactly what I was looking for right from my childhood.

When we meet a perfect Master and when we become receptive to the purity of the Master, He has His own ways of giving things to us and He gives to us according to our need. The pain of separation is like an emperor. Only he can welcome the pain of separation who has become pure within and who has become receptive to the grace of the Master. If you want to welcome an emperor, you must become an emperor; because only an emperor can take care of another emperor. So unless we become as pure as the Master is, unless we become receptive to the grace of the Master, we cannot welcome, we cannot appreciate, we cannot take advantage of the pain of separation from the Master.

Once there was an initiate, a very devoted, very loving disciple of a perfect Master. He used to do his meditation and he was progressing. His Master became pleased with him and He appeared to him and said, "Today I have come to bless you with whatever you ask. So ask for whatever you want and you will be given that. Today I have come only to give you that, and I will not go back without giving it to you." That disciple who was very devoted to the Master replied, "Master, I sacrifice my head on all of those steps You have taken from Sach Khand in order to come here. I want only the pain of separation; I want only separation from You; because if You will give me this gift of separation, only then will I remember You, will I love You. And when I remember You, the love will be developed within me, and then I will be able to do more of Your devotion." So the pain of separation is like an emperor, and by utilizing the pain of separation we can gain a lot, because Masters have their own ways of giving things to the disciples. It depends upon the disciple and how he receives things from Him.

I never criticize anyone, and God forbid me from ever criticizing anyone in my life, because I am always against criticizing others. But it is a pity to see the condition of the *Acharyas* and the so-called mahatmas or masters visiting America, how they go from here and get married to some of their disciples and stay there and become the worm of lust. It is a very great pity to see the condition of such people, those who work in the garb of godmen and who are visiting people like that.

When I went to Sant Bani Ashram for the first time, there was one woman satsangi who thought that maybe I was also like those "mahatmas." While I was giving the Satsang she was thinking about me in her own way. She was thinking that maybe after the Satsang I would go to my room and turn on the television and enjoy it. There was no television in my room, but she had her own idea that I was one of those so-called godmen coming from India and I would be doing the same things they were. Next day she confessed and apologized for having those thoughts, but again she had some doubts, so she asked me whether I would get married and settle in America. I said, "It is possible, but let me first tell you about my condition. Let me first tell you this — how I see a woman's body. I see that the physical woman is just a bag of dirt, because dirt is coming out from the eyes, from the nose, from the mouth, and from all parts of the body. For me, it is not more than a bag of dirt; and so is the body of a man, because from the body of the man also dirt is coming. I do not find any attraction in looking at the body of a woman, because Baba Bishan Das told me that if you look at the body of a man or a woman, you will find that bodies are not more than bags of dirt. So that is why I do not find any attraction; I don't even like to look at the feet of a woman. So that is why there is no chance that I would get attracted to a woman and get married."

When Vashist, the teacher of Lord Rama, was giving him the teachings, he said, "Look here, Rama, God has created the bodies of both man and woman, and from the body of the woman as well as from the body of the man dirt is coming out. You should not go after the physical beauty of a woman. You should do the devotion of God, and you should always keep the goal in front of you, of what you have been sent to do, in this world. You should not get attracted or attached to this outer beauty of a woman's body."

So I am very grateful that my great Master, Baba Bishan Das, gave me this boon of seeing only dirt coming out of the body, so that I do not feel any attraction towards the body. I told her this, and when we came back from Satsang, a very dear friend of mine requested, "Master, give me that boon which Baba Bishan Das had given to you of seeing only dirt coming from the body and not getting attracted to the body." I said, "Dear One, this is not something which we ask for. This is something which we earn. If we do meditation, if we keep our lives pure, and if we obey the Master, then we do not need to ask for all these things. Master will give this boon to us by Himself because we will have made our minds so that we can see the realities within. This is not something which we request or beg. This is something which we have to earn, and we can do that only by doing meditation and keeping the mind pure and having faith in the Master."

So Dear Ones, I would like to tell all of you: keep your lives pure, don't get attached to the body, maintain faith in the Master, do your meditations, so that you may also be given the same kind of boon and you may also have the same insight of seeing only dirt coming out from the bodies, and you may become detached from the body. We are very fortunate ones that we have got this human body, and we have got the perfect Master. We do not know, before coming into this body, how many times we came into this body, how many times we got married, how many times we had husbands and wives, how many children we had. We have no idea; and we do not know how many more times we would have come if we had not gotten the perfect Master.

So we are very grateful to the Master Who has given us Initiation and Who has given us the secret which enables us to go back to our real home, Sach Khand. We need not even ask for going back to the real home; we need not ask Him to come. If we do our job, if we do our Bhajan and Simran, if we keep our minds pure and have faith in the Master, then He Himself will come to help us. He Himself will pull us up. Because if we are devoted to the Master and if we have faith in the Master, the Master works for us. It is possible that you may witness Him and when you are sick, when you need air, or are in need of anything, He will come to help you; because He is always there to help.

The emperor of purity, Kabir Sahib, has said, "The devotion of God cannot be done by unchaste, angry, or greedy persons. Only a brave one who is above all these things and who rises above caste, creed, and all outer attachments can do the devotion of God."

15

Faith, Love, Devotion & Effort

Sant Ajaib Singh Ji

a question and answer session given September 25, 1988, at Sant Bani Ashram, Village 16 PS, Rajasthan

Dear Master, I was initiated eight years ago but through my efforts I can't obtain any progress . . . My meditation doesn't light up the Path and my path doesn't light up the meditations. This is very evident and somebody criticizes me and You for this. I have suffered it alone but now I ask why? Is my temper too bad or my karma too heavy or is there some other reason? How much can You suffer for my safety? What should I expect?

Every satsangi should think about this question patiently. Maharaj Sawan Singh Ji used to say that not even the experiences of the husband and wife are alike, because they have their own karmas, different karmas to pay off. We do have the effect of our bad karmas just as we also have the effect of the good karmas on our soul. As our good karma has a good effect, the bad karma also effects us very badly and has a direct effect on our meditations. Often I have said that, "It is worse to surrender than to be defeated. You should not surrender to your mind." You should continue your struggle and when your karmas are paid off, then you will get all the experiences and then your path will brighten up and you will make progress. But you should not be disappointed. You should not surrender yourself to the mind. You should go on doing the meditation.

It has been my experience that out of hundreds of people

who get the Initiation, everyone's experience differs. There are many people, even after being given two or three different sittings, who don't get any experience at all. But the grace of the Master is equal for everyone.

For those people who did not get any experience or those who do not yet have the experience after meditating for so long, or after being on the Path for so many years, I would like to advise that they should continue doing their meditation practices with love, faith and devotion for the Master. If you will maintain your faith and devotion for the Master, sooner or later, after your karmas are paid off, you will definitely get what you are looking for.

Many times when the good souls come to get Initiation they do not need to have so much explained, they just sit there and when they get the Master's attention they confess that they have received very high experiences and thus there is no need to spend much time explaining the theory to them. They accept the attention of the Master and they do not have any difficulty in getting the experiences. Many times it happens that our mind will not let us confess our mistakes. As a result, even though we know deep in our heart the reason why we are not getting the experience, still, because of the influence of the mind, we are not able to understand. We do not believe that it is the mistake of our mind, that it is our mistake, that we have not received the experiences at the time of Initiation.

During the first world tour, at Sant Bani Ashram many people were initiated and one dear one came from South Africa to receive the Initiation. She was a good soul but she did not get any experience of Light or Sound at the time of Initiation. She was a good soul and she knew what her mistake was. She told me with love and patience that she knew why she did not get any experience at the Initiation and that she was sure with Master's grace everything would be all right. I was very impressed by her patience and by her devotion. She continued doing her meditation after the Initiation and even though she did not get any experience she continued doing her practices with love, faith and devotion for the Master. All the dear ones in her area, including her husband, were so impressed by her faith and devotion for the Master that they also were drawn to the Path. Later on they received Initiation and, because of her, now there are now many initiates over there. That dear one knew about her mistake and she gradually removed it and after a year she got the experiences and everything became all right and now she is a good, leading satsangi over there.

Another dear one, from the same area, came for the Initiation and he was given two sittings at the Initiation but he did not get any experience at all. He had done something wrong before coming for Initiation and even though he knew that he had made some mistake, his mind did not allow him to put the blame on himself, and he did not confess that it was his own fault. Instead he was putting the blame on the Master. About six or seven months later he realized his own mistake, then he wrote a letter and told me, "Now I realize why I was not having any experience at the time of Initiation. I had done this thing wrong, and I was so embarrassed to admit that in front of all the people that I did not tell you. My mind did not let me confess it at that time, but now I confess my mistake, and now you should shower grace on me." Later on he also got the experience.

So I mean to say that many times our mind is so powerful that he will not let us believe that it is our own mistake; and under the influence of mind, we lose faith in the Master. If we would continue doing the meditation with faith and love for the Master and with all our devotion, then after some time everything becomes all right.

Once Master Sawan Singh Ji went to the Dhiri area and over there many people came to hear His Satsang and they got Initiation from Him. Master Sawan Singh Ji used to say that those people were so innocent and such good souls that they all got very good experiences at the time of the Initiation and they became very devoted to the Path of the Masters.

In the same way, last year in Bangalore many people came to attend the Satsang and many people got the Initiation. Those poor people did not understand the Hindi language very clearly but they were such good souls that I did not have to give another sitting to anyone because everyone got very good, very high, experiences at the time of the first Initiation sitting.

Last time when I went to Colombia many dear souls came there for the Satsang and they attended the Satsang for many days and they understood the Satsang, they understood the Path. Afterwards when they received the Initiation they got very beautiful experiences and I did not have to give another sitting to anyone over there.

This Path of the Masters is not like government service where if you serve for many years you get a promotion; it all depends upon your faith, your love, your devotion and how much effort you put in doing your practices.

Dear Ones, this is something which needs your consideration. Many times it happens that we do our meditation wholeheartedly and we do all the things which are required of us, but we do not give up those things which we are supposed to give up, and that is why we do not get anywhere in the meditation, we do not make any progress.

Master Sawan Singh Ji used to say that if a sick person goes to the doctor, the doctor gives him some medicine. If he takes that medicine, but does not abstain from the things which the doctor told him to, then that medicine will not work for him.

Swami Ji Maharaj also says the same thing, "The disciple does not abstain from the things which he has been told to, but instead he blames the Master for not getting any progress."

As far as getting criticism of our own self and also of the Master this is because of our own ignorance; because we do not understand our responsibility to do the Path. It is the responsibility of all the dear ones, all the satsangis, to present an example for the people in their home and in their neighborhoods, so that, looking at the satsangi's way of living, people may be impressed and they may also come to the Path and improve their lives.

I will tell you an interesting story about my father. We were born in a Sikh family and it is considered that those who read the *Jap Ji Sahib* early in the morning are doing a good deed. So my father, because he was a Sikh, read the Jap Ji Sahib in the early morning. Once he met a mahatma who didn't have any knowledge of going within or the secret of the inner worlds, but he was a good mahatma and he gave my father a rosary to move. He told my father, "If you will move the rosary along with the reading of Jap Ji Sahib, then all of your difficulties will go away." So my father used to read Jap Ji Sahib in the morning along with moving the rosary. You know that in the home there are many problems and difficulties, and even if there are none, we ourselves create many difficulties and problems. My father had a habit of calling names at his servants every morning when they were working. One side he would be reading Jap Ji Sahib and moving the rosary and he would also put the feed in front of the cattle and at the same time he would be calling names at the servants and he would be rebuking everyone in the family.

Both my mother and I would ask him to tell us what he thought God would accept — "Will He accept your reading of Jap Ji Sahib, your moving the rosary, or your calling your servants names?"

So when my father went to Baba Bishan Das, Baba Bishan Das told him, "Instead of moving the rosary and reading Jap Ji Sahib and doing everything all at the same time, you should sit at one place quietly, read Jap Ji Sahib and move the rosary. Then all your difficulties will go away and the people who see you doing that may also get impressed that you are not fighting with anyone, that you are not rebuking anyone, and in that way they will see that you have improved your life.

Dear Ones, the fragrance of Naam should come out from the satsangis. *Each satsangi should always be determined to do the meditation; he should not go after getting experiences, he should only be determined to do his meditations regularly and wholeheartedly.* The Light is within you, the Sound is within you, all the stars, suns, moons and all the beautiful glimpses, all the beautiful things are within you. Your Master is also within you. He is the Form of the Shabd, He is sitting there within you and you should only be determined to do the meditation and you should not worry about getting any experience.

We complain only when we do not sit for the meditation. If we abstain from the things which our Master has told us to, and if we would sit for meditation, withdrawing our attention from the outside world, and concentrate at the Eye Center — if we do all these things — it is not difficult. Our mind has made it difficult but in fact it is not that difficult if you would only obey the commandments of the Master and do the meditation.

Should a satsangi ask for, or yearn for, the darshan of the Master?

We ask for the darshan of the Master only when our mind is quiet and when we are concentrating at the Eye Center. If we are asking for the darshan in that condition we are not the thief. In fact whenever this condition comes we should take advantage of it and we should at once sit in meditation and ask for the real darshan of the Master.

Regarding the darshan of the Master, I would like to tell you a story of the sixth Guru, Har Gobind, and His disciple. The Master is residing in us, He is present in every single cell of our body in the form of the Shabd and He is not unjust. Whenever the disciple longs for His darshan He always supplies it. He always provides the disciple with whatever he needs and whenever the disciple longs for the darshan He is always there to give it.

Bhai Rukhchand was an initiate of Guru Har Gobind; he had one brother and both of them were farmers. It was the month of April or May and it was very hot and they were harvesting wheat. In those days there were no refrigerators so there was no way of cooling the drinking water. As they were working they became thirsty, and they came to a place where the water was very cold. Bhai Rukhchand at once said, "We should not drink this water. Our Master should be the one who drinks this water because it is very cold."

They were about fifty or sixty miles from where Guru Har Gobind was doing the Satsang. Bhai Rukhchand was doing the farming, but he had the desire of taking that water to his Master. He had the desire of having the darshan of his Master, even though there was no means of traveling the distance to his Master at that time of day, but still he had this desire.

Guru Gobind Singh was sitting among the other dear ones of the sangat and He was giving Satsang. He became thirsty but He did not drink any water. Suddenly He said, "I have to go to a place where one of my disciples is very thirsty." Bhai Rukhchand was very thirsty, because it was very hot, but he had not drunk the water because he wanted his Master to drink that water. On the other side Guru Har Gobind also did not drink the water and suddenly He left the Sangat. Guru Har Gobind was a very good horse rider and at once He took His horse and He rode all the way to the place where Bhai Rukhchand had by then become unconscious from the heat.

Guru Har Gobind went there and He Himself made Bhai Rukhchand drink that water.

So now you imagine, was there any telephone there, was there any cable system there? There was no telephone, there was no outer way of communicating. It was in the heart of Bhai Rukhchand that his Master should come and drink that water and he had the pangs of separation and he wanted to have the darshan of the Master. The Masters are All-Conscious, that is why Guru Har Gobind knew what was in the heart of His disciple. He left the sangat and went at once to Bhai Rukhchand and made him drink the water; in that way He not only quenched his physical thirst but He also quenched the thirst of his soul.

Raja Ram Sahib was a very devoted dear one of Master Sawan Singh Ji and Master Kirpal Singh Ji often used to talk about him. Once he bought a piece of melon. It was very sweet and as he was about to eat it he tasted that it was very sweet and at once a thought came in his mind, "My Master Sawan

Singh should eat this melon because it is so very sweet." And right then he drove all the way from Husan (which was very far from Dera Beas) to the Dera to give that melon to Master Sawan Singh. When he reached Dera Beas, Master Sawan Singh had gone to Peshawar to give Satsang. So Raja Ram Sahib continued on to Peshawar and on the way it was very stormy, and many trees were uprooted. Still he was not stopped by any barriers; he went straight to the place where Master Sawan Singh was and he presented that melon to the Master. As soon as Master Sawan Singh saw Raja Ram bringing the melon He said, "Raja Ram, why did you take so much trouble in bringing this melon all the way from Husan? I got this melon as soon as you thought about me having it."

So you see, Who will fulfill the longing of the disciple? Only He who has created that longing in the disciple. Whenever we have the longing, whenever we have the thirst for the Master, He has inflamed that love within us and He is the only one who will extinguish that fire of love. He is the only one who will fulfill our longing because He is the one who has created that longing within us.

Guru Nanak Sahib said, "He knows everything without your asking. To whom are you praying?" He knows your every single need and He gives you whatever is appropriate and whatever is good for you.

We become disappointed after praying to our Master only when the thing which we are praying for, which we are asking for, from the Master is not feasible, is not appropriate or is not good for us. But we do not know what is good or not good for us. That is why if we pray for something from the Master and if it is not given to us, then we become disappointed and we think that Master has not heard our prayer. Master knows everything and only He knows what is good for us. Many times we think something would be a good thing for us but eventually we find that it was not good after all. Master always protects us and He knows, "This thing is not good for my disciple." That is why even though we pray for it, sometimes He does not give it to us.

He knows our every single thought and He always gives us those things which are good for us.

When we ask for the darshan of the Master He always comes to give us the darshan provided our asking is sincere and it is coming from our heart. This place where you are sitting is now full of all the conveniences. We have an orchard here, we have good roads, and we have all kinds of things here. When beloved Master Kirpal used to come here to give me His darshan, at that time there was nothing here. We did not have anything, we did not even have good roads for Him to travel, it was all sand everywhere, and it was very difficult for Him to come here physically, but still whenever He was remembered with love, He would come here to give the darshan.

I often used to say that there is no enjoyment or happiness in weeping if you do not have someone to wipe off your tears. And it is true that whenever this poor soul would remember Him, whenever this poor soul would cry in His remembrance, He would come here to give me darshan and He would wipe off those tears of the pain of separation. He would give whatever this poor soul needed at that time. This small place which you go to see, the Underground Room, was also made according to Master Kirpal's orders. Otherwise we had nothing here; but still He used to come here to quench the thirst of my soul and He used to come here to give His darshan.

I would like to tell you that Master always gives us whatever thing is being asked from Him but the thing is that we should be also doing our part. We should obey His commandments. It all depends upon our faith, love and devotion and it also depends upon how much we have devoted ourself to obeying the commandments of the Master.

Dear Ones, if you would go in the within, after doing the meditation, if you would remove all the three covers from your soul, then you would see the Real Form of the Master. Then you would understand that Master is not the body. He has assumed the body only for this world, only for this plane and He is going to leave this body here in this plane. The Real

Form of the Master is the Shabd, which will go with us. Then we realize that Master does not have to come from anywhere outside to give us the darshan, He is within us and whenever we remember Him in our within, He is there to give us the darshan.

Very often such things happen between the Master and the disciple. Many times Master helps us through some other people. The dear devoted souls at once recognize that it was the Master Himself who has worked through this person; and whatever sympathy or whatever help we have received, from this person, is in fact coming from our Master. Baba Jaimal Singh told Master Sawan Singh, "Many times the Master gives us comfort, He gives us happiness and help, through other people."

Sometimes it happens that if you are lost in the wilderness and it is dark and you do not know which way you should go, Master will appear there, not in His Real Form, but in the form of somebody else to guide you on your way. If you are remembering the Master, if your attention is toward the Master, then it is possible Master would appear there in His Real Form and show you your way. But because our attention is not there, since we are very much confused and afraid at that time, that is why He appears there, in somebody else's form, to give us the right direction and to guide us to a safe place. He does not perform any miracles, but we take it to be a miracle because we have this realization that it was the Master who helped us.

If the Master appeared in His Real Form without our remembering Him, without our paying attention to Him, then it would be considered as a miracle. Then we would make His life very difficult, because we would go on telling people how Master appeared there, and in this way we would make His life difficult. That is why He never performs such miracles. But because He has taken responsibility for us, that is why whenever we are in difficulty He appears there in some form to guide us to our destination.

Once we were driving along the canal of the River Mali near Nervankar and suddenly it started to rain, as it rained today, and it was an unexpected and very heavy rain. There were many ditches along the road where we were driving and they all filled up with water and we did not know which way to go. One of the tires of our jeep fell in a ditch and our jeep got stuck. I told the driver that I would try to lift up the side of the jeep and that he should start the engine and try to move the jeep, "And with His grace, everything will be all right, and we will continue our journey." At that time I was just initiated, I remembered my Master and told Him, "Help me, just like you saved the honor of Draupadi."

You might have heard the story of Draupadi, how Duryodhana was trying to take off all of her clothes. But she was the disciple of Lord Krishna and she remembered Lord Krishna saying, "Today my honor is at stake and it is in your hands, you have to take care of me." So at that place Duryodhana tried his best but still he could not take off her clothes, he couldn't unwind her sari, because Lord Krishna from the other side was making the sari cloth longer and longer, and in that way her honor was saved.

So I remembered my Beloved Master in that way and we were saved from the difficulty. You see that it was not my miracle; I had just recently been initiated, and I just remembered my Master, so who did that? It was the Master who was doing everything from behind the curtain. Master does many different things to protect the honor of the disciple. But the thing is that you have to remember Him. If you remember Him, surrendering yourself completely to His Feet, then He will take care of your every need.

Master Sawan Singh Ji used to say that ordinarily if our son gets sick we at once request and pray to the Master to make him all right, because we do not have any idea of how many karmas were involved in that, we only see our son suffering. We have prayed to the Master and if he does not become all right, then we lose our faith in the Master. Or suppose we are involved in some lawsuit and we pray to the Master; if we do not win that case, then we lose faith in the Master. Suppose we do not have a child and we pray to the Master, even though we do not know whether we are meant to have a child or not, or whether it is good for us or not. But if we do not get the child then our faith in the Master breaks. If with His grace we do get the child and the child cries a lot, then we request the Master to make him quiet. If that does not happen then we lose our faith in the Master.

So we go on asking for such small things, and if they are not done, then our faith in the Master breaks. Master Sawan Singh Ji used to say, "Such people who come to the Path, and who request the Master to fulfill all their small desires without knowing whether they are good or bad for them — such people should not come to the Master, they should not come to the Path, it is better for them to stay in their homes." Only those people who have the desire to do the devotion of the Lord, who are here to surrender themselves to the feet of the Master, only they should come to the Path. Only those who really understand the Path can get the benefit from the Master by surrendering themselves to the Master.

All the world dances to the tune of the mind — whether one is a warrior, a ruler or a poor person, all dance to the tune of the mind. Mind is the only thing which dances to the tune of the Shabd. Shabd is present within us and He is present within every single cell of our body and He is present everywhere in this world.

The relationship of the disciple with the Master is unbreakable, it does not end only in this lifetime, only in this world; it continues even after we leave this world. It is permanent and it always remains there until our Master takes us to our Real Home.

16

To Be Steadfast on the Path

Sant Ajaib Singh Ji

a question and answer session given March 2, 1988, at Sant Bani Ashram, Village 16 PS, Rajasthan

Would it please Sant Ji to comment on the disciple's attitude toward earthly life, in connection to true submission to God and the Master?

It is a good question. We hear in Satsang and we read in the Masters' writings that we must submit ourselves to God. When the Masters come into this world They live that exemplary kind of life in which They give full importance to meditation. They live that life to teach us that, along with doing all the worldly things, we have to obey the Master. We have to give importance to the commandments of the Master, and do the Bhajan and Simran. Since They Themselves live a life like that, They inspire us also to live the same kind of life.

Yesterday we had a Satsang on Guru Nanak's bani in which we heard how Guru Angad, along with attending to the responsibilities of His earthly life, did His job towards His Master. We heard how He pleased His Master, how He obeyed the commandments of His Master, how He surrendered to His Master and how He became as the part of the body of the Master.

Swami Ji Maharaj said, "When the dear one comes to the Master he should chase away all the religious deeds which he has been doing. Whatever Path the Master puts the disciple on, that Path should become his religion, his everything, and he should remain true to the devotion of the Master." I have often said, "Before you come to the Master, search as much as you want, read the history of the Master, see if He has done any meditation or not; but after you have taken Him as your Master, whatever the Master tells you to do you should do it. After that, it is not good for you to be wishy-washy; you should be steadfast on the Path which your Master has put you on."

Master Sawan Singh Ji served in the army, and He did many other things in this world, but He gave most importance to meditation, love of the Master, and obedience to the commandments of the Master.

What is our lacking? We do not give that place to the love of the Master which we should be giving. We are not ready to refuse the orders of the mind. We are always eager to refuse the order of the Master, because we have understood the mind as our owner.

Once there was an initiate of Kabir Sahib who after receiving Initiation from Him went on different Paths, he did many other things, but finally when he was in trouble he remembered his Master, Kabir Sahib. And when he came to Him, Kabir Sahib said, "Why did you wander here and there and give so much suffering to your soul? If you had done what I told you in the beginning, if you had given your soul the great Elixir of Naam to drink, you would not have gone through all these sufferings." Even after that — Saints are very gracious — He lovingly accepted him; He embraced him and gave him all His grace.

Master Kirpal often used to talk about the love of Laila and Majnu. He used to say that they did not have a worldly love, they had a very pure and high kind of love. When people hear stories of the lovers they are eager to go and see them, so once a prince came to see Majnu; he wanted to see the person who had become emaciated in the remembrance, in the separation, of his beloved. When the prince came, somebody told Majnu, "A prince has come to see you," Majnu replied, "Yes, I will see him, but he should come in the form of Laila." So do you think we have even that much strength? Do you think we have that much love and affection for the Master?

Usually people go to the courts to sue for the *deras* or the ashrams [when their Master leaves the body], but Param Sant Kirpal was the only great Saint Who did not fight for His Master's Ashram. He left everything there. I have seen the house that Master Kirpal had made in the dera. He did not even go there for that, because He had completely surrendered Himself to His Master and He did not care for those things. He used to say, "Whatever I have done, I have done only for my Master." Because He had completely surrendered Himself to the Master, He did not look for anything, He wanted only His Master. This is called the total submission, the total sacrifice, for the Master.

Dear Ones, we can sacrifice or surrender ourselves to the Master completely, only when we give first preference to meditation, and obedience to the commandments of the Master. If we consider the world second, only then can we become successful. Master Kirpal always used to say, "I became successful only because I gave first preference to God, and the world came next."

Dear Ones, when we understand our Master as our everything then we always give first preference to Him. Master does not want us to change our society. He does not want us to change anything of this world. Guru Nanak Sahib says, "We have met the perfect Master and, along with living happily in the family life, He is making us achieve liberation." Master does not want us to leave our families, our home, or our society. It is a fact that we may not be willing to attend to the responsibilities which we ourselves have taken on our shoulders. But the Master always inspires us to attend to the responsibilities of the world, and He always showers grace upon us. But what is the reason that love for the Master is not awakened within us? What is the reason why we have not surrendered ourselves completely to the Master? Only because we do not give the first preference to the Master and to meditation. We always give preference to the passions and things of the world. We have fallen into the swamp of lust, anger, and the other passions, and because we have given preference to them and not to meditation, to the Master, that is why our condition is like this. If we were to give first preference to the Master, if we were to completely surrender ourselves to the Master and to the Bhajan and Simran, then we would not have any difficulties.

Master Sawan Singh Ji often quoted a saying in Punjabi which meant, "Your hands to work and heart to the Beloved." How many of us have adopted or have developed this quality of remembering our Master when we are working in the world? Almost all of us bring the worldly thoughts when we sit for meditation; when we are supposed to be remembering the Master, then we are thinking about the worldly things. But how many are there who bring the Form of the Master in front of them or remember the Master when they are working in the world?

Dharam Das was an initiate of Kabir Sahib whose questions and answers you may read in the book *Anurag Sagar* [*The Ocean of Love*]. He was very wealthy. At that time in India, the currency had greater value, and he was so wealthy that he was called by the name "Wealthy" Dharam Das, because he had fourteen billion rupees. You can imagine that, since he had so much money, he must have had so many different kinds of businesses to attend to; you can imagine how many responsibilities he might have had at that time. But when he met Kabir Sahib he got Initiation from Him. After that when he went within he said, "O Master, I swear by You, that I don't have any desire except for Your Will, even in the state of dream."

You see that if one is a true disciple of the Master he will never swear by the name of the Master. He would be ready to incur any kind of loss, but he would never swear by the Master, because he understands that the Master is God. But only to express his true condition he said, "I swear by You, O Lord, that I do not have any desire of lust or any other thing. I have only desire for You even in dreams." If the beautiful Form of the Master is in front of us while we are awake and while we are doing the worldly work, do you think that we will not have the darshan of the Master when we are asleep? Only those who remember the Form of the Master during the day get the darshan of the Master while asleep. If we have any desire of the world during the day, those same desires come in the form of bad dreams. But if we have only desire for the Master during the day, and if we have only remembered Him and His beautiful Form, in the night also He will show us His beautiful darshan.

Dear Ones, the creation of this world is such that the Negative Power has spread His snares all over. Not even the Saints and Mahatmas can tell you about any place on this physical world where you can go and not get involved in the worldly affairs or where you can get the completely pure love. But it is the personal experience of the Master that if you go within, if you rise above the physical body, remove the physical veil from your soul, and then if you go to the Astral plane and remove the Astral cover from your soul, and then further if you cross the Causal plane and remove the Causal cover from your soul, then you can reach a place where the creation of love starts, where there is no difference between male and female, where there is no enmity, where there is nothing of the worldly nature, only love exists over there. When we reach there, after removing all these covers from our soul, only then do we know how to become grateful to our Master and only then can we learn how to completely surrender to the Feet of the Master.

When we reach the plane of love then we see how long we have been attending to the responsibilities of this world. Then we understand why we have to do our real work of meditation. Master Sawan Singh Ji used to tell a very beautiful story in this context. There was a person going someplace on a horse. On the way his horse became thirsty and he wanted the horse to get some water. He came to a place where a farmer was taking out water from a well, using a pump operated by a bullock. He asked the farmer to give his horse some water. The farmer told him to bring his horse near where the bullock was pumping but he was making a lot of noise. When he moved and made noise the horse became afraid and shied away and he would not drink the water. So the rider said, "Why don't you stop the bullock?" But when the farmer stopped the bullock the water stopped flowing, and when he moved, the horse would not go there to drink the water, because he was afraid of the noise. The farmer said, "The water will not come out unless the bullock moves and your horse will have to drink the water bearing this noise of the pump."

In the same way, we have to live in this world, attending to the responsibilities of the world, and we will have to do our Bhajan and Simran attending to the responsibilities of the world, no matter how difficult they may be. But we should give first preference to our real work, which is the Bhajan and Simran.

Guru Nanak Sahib says, "He may be talking with the people of the world with his mouth, but within he has manifested his beloved Lord." He says, "The life of a gurumukh or of a satsangi should be like this: outwardly he may be talking or doing the things of the world, but within he is always remembering his beloved Master."

In one of the bhajans it is written: "This is the call of Ajaib, the heart-string is moving within." What is called the moving of the string is that on your tongue the Simran of the Master should be going on. In your eyes the beautiful Form of the Master should be installed and all the time you should be remembering His beautiful Face.

Mahatmas tell us that in order to get the darshan of the Beautiful One people do so many things. They leave their homes; they go to the forest and they do so many other kinds of practices. They even make their body very thin, suffering hunger and thirst. But doing all these things they do not get the beloved Lord. Finally when they get nothing from outside they come back to their home. When they left their home in search of Almighty God they did every single practice; but by doing those practices neither their lust was decreased nor their anger was removed. They could not get rid of any of their passions. When they did not realize the Almighty Lord they came back to their home and had to face embarrassment, because when they came back without success, people laughed at them and again they had the same passions, the same difficulties. Even though they left their homes still they did not become successful. But the perfect Saints don't tell us to leave our homes; They do not tell us to become renunciates. They tell us, "Every morning get up and do your meditation for two or three hours, live a pure life, earn your livelihood by honest means, and attend to the worldly responsibilities which you have been given, lovingly and happily. And you can still get the liberation, while doing all the things of the world, if you would give first preference to meditation, and if you would surrender yourself to the Master."

I will tell you an interesting story which happened when I was in the army. Once I came home on two days leave, with me there were three or four friends also. We all had to go back on the same train — the other people also lived in the same area — and at exactly twelve noon the train would come to the station of our village. But we did not go to the station at twelve o'clock, instead we left our homes at one-thirty, and when we got there the train had already left. As a result we got back late to the army. When we got there late they told us that we will be questioned because we had not come back on the exact time. Next day we were summoned by the officer and he asked all of us, "Why were you late, why didn't you inform us? Why didn't you send a cable?" That was our first mistake and usually for the first mistake you are forgiven just by being given a little warning. So we were not very worried, but still since the officer was going to ask us questions we were very confused, and we did not know what to do. He started asking each one of us why we did not come on time. All the other four friends said that the train was delayed, but when that officer came to me I felt that I should be telling him the truth. I told him, "Dear Sir, the train did come on time but we left our home late. That is why we missed the train. Now it is up to you, whatever punishment you want to give us you can give us." So because I had told him the truth and I had surrendered to him, he became very pleased and he forgave us. At that time I learned this lesson: that if we had left our home at eleven o'clock, an hour earlier than the train, we would have got to our duty on time; then nobody would have questioned us. Nobody would be scared of any punishment, there would be no reason for us to be confused and perturbed, and there would be no reason for anyone to speak a lie. It was only because we wanted to rest one hour more at home that we had to go through all that difficult time.

Then I thought, "As we were afraid of that officer — we were confused and the other people were not even able to speak the truth — are we ever afraid of our Master like this? Do we ever take our meditation so seriously?" There are many dear ones who do not do meditation for many days, who don't remember the Simran for many months, but do they ever think that they will be questioned by the Master? And when the Master summons them, when the Master asks them the questions, what will they say? Will they be strong enough to tell Him the truth? Remembering that incident, I always think that we people always give preference to the worldly things, but we never give preference to meditation, to the Simran. We never care for the Master as much as we care for a worldly officer.

In the book which Mr. Oberoi has written [*Support for the Shaken Sangat*], the stories of Sunder Das are written. Sunder Das was a person who got many opportunities to be in the company of Master Sawan Singh and he paid off many karmas which Master Sawan Singh told him about well in advance.

We used to live in the same house; we used to eat together and meditate together. He used to say that if we remember the Simran for one moment, it means that we have gotten the Simran for twenty-one moments. And he used to say that if we have forgotten the Master for one day, that means we have forgotten the Master for twenty-one days. Similarly he used to say that if we had not had the darshan of the Master for one year, it means we have not had His darshan for twenty-one years. And we don't know if we are going to live that long or not, so how are we going to fill up that gap which is created by not having the darshan and not remembering the Master for those many days and years. He had given preference to his meditation, and we used to meditate together.

Once when we were sitting in the field meditating we were sitting around a fire. We sat continuously for eight hours and during that sitting a piece of burning wood fell on his leg. That piece of wood burned his leg but he was not aware of it burning. You know how painful it is when your body burns but he did not feel any pain; because when the soul is withdrawn, when you are enjoying the inner planes then you forget all the pains and everything like that. So he did not feel any pain. Afterwards when his meditation was completed, when he came back to physical consciousness, he said, "I have never before gotten such a taste in my meditation, as I have got today."

The doctors said that his leg was so badly burned that it needed to be amputated, but it was the grace of Supreme Father Kirpal who told him not to get his leg cut off. When Master Kirpal came to my ashram, along with the other dear ones with Him, He said, "You see, this is the devotion, this is called meditation. Is there anyone from you who does meditation like this? Is there anyone among you who forgets his body and everything and remains attached to the Feet of the Master in meditation like this?"

So you see this is what it means to attend to the responsibilities of the world while giving preference to the Master, surrendering completely to the Master. Sunder Das used to attend to all his worldly responsibilities, all his worldly obligations, but he had given the first preference to his Master, to the Bhajan and Simran, that is why he was successful in his meditations.

Dear Ones, nowadays we have tractors and other machinery to plow the fields, but at that time we had only one camel and two bullocks with which we used to plow the fields. We both used to work together; we used to plow the fields and grow the crops. The people who used to live around us would hide and try to listen to what kind of conversation we used to have. And when they heard that we only used to talk about the Master and the love of the Master they were very impressed and they wondered how we had so much love and devotion for our Master? We used to do our Simran; and we used to do our meditation without missing it; and we also used to do a wonderful job at the farming. Just he and I were there. Some people would even say, "They do not have any worries, they have no worldly things to do, that's why they are always talking about the love of the Master." Sunder Das was an old man, so people used to say, "His family has died, that is why he doesn't have any worries, and the other person —" referring to me, they used to say, "He never got married, so he has no family to take care of, that is why they are always devoted to their Master and they are doing the devotion of God."

Since I was younger than Sunder Das I would get up every morning and after taking a shower I would make tea, and then I would call Sunder Das to get up. I would say, "Sunder Das are you awake?" He would say, "Yes, I am awake; but I am lazy and don't want to get up, that is why I am pretending as if I was asleep; but I am awake." So then he would get up, drink the tea and then he would say this hymn from Tulsi Sahib's writing, "For doing the Bhajan and Simran, for doing meditation and the things of the Lord, I am always very lazy but for eating, drinking, and all sorts of worldly things, I am always awake." After saying this and drinking the tea he would start doing his work, and then he would do his meditation also. So both of us used to work very hard and we never allowed any third person to come and live with us because Sunder Das used to say, "If we will let another person live here, he will create problems and then we will not be able to do anything." So just between him and me, we used to finish all the work of the farming, and along with that we also used to do our Bhajan and Simran. At that time I had the Initiation into the Two Words and I used to do meditation on those Two Words. Sunder Das was an initiate of Baba Sawan Singh and he had the knowledge of all the Five Words and he used to do meditation of Five Words.

Right from my childhood people used to come to see me, saying that I was a Saint; and they always wanted to come and see me. Even though we were not allowing people to come to see us — but as Master used to say, "Even if the perfume seller does not want to sell his perfume, but still sometimes one of the bottles of perfume remains open which attracts the people." Sometimes people would come and they would want to see the Saints they had heard so much about, and when they would see me working in the field in my work clothes and I would be pushing a plow or something like that they would not think that I was a Saint or the person whom they had come to see. So they would say, "We want to see the Saint." And I would say, "Okay, let us sit here and wait and he will come." And then they would start talking to me and then they would realize that I was the person they had come to see. So I never wore good clothes and I never pretended I was a Mahatma, even though people used to call me a Mahatma. I always remained very humble and very simple, and I used to do all the worldly things, all the farming and all the other things, and still our Simran and Bhajan was going on with all the other things. We never missed our meditations. Many times if there was too much work to do we would stay up in the night and finish that work, but we never allowed anyone else to come there and we never missed our meditation. We did our meditations and we also did all the worldly things.

There is so much to say in this matter, but since time is running out I won't say anything more, but I would like to make a request to all the dear ones, that you should follow the schedule of meditation we have made here. Before coming here you should prepare yourself. Those dear ones who do not have the habit of meditating for long hours in their homes, when they come here and see other people meditating for many hours, they also want to follow them, that is why they do not take enough sleep. And since they have not slept enough, then when they come here to the Satsang some people are having a difficult time staying awake. So you should follow the schedule of meditation which is made for you. You should not sit for meditation right after eating food, because that affects the digestive system. And if you are feeling sleepy here in the Satsang, it is natural that you will be sleeping even during meditation. So please follow the schedule of meditation, and sleep according to the schedule, so that you will not have any difficulty getting up early in the morning.

17
The Enemy Within
Sant Ajaib Singh Ji

a talk given by Sant Ji to the sevadars of Sant Bani Ashram, Sanbornton, New Hampshire, in May 1977

Swami Ji Maharaj says, "How can I tell you all the tricks of the mind? The mind has so many ways in which he can deceive us that we cannot describe all his tricks." What does he do? He destroys the love in the satsangis, and instead of that love, he fills them from within with jealousy, with duality, and people start hating each other.

What does Maya do? Maya brings illusion within us, and Kal colors that with the color of dirt. And then we also behave like ordinary worldly people, after giving up our meditations.

What does Kal do with us? Whatever good thoughts we have had by attending the Satsang, whatever meditation we have done, whatever knowledge we have achieved through the Satsang — when the time comes, the Negative Power tries his level best and plays all his tricks to take those things away from us.

If someone has achieved a little bit of love and the Will of the Master or Saint, the Negative Power tries to take that away from him also in due course of time.

Swami Ji Maharaj says, "It is a surprising thing that when the Negative Power attacks us, we forget the forgiveness which we have received after attending the Satsangs."

How does Kal or the Negative Power affect us? We are

called satsangis and we are satsangis, and we are all brothers and sisters in Master. But Kal sits in us and makes us fight among our brothers and sisters. He creates dryness within us and tells us, "What is in meditation?" Coming into the Satsang also he disturbs us. He does not leave us even for a minute.

Once the Negative Power came to Guru Nanak and said, "You are giving grace to many people and liberating them. So give me some room in your sangat so that I can also get something from you." Guru Nanak said, "No, there is no room for you. But if you still want, you can sit in the place where the shoes of all the people are kept." That is why, when we are sitting in Satsang, after hearing the talk of the Master, we make up our mind that we will do whatever Master has told us to do. But as soon as we come to the place where the shoes are kept and we put on our shoes, the Negative Power starts affecting us, and we forget everything we have learned in Satsang.

If the satsangis are loving and respecting each other and doing their meditation, then if the Negative Power cannot do anything to the meditators, he goes to the sevadars. And sitting in the sevadars, he will pull their minds in different directions. He will tear the sevadars apart, and he will not allow them to make their seva successful. If he is not successful in using any of his tricks on us, then what does he do? He takes whatever seva we have done. Guru Nanak says, "It is easy to do seva, but it is difficult to maintain it."

How does he dwell in the sevadars? He comes and sits in the minds of the sevadars, and that's why some of them think that they are very good sevadars, that they are doing very good seva, and that nobody else is competent like them. And some people think that they are very good at organizing.

So sitting in their mind he creates this type of thing within the sevadars. Because if a few people start praising us and folding hands to us, then we do not want to stay on the ground; we start flying. We think, "We are also something."

Now when the sevadars go in different directions and start fighting with one another, Master warns us and rebukes us,

"What have you done? You should not do that." And then the satsangis realize and they repent. But they do not understand the tricks of the Negative Power.

When the sevadars start fighting with each other and becoming angry with each other, Master rebukes us and tells us, "Your work is to do seva, and you have to set an example for other people." When Master is telling us that, then our mind starts making excuses to the Master and people start arguing and explaining to the Master, "No, this is right," or "this is wrong."

This is the Law of Nature: the soul which is affected by the tricks of the Negative Power, and who starts finding faults in Master, goes back into the cycle of eighty-four lakhs births and deaths.

Swami Ji Maharaj says, "It is a pity that ten years, five years, twenty years have passed by doing Satsang, but we have never recognized our Master as the Form of God. We have never had love and respect for each other, and we have never had any effect from the Satsangs which we have been doing. We were supposed to make our minds humble by doing seva; but instead of that we have got egoism in our minds."

If you cannot do anything, at least request your Master, "O Master, we are helpless in front of Negative Power, but the Negative Power is not stronger than You. You help us, save us from the effect of the Negative Power." Do the Simran which He has given to you, take the medicine which He tells you to take, keep the abstinence which He is telling you to keep, and the disease will go away.

When we call our Master, what does Master do? He purifies the minds of the satsangis who are torn apart and are fighting with each other. When Master makes their minds pure, they start loving each other, and everything becomes as it was before. And when we do meditation, we again get the same love for each other, and we start living in love as we were doing before.

Swami Ji Maharaj says, "What is the duty of satsangis? To

live in love for each other, and to always maintain that love. This is the order for all satsangis: to love each other, to be united, and to meditate. If the satsangis are not loving each other, if they are not remaining united, if they are not meditating, that means that they are surrendering to the Negative Power."

So Swami Ji Maharaj says, "If, obeying our requests, all the satsangis could love other satsangis and meditate, they will go to the Court of Sat Purush, and there is no obstacle which will prevent them from going to His Court." So don't let your intellect come between you and God, do the devotion of Satguru, and don't keep any worries in your mind. Because now you have the Naam Initiation, and Satguru has given you the opportunity to do the seva, to meditate and earn that Naam. So do the seva, and always remember Satguru with each and every breath.

But if you have any skill with which you can do seva, don't let egoism come in your mind. When you do any seva, always understand yourself as the low one, and always understand another as the higher person. Don't expect that after doing seva, people should pay you. And you should never think about praise from people. You should never go on repeating your own praise to the people about your seva, that you have done this seva; but always keep humility in your mind. Many people have this habit, that unless they repeat their own praise, it goes on increasing in their stomach and they can't digest it.

Baba Bishan Das used to tell this story. There was a king who had two horns on his head. He had a special barber who did not tell anyone about the horns, because that was the question of his trust. But when that barber left the body, the king was very concerned. He thought, "Now another barber will not be able to digest this information; he will tell other people, and that is not good." So he called another barber, whose name was Vir Barbaru. He asked him, "Do you know why I have called you?" Vir Barbaru replied, "Yes. Because I am a very good barber and I can cut your hair beautifully; that's why you have called me." The King said, "Well, that is one thing, but there is one more reason why I have called you here." Vir Barbaru replied, "I don't know that other reason." So the King took off his cap and showed him: "You see, I have two horns; but you should not tell this to anyone. If you tell it to anyone, I will kill you, also your family, plus the person to whom you tell this secret. So beware that you don't tell this to anyone." Vir Barbaru said, "Okay, I will do that."

But that man had the habit that if he could not tell something to others he would not feel good and he could not hold anything else in his stomach. When he went back to his home, and he was not allowed to tell this thing to others, his stomach went on increasing and increasing, because that thing was still in his stomach. Eventually he became sick, because he could not tell it to anyone. Many doctors were called, but that was not a disease that a doctor could cure. Some wise people were called, and they thought that it had something to do with his mind. They asked him, "Tell us the truth. Why is this?" He said, "I have one thing; but if I tell this thing to anyone, then I will be killed, and my family will also die. But if I don't tell it, then you see my condition, and I will die in either case."

So one of the wise men told him (he was lying on a bed, he could not walk) to tell four people to take his bed into the forest and then go away from him; and, facing any tree, he could tell it whatever he had on his mind. In that way he could get rid of it, and his stomach would become all right.

So he went there and facing toward one tree he said, in a very impressive chant, "Vir Barbaru says this: The king has two horns." It so happened that later that tree was cut down, and the wood was used in making a harmonium and tabla. Then the king's wife gave birth to a son, so the king called all the musicians to celebrate. It so happened that the musicians were using the same harmonium and tabla. Before starting a program, they tuned their instruments, and when they started tuning the harmonium, the sound came — "The king has two horns!" The people were amazed and asked, "Who says this?" And when the tabla player started tuning, it said, "Vir Barbaru."

The harmonium was sounding like, "The king has two horns!" And the people would say, "Who is saying this?" And the tabla would sound like "Vir Barbaru." So then the king took off his hat and said, "It is true, I have two horns." So people like Vir Barbaru cannot hold anything in their stomachs, and this thing happened.

If we people get the opportunity from God to do the seva, we should hold everything within us, but not like Vir Barbaru, we should not let our stomach go on increasing and increasing; we should digest it.

Swami Ji Maharaj says, "Why are you proud? Who knows at what moment death will come? Whatever seva we do, only that is counted in our devotion. You see the beggar, how much people are taunting him and giving him a very hard time. But he is so humble that he never replies to that treatment. No matter what anybody says, the beggar will not give any place to that bad feeling in his mind."

Without Satguru's grace a soul cannot be successful. That's why we should always remember that it is Satguru's grace which is working and helping us in our every single work.

One other thing also comes up here — some people show love and humility from outside, but from within they are jealous and hate others. For them, purification is almost impossible.

Master Sawan Singh Ji used to say that it is not a good thing to remove one veil, and hide in another veil. It is not good to purify from outside, but from inside leave all the dirt uncleared.

That beggar has not attended any Satsangs but still he is pure. But you have attended many Satsangs, you have done many things, but still you have not given up your egoism, still you have not developed humility. Then what have you done after attending so many Satsangs?

First of all, develop humility, and keep that humility within you. And if anybody commits any mistake, others should try to forgive him, and the person who is doing the mistake should repent. If anyone is doing something wrong — talking or saying bitter words towards others — it is the work of the one who has done that to go and ask for forgiveness from the others.

Any heart in which jealousy and enmity is there, when looking at other people's seva and meditation, is very difficult to purify. That heart himself feels that pain, and it is very difficult to get rid of that pain.

Whoever has jealousy in him, he should understand that he is losing too much. If he himself cannot do anything about that, he should ask for Satguru's help, and only with the Satguru's help and grace, he can resolve that problem. But he who has this thing in his heart, he himself should give some attention to purification. And we can purify ourselves from within only with the help of Simran; Simran can do that.

If the satsangi cannot be successful by using his own efforts, he should start requesting Satguru: "I am helpless, I am powerless; please help me." He is our eternal grace; He definitely helps us.

You should not hide any faults from the Satguru, because He is All-Conscious and knows everything. Whatever faults you have, you should tell Satguru, and you should always feel the presence of the Satguru around you, and when you confess in front of Satguru, make up your mind that you will not repeat those faults again. It's not good to request from one side, and then keep repeating the same thing on the other side.

Request to Satguru in this way: "O Satguru, Swami, I am blessed in front of You, and You are Light; You help me, and You enlighten me. O Satguru, when You shower grace on me, only then I can be successful." There is no other remedy for this; without Satguru's grace no soul can become successful.

Swami Ji Maharaj says, "You don't understand that no enemy is coming from outside; mind, our enemy, is residing within us." Mind is within everyone. You should not think that only the other person has the enemy, the mind, and that you don't. Everybody has the mind, everybody has his enemy within. And that enemy is the agent of Kal, and he has the duty from Kal not to allow any soul to do Satguru's work. That's why he is holding us.

So what is the medicine for this? Do Satsang and get the earnings of the meditation of Naam, and receive the grace of Master. With the help of and grace of the Master, all our bad deeds and thoughts will go away from us, and we will become pure. But those who hide everything from their Satguru, and after going to the Satguru, even if they have many faults, still say, "I have not done any mistake, and I am doing so much meditation —" for such people, what can be done?

Such a person never understands that Master is looking at his every thought, his every action. He always takes the Master as an ordinary human being, and that is why he goes on committing mistakes, under the impression that nobody is there to see them.

Swami Ji Maharaj says that those who understand Master as an ordinary human being and do not understand Him as God, and those who always think that Master is not looking at their bad deeds, for them there is no remedy. They have that kind of disease that is incurable.

Truly speaking, such people are not able to attend Satsang. And those who have the perfect Master, and after attending their Satsang, if they understand the reality of the Master, and if they obey the commandments of the Master, and copy the example or the life of the Masters — then one day they will also become pure, and will also be able to get rid of all the evils which they have within them at present.

Satsang is very pure water, and one who bathes in this water will get rid of all the filth he has within him. That's why Master Kirpal always used to say, "Give up a hundred urgent works to attend Satsang." Guru Nanak says, "Without Satsang, whatever effort we are doing is like taking the pure water from one side and putting in dirt from the other." Swami Ji Maharaj says, "We cannot praise Satsang; there is no other means to purify our mind except Satsang. God says, 'No one can attain me through japa, tapa or any other practice; He can realize me only with the help of Satsang.' " There is no other way for the liberation of the soul. You cannot be liberated if you will not attend Satsang. Swami Ji Maharaj says, "In the Kali Yuga there are only three means for liberation: Satsang, Naam and the perfect Master. Those who have the perfect Master, and those who are meditating on Naam, and those who have made their Satsang, they should understand that now they are redeemed." But if we are doing any japa, tapa, or any other practice, instead of making our minds small and thin, we make our minds stronger; because after doing all those things, we become full of ego.

It is true that in the previous yugas or ages, the japas, tapas, and austerities were the worship of the time, and the Rishis and Munis performed them. But we cannot do them because now we don't live long enough; if we somehow manage to do a little bit of them, then we cannot get the real truth. The scriptures say the austerities and the worship of the Rishis and Munis were meant for the Golden Age, and in this Iron Age, if we practice them, they won't work for us because we have less life and less health.

That's why, in this Age, Saints came and They discovered Satsang and set up Satsang for the benefit of the souls.

18

Go Ahead and Do It

Baba Sawan Singh Ji

a letter to an American disciple

I assure you that I do not mean to neglect any of our American Satsangis. I think I answered your last letter. It may have gone astray. But in any case, you should write to me every few months and give full account of your progress and ask any questions you may wish to ask. I shall be glad to hear of your inner progress on the Path. No doubt you are making some headway, and I am anxious to see you go inside truly, and find the Great Light and Joy which awaits you there.

There is nothing equal to this Way, and it gives more real joy and satisfaction than all else in the world. But to get that you have to go inside. It cannot be realized outside. All the world is seeking it in books, holy places, and association with people, but it has to be found inside. That is gained by steadfast meditation and holding your attention in the Eye Focus, without wavering. When you learn to do this, the Treasure, which is yours already, will come into conscious possession and you will realize more than you can dream of. Let nothing stop or hinder you. Let no earthly obstacles stand in your way of going inside. Set your mind steadfastly upon that and make all else subordinate to that, and other things will melt away and leave you free.

I am well aware that you have struggles. You have some things within yourself to overcome and some things outside of yourself which must be surmounted. But you can do it. If you have full confidence in the inner Master, He will always help you. Often when you find the difficulties greatest and the hour darkest, the light will appear and you will see that you are free. Let nothing discourage you. This is no light proposition, but your getting Naam means more than if you had inherited a million dollars, or many millions. You are one of the luckiest sons of Sat Purush, and He has chosen you to get Naam and go with the Master to Sach Khand. You must reach there. Nothing can prevent you. But you can hasten the progress or retard it, as you like.

Do your utmost now to remove all difficulties within and without yourself, and then sit as many hours as you possibly can. Hold your attention fixed at the focus, not allowing the mind to run away or to waver in the least. If the mind runs away, bring it back instantly and hold it at the focus. By and by, if your attention is steadfast, you will see a blue sky and the stars and suns and moon, and then you will see the great Jot, the thousand-petaled lotus and the Master's Radiant Form. You must see these things. Look steadily for them and permit no doubt or question to enter your mind. It is certain.

When you have entered the first region, you will get the full benefit of the Sound Current. It will come to you clear and sweet, and its music will fill you with joy, and that of itself will enable you to overcome all your remaining difficulties and weaknesses. That is the one thing that makes you strong against all foes and makes your victory absolutely certain. With the melodious sounds ringing in your ears, your success is absolutely certain.

You must reach the Supreme Goal in due time. Some reach it sooner, others later, according to their own individual efforts and the karma they have to overcome. But you should not have a long battle. You have already overcome much, and the Inner Master is always within, to receive and welcome you. When you meet Him inside and talk to Him face to face, as man to man, He will always be ready to answer all your questions and to guide you along the Path. He is there now, but you cannot see Him until you remove the intervening curtains. But you can easily do that. Go ahead and do it. Great will be your reward.

19

Live in Love and Harmony

Sant Ajaib Singh Ji

This is the farewell Satsang given in South Africa, September 7, 1994.

First of all, I thank Beloved Lords Sawan and Kirpal, who united us, the separated ones. He brought us from far and near, and He connected us with His Sound, with His Sound within, and He brought us together. So first of all I am grateful to Him for doing this.

Only because of His grace, only because of His permission, only because of His orders, and only because He has told me to do this, I came into this world. Often I have said that I do not have any mission of my own. The mission is His. I come here only to give His message to the souls.

You know that it is not an easy task to take the message of the Master from home to home, from door to door. You have to suffer a great deal in doing this work. You have to bear hunger and thirst. You have to take so much upon your body. It is not a very easy thing to do. But that Almighty One, that omnipotent Master, is very powerful, very strong. Whatever He wants His disciples to do, He can make them do that. Master used to say that if the Master wants, He can even make a wooden stick work for Him.

His message is to give up hundreds of important works to go to Satsang, and to give up thousands of important works to sit for meditation. He used to say that we should not feed our body until we have fed our soul with meditation. You know that we need to feed our body, because we are aware that if we do not feed our body it will become weak and we won't be able to do the things of the world. That is why we understand it is very important and very necessary to feed our body, and we always feed our body with good kinds of food. But we have never paid any attention to the issue of feeding our soul. In fact, our soul needs even more food than our body does, because our soul has been hungry for birth after birth. We do not know for how many births our soul has not gotten any food of meditation to eat, and that is why she has become very weak, very feeble. It is only because of the weakness of our soul that she is not able to stand in front of the mind. You know how the mind is bothering us, and he has made our soul like a servant. Whatever he wants us to do, we do. It is only because we have not made our soul strong. That is why our condition is like this.

The reason why we easily get anxious and nervous is the weakness of our soul. So just as we need food for our body, we need the food for our soul even more than that.

Why is it necessary for us to go to Satsang? Last night in the Satsang I said also that when our mind sees that his freedom is going to end, he cannot bear that. He cannot give up his tendency of remaining free. So he does not like to go to Satsang, that is why he creates all sorts of obstacles to keep us away from the Satsang.

But if we somehow keep ourselves in the Satsang, then we start to enjoy the Satsang. In the beginning, just as it is difficult for us to go to and enjoy Satsang, once we start getting the enjoyment, the pleasure, from attending Satsang then it becomes very difficult for us to give up going to Satsang.

There are only two people who can tell us about the weaknesses which our mind has created within us. Either the Masters can tell us about the weaknesses which we have, or the one who opposes us can tell us. Our opponent, or our enemy, will say that we have this fault or we have this weakness within us.

We should not mind the words of the Master, and also we should not mind if our enemy or our opponent tells us about our weakness. We should not go into detail about who has told Master this, or who has told that person about this. Instead of getting into that kind of argument, we should look within ourselves and we should remove that weakness, we should remove that lacking, because we have to look within our own selves and we have to become free from that lacking or that weakness.

The difference between the enemies telling us about our weakness and the Master telling us about our weakness is that our enemy, our opponent, will tell us to our face, "You have this fault in you," whereas the Master will tell us stories and parables to make us understand that we have this lacking within us.

This is why the Masters always praise Their opponents, Their critics, and They even pray for their long life. They always become grateful to Their critic for telling Them about the weaknesses or the lackings. Even though the Masters do not have any weakness or any lacking in Them, God Almighty has created the critics or the opponents of the Masters only to remove the dirt which They have accumulated. Paltu Sahib says, "How could the Saints get liberation if the critics had not worked very hard in purifying Them by criticizing Them?"

Many Satsangis misunderstand this statement, and they just say, "Well, it is okay that the other person is criticizing us." Dear one, the criticism is that you don't have that particular fault in you and [still] you are criticized for that. If you do have that fault, that weakness or lacking within you, then it is better for you to give up that fault, once you know that you have it.

Kabir Sahib says that if your heart is pure, and still you are criticized, you should be grateful that the critic is washing your dirt. Sufi Saint Farid Sahib has said that in the domain of Negative Power where even the innocents are punished, how will those who are committing the sins be forgiven? He gives the example of a bell. In the ancient times they used to ring bells, in a way it was like beating the bell, so using that example He says that in the domain of the Negative Power where even the innocent ones are getting a beating, what will happen to us who are always committing sins?

If we practice the things we hear about in the Satsang, only then is our attending the Satsang useful. If we meditate — as Master has said, "we should give up thousands of works to meditate" — if we meditate, only then is our attending the Satsang useful.

Master Kirpal showered so much grace upon us, and He gave us this diary form. Even though all the Masters have in Their own ways told us to keep the account of our deeds, but Lord Kirpal showered so much grace upon us and gave us this diary form, in which we can write down all that we do and all that we think, and where we stand. The diary is like a daybook in which we can write down every day what our thoughts were, how much work we have done, where we stand, and what our faults are. So Master showered so much grace upon us, and He gave us this form to keep so that we may know where we are.

I get so many dear ones' diaries in which I see that they go on repeating the same faults, the same mistakes, again and again. Often in Satsang I say, "Dear ones, once you have made a mistake, why should you make that mistake again?" Because once *you realize* that it was a mistake, and when you yourself have confessed it, when you yourself have written down in the diary that it was a mistake which you have made, then why do it again? Just one mistake in your life can ruin your entire life. So when you know that you have made that mistake, why go on doing it again and again? Why go on committing the same sins again and again?

Just as in the evening before we go to bed we fill up the diary about our activities during the day, in the same way in the army also, before you go to bed, you are supposed to mark the attendance and write down what you did during the day.

We are very fortunate ones that through the diary He has given us this opportunity through which we can improve our life. So we should keep the diary, we should fill out the diary, according to the different sections which are there, and we should fill that out sincerely.

If you keep the diary even for one week with the feeling for which the diary has been given to us, I am sure that you will be able to divert your attention from the pleasures of the senses, and you will be able to go within. If a Satsangi is able to go within even once, if he is able to make his soul drink the Inner Nectar, he will never want to drink the useless water of the pleasures of the sense organs. So if you keep the diary sincerely, even for one week, understanding the idea why we have to keep the diary, I am sure that you can improve a lot.

Saints and Mahatmas are not social reformers, nor are They here to improve our financial condition, etc. Their job, which They have from God Almighty, is to come into this world and collect the separated souls and connect those souls with the Light and Sound of God.

I have not told you anything from hearsay. I only talk about those things which I have done in my own life. I met with my Master, I met with God Almighty; I got hold of my Master, I got hold of God.

So He has showered so much grace upon us. He knows what is going on within us, He knows about our yearning. So if we will sit in His remembrance, if we will sit with yearning for Him, then He will also make every possible effort to pull us up. This is a kind of competition which goes on within us between the disciple and the Master. The disciple who does the Simran and remembers the Master with all his yearning thinks that he is remembering the Master and he has all this yearning. But when he does that, when he goes within, then he realizes that it was the Master Who was yearning for him, remembering him and pulling him towards Him.

Bikha Sahib has said, "O Bikha, no one is hungry. No one is empty. Everyone has the precious ruby within him. But they do not know how to untie the knot. That is why they are living like a pauper."

Kabir Sahib says that sitting in His window, God Almighty is looking at us, and according to our devotion and service, He is giving us the rewards.

The other thing the Master teaches us is humility. In the same way, I saw Master Kirpal Singh, and He also was so humble that I cannot describe His humility in words. The Masters bring a lot of humility, and They express that to us.

We satsangis must adopt this quality of being humble. This is the highest quality and we must adopt this quality. You know that if you are standing on a lower place, all the water will come to you. In the same way, if you are humble and lowly in your own self, you get everything.

Regarding humility sometimes I have told this story which Baba Bishan Das often told. It is about a Master and His disciple. Once a Master and His disciple were both going somewhere, and the disciple requested the Master to give him some good piece of advice or teaching which would be very pleasing to him, and which would bring some peace to the disciple. The Master said, "Dear one, don't become anything."

Now the disciple was expecting that the Master would tell him a very long story or give him many teachings, but the Master kept quiet after saying, "Dear one, don't become anything."

On the way they came to a garden of the king, where the king used to come once in a while to rest. The disciple saw a very nice bed there which was scented with different kinds of flowers and perfumes. It looked very comfortable, so he just went there. He thought, "Well I should rest a little bit here before continuing our journey." So he fell asleep on that bed. Meanwhile the Master was not tempted by those comforts; He just went to one side and sat somewhere on the ground in meditation.

After some time the guards came there, and when they saw a fellow sleeping there, they woke him up, and they asked him what he was doing there and who he was. So he said, "I am a sadhu." Hearing that the guards started beating him, and they said, "You call yourself a sadhu, and still you are sleeping on this comfortable bed?" So they gave him a thorough beating.

When he got that beating, he ran to his Master and told Him, "Master, they gave me a beating." So the Master said, "Well, you must have done something wrong." He said, "No, Master, I didn't do anything." Master said, "Well then, what happened? Why did they beat you?" He replied, "Master, they asked me who I was and I said, 'I am a sadhu.' And they started beating me."

So the Master said, "Yes, dear one, you became a sadhu. That is why you got the beating. I told you that you should not become anything. Because you said that you were a sadhu, that is why you got all this beating." The Master knew that one becomes a sadhu only after rising above the physical, astral, and causal bodies, and reaching Par Brahm.

And this disciple of His had not yet learned how to remain still at the Eye Center, but still he had the pride of being a sadhu because he was with the Master. So that is why he got the beating. So dear ones, in the same way, if God Almighty has showered grace upon us, and if in meditation He gives us a little ray of Light, if He gives us anything inside, we should not be puffed up with this pride that we have become something. Even if He showers so much grace upon us, still we should always remain humble, we should never become anything, because we invite all the troubles only when we say that we are this or we are that.

Usually what do we do? When our Master showers grace upon us, we start allowing people to bow down at our feet, we let them touch our feet, we go on giving them blessings. And either we announce it in the newspapers that we have become something, or we somehow make it known to people that we have got the grace of the Master. We even climb on elephants and go around the city, and in this way we go on collecting the praise and glory of the world. We even give blessings to people; those who do not have children, they come and ask us to shower grace and we say, "Okay, God did not write in your destiny that you should have children, but we are giving you this." By doing all this we may be doing some good to the people, but we are not left with anything. Kabir Sahib says, "Only one who is always very humble, and who always speaks humble words, realizes God Almighty, because God Almighty always resides in the heart which is very humble."

As you all know, this program is now finished. The organizers worked hard and made very good arrangements, and I am very pleased with all of them. I hope you will follow and do all that I have told you in the Satsangs. We all are souls, we are brothers and sisters, and we should always love and respect each other. We should keep attending the Satsangs and should always do the meditation. Since we are the children of the same Shabd Master, we all should have love and harmony. We should all live in love and harmony.

PART II

Seclusion: Spending Time in the Company of a Saint

The fortunate one gets the company of Saints.
The meditation on Naam is the service of Saints.

GURU ARJAN DEV

Only those with very good fortune have the company of Saints and Masters. And when we go in Their company, and when we start serving them, They will tell us to do meditation on Shabd Naam. And when we start meditating on Shabd Naam, by Their grace we start taking advantage of being in Their company.

SANT JI

20

The Value of Seclusion

Sant Ajaib Singh Ji

a question & answer talk given on January 31, 1988, at Sant Bani Ashram, Village 16 PS, Rajasthan, India

In the instructions for the India groups it is emphasized that we should remain in seclusion as much as possible while we are here. Could You please comment on the importance of refraining from conversation while we are here for these ten days?

Before we are going to do something we start thinking about it and making preparations for it; and we *should* do that if we want to achieve success in that work. The first time I said things regarding coming to India, I said that before coming here everyone should plan their trip here, and in that preparation, you should start sitting in meditation, so that as you are preparing yourself for the trip by doing the meditation, your attention will always remain here and when you come here you do not have to struggle so hard to sit for meditation. If you have developed the habit of sitting for longer hours in meditation at your home, then when you come here, you can progress more in the direction of doing constant Simran, and you will not have to struggle very hard to meditate here. As far as keeping quiet or secluded is concerned, that also plays a very important part in achieving success in the trip here.

Master Kirpal Ji emphasized a lot about remaining in seclusion; Master Sawan Singh Ji also said a lot regarding remaining in seclusion. All the Saints have emphasized this a lot, because we cannot gain, we cannot achieve God Almighty by talking.

The more we talk, the more we become extroverted.

In the beginning it seems very difficult for us to remain in seclusion and refrain from talking because we have the taste of the worldly talks and we are habituated to talk about worldly things. That is why it is very difficult for us to have control over our thoughts and over our tongue. But if we start keeping quiet and remaining in seclusion, controlling our conversation, then it becomes our habit, it becomes our nature. After that, in our heart we always find seclusion, we always find peace. Whether we are standing, sitting, walking, or doing anything, we will develop a habit such that either we will think about God or we will remember Him; then we do not enjoy the talking of the world.

When the dear ones are planning their trip here, first of all they work hard and save the money to buy the tickets and pay the other expenses, because I have always told people that they should not borrow money to come here. They should work hard, save the money, and they should come using their own money. At that time they think about the Master and all their attention is directed toward the Master. When I welcome the dear ones I tell them, "You should always remain involved in the work for which you have come here; you should always remember the purpose for which you have come here." You know that it is not easy to come here; there are so many attachments binding you to your families and the world. You people come here, leaving all those things behind, and if you do not do the work for which you have travelled so far, then what is the use of your coming here? If you spend your time in talking then what was the use of your coming so far? You could have easily talked and done all those things back at your home. So you should always remember that you have come here for some definite purpose. You have come here to get the advantage of the Presence of the Master. You have come to do Bhajan and Simran and remain in seclusion.

All the dear ones who come here should understand the importance of remaining in seclusion and keeping quiet, so that they may gain the benefit of the presence of the Master. Those dear ones who obey the instructions of the Master, who remain in seclusion, and do their Bhajan and Simran, tell me about their progress and beautiful experiences. Do not think that those who keep quiet, or those who do the Bhajan and Simran do not get anything. They get a lot of benefit, a lot of grace, and they report that in their interviews.

Master Sawan Singh Ji used to lay a lot of emphasis on this matter. He used to say that when you are attending the Satsang of the Master, your attention should be so concentrated on the Form of the Master that you are not even aware of the party sitting next to you. Even when the Master is talking to someone during the Satsang, you should not be paying any attention to the person to whom the Master is talking. Your attention should be fixed at the forehead of the Master; you should be fully absorbed in having the darshan of the Master. Since in the Satsang and the meditation your heart is filled up with the grace of the Master if, after the Satsang or the meditation, you start talking with or making contacts with other people, what will happen? All the Spirituality and grace, with which your heart is filled, will start going out and instead of the Spirituality, all the worldly things will come back into your heart. That is why Master Sawan Singh always used to say that after attending the Satsang or doing the meditation you should not talk with anyone; you should remain in meditation.

All the Saints have emphasized about remaining in seclusion, but They have not told us that we should leave the world and go into the jungles and the forests. They have said, "No, you do not need to go into the forest, you do not need to leave your family. You have to live in this world, but along with living in the world with your families, still you have to maintain the seclusion."

We can make our home itself a jungle. When I got Initiation from Baba Bishan Das, when I was doing the meditation on the first Two Words, as you all know, I did the meditation of those Two Words for eighteen years. And the ashram where I was sitting and doing the meditation also had the same kind of boundary wall as we have here. I remained in seclusion for all those years; no one was allowed to come and see me and not everyone was allowed even to come into the ashram. There was a person sitting at the gate and he would not allow anyone in and I would not go out of my room to meet the people. I would come out only for necessary or very important things, otherwise I would remain inside and do the meditation. Here at this ashram there are many dear ones who know about my seclusion and about the way I did the meditation at that time, and even now living in this ashram, I remain in seclusion. Sometimes for weeks together I do not come out and I don't see the dear ones who are living in the ashram itself. I come out and meet only those people who come from far away, those who have come for a spiritual purpose. Otherwise I always remain in seclusion; I don't go out and see people.

It is not that I am not attending to my responsibilities towards the ashram. I am attending my responsibilities towards the ashram and also, since I am a farmer, I help Gurmel with the farming, and even in the smallest details of the farming work I help and guide him.

It is good that Judith has been instructing the dear ones concerning the trips to India, if we will understand and obey these instructions it is for our own good.

I said that in the beginning it seems difficult because we are habituated to talk in the outer world, that is why it is difficult for us to do this, but later on, when we develop the habit of remaining introverted and remaining in seclusion, then it becomes very easy for us and then our condition becomes like this — our hands are at work but our heart is towards our Beloved.

Guru Nanak Sahib said, "Those who develop this habit, they talk with the people of the world outwardly, but within them, they are always connected with God Almighty."

21

The Importance of Ashrams

Sant Ajaib Singh Ji

a walk talk given on February 26, 1980, at Sant Ji's former ashram at Village 77 RB, Rajasthan, India

Sant Ji, could you say something about the importance of ashrams?

When we are living with our families sometimes it is very difficult for us to do the devotion of God. In the world it is very difficult to stop worrying about our problems and meditate on Naam. That is why ashrams are made; they are made for the purpose of meditation. The meditation which we cannot do while living with our family we can easily do when we go to the ashram for that purpose. When we are living with our families we have to think about many things and we have to face many problems; while doing all those things it is difficult for us to spare much time for meditation. But if we go to the ashram, for the purpose of meditating, after a certain period of time we can gain a lot of benefit from that.

And those who are living in the ashram are the most fortunate ones, because not only are they meditating, but they are also helping others who come to the ashram to meditate. They understand their responsibility of doing more meditation there and moreover they take care of the dear ones who come to the ashram for the benefit of their souls. The people who live in the ashrams get the opportunity of serving other people and that is a helping factor also. They are more fortunate than the people who visit the ashram. So the ashram is very important, if you understand that meditation is very important for your soul. In the same way, in order to do more meditation it is very important for us to go to the ashram.

Many times those who have Satsang in their homes postpone it because of laziness, and many times they even postpone their meditations. But when they go to the ashram to meditate or to attend Satsang, they cannot do that. Two or three days before the scheduled time they start thinking about going to the ashram on that certain day for meditation and Satsang. And whether they have to drive for seven hours, or an hour and a half, during the time they spend travelling to the ashram they always remember where and for what purpose they are going; all that time is also counted in the remembrance of the Master. So going to the ashram brings many benefits for the Satsangis.

As the melon changes it's color in the company of the other melons, in the same way, when we sit in the ashram in the company of other people who are meditating, our mind also gets the inspiration to meditate. At our homes we do not get inspired to meditate and we become lazy. But when we come to the ashram and we see that other people are meditating, we also feel like sitting down to meditate. At the ashram we spend a couple of days doing meditation, whereas in our homes we cannot even spend a couple of hours in meditation.

Moreover, if there is any ashram and people are visiting the ashram, many people get the opportunity to do physical seva, many people get the opportunity to do the mental seva — that is doing the Simran — and many people get the opportunity to help the ashram with money. Many people get the opportunity to do the seva which they can do by doing meditation.

Master Sawan Singh had made a very big Satsang hall and He used to say, "Those who have contributed in making this hall, whether physically, mentally, or financially, no matter if they have left this world, but still they will get the benefit of the service in making this hall, because they will get a share of the meditation of the people who will be using the hall for it."

Saints do not make the ashrams for Their own benefit nor do

They make the ashrams for Their children or Their relatives; They make the ashrams for the benefit of the sangat. They do not accept any money from the sangat for Their own use; whatever donations They get They spend for making the ashram for the sangat. For Their own needs either They do farming, or work somewhere, or have a shop or something like that. They earn Their own livelihood and moreover from Their own income They contribute also to the making of the ashram.

Whenever we go to any ashram we should spend the maximum time in doing more Bhajan and Simran, and we should always remain in the discipline when we go to the ashram. Remaining in the discipline means that we should spend maximum time in meditation and not waste our time in gossiping and just talking about useless things. We should have respect for the ashram in our heart, and we should do more meditation there so that only the fragrance of meditation will come out from that place. And we should always maintain the purity of the ashram.

This is a fact that the Saints are never attached to any of the ashrams because They are attached only with God or They are attached to the sangat whom They have initiated. They always look forward to the day when the initiates will understand Their message and will go back to their Real Home.

There is not even one moment when the Masters are not thinking about the benefit of Their disciples. They are always waiting for the disciples to come back to Them and They are always waiting for the disciples to obey Their commandments. As a mother is always thinking about the welfare of her children — she is always worrying about her child and she is always taking care that her child does not put his hand in the dirt or put his hand in the fire. If the child gets into any trouble and it cries for help, or even if he doesn't cry for help, but when the mother sees that the child is in trouble she leaves off all the works she is doing and at once she goes and helps her child.

In the same way Master's attention towards the disciple is

constant. He is always watching what the disciple is doing. If the disciple creates any problem for himself, and if the disciple cries for help, Master goes there, and from behind the veil, He always helps the disciple. The disciple may not be aware that he is getting help from the Master but Master always helps him.

Saints are not interested in running big *langars* (free kitchens), and They are not even interested in making big buildings. They do that only because They want to utilize the money of the dear ones in the right place for the right purpose. Master Sawan Singh Ji used to say, "In the langars of the Master the rich people donate from their earnings which is distributed among the poor and rich equally, and in that way the earnings of the rich people become successful if used at the right place."

Swami Ji Maharaj also said, "Master is not hungry for your wealth, but He is using it for your benefit. He is feeding the hungry and thirsty with your money, and in that way He is utilizing your money in the right place. When you are giving money to Him which He gives to the poor and needy people, you are gaining His pleasure without paying anything, and when He is pleased Sat Purush is pleased."

Kabir Sahib says, "Those who move the rosary, and those who give the donations, without the guidance of the Master, all their efforts are useless, because only the Master knows what practice will bring the benefit for the dear ones." They know which is the right place where Their disciples should donate their money, that is why only when the money is donated under the guidance of the Master does it bring good fruit to us.

My personal experience is that many people wanted to give money to Master but only the fortunate ones were allowed to do that. Many other people who had money and wanted to give it to the Master were not allowed.

Master Sawan Singh Ji used to tell one very beautiful story about a mahatma who would only eat food at the house of a person who was earning his livelihood righteously and honestly. Once he went to a village and asked, "Who is the person in this village who earns his living honestly and who feeds the mahatmas?" They told him that there was one trader in that village who was a very righteous man. He earned his livelihood honestly and was always interested in serving the dear ones of God.

The mahatma asked how much property and how many children the trader had. He was told, "He has four sons and about a hundred thousand rupees."

When the mahatma went there, the trader welcomed him with very much respect and honor, and the mahatma told him, "I want to eat food in your home."

The trader replied, "Yes, have a seat and wait, I will tell my family to make the food for you."

While the food was being prepared the mahatma asked the trader, "How many children do you have?" and "How much wealth have you collected?"

The trader replied, "I have only one son, and I have collected only fifty thousand rupees."

The mahatma got very upset and he started to leave that place without eating any food. So the trader asked him what was the reason why he was not sitting and waiting for the food, and why was he so upset?

The mahatma replied, "I have heard that you have collected a hundred thousand rupees and you have four sons, but here you are lying, so it shows that you are not an honest man; I do not want to eat in your home." That trader said, "Well Mahatma Ji, sit down, let me explain to you. Whatever you have heard is correct: I do have four sons. But only one of them is helping me in the Path of Spirituality, so I call only that son as my own. The other three sons who are not helping me in Spirituality, in realizing God, how can I count on them? How can I say that they are my very own when they are not practicing the Path that I am practicing?

"About the money: no doubt I have a hundred thousand rupees, but I have kept fifty thousand rupees separate. I have spent fifty thousand rupees in the Path of Spirituality; I have given that money for the needy people. I used that for the cause of the Master and I am sure that I will get the benefit of that money. I don't know what will happen to the balance, the other fifty thousand rupees. Where will I spend that money? I don't know whether that will be given to lawyers or doctors, so how can I say that money is my own? Only that money which I have spent in the cause of the Master is my own, because I will get the benefit of it." When that trader gave such an explanation, the mahatma was satisfied and he ate the food.

So only the money or materials we spend or use in the Path of the Master can be called as our very own. Who knows what will happen to the money which we have not spent in the cause of the Master? It may be spent in settling our lawsuits; who knows what will happen to it? But whatever we have spent in the cause of Master, we will definitely get the benefit of it.

Suthra Shah, one fearless Fakir, has said, "We should serve the Master with our hands, and we will get the benefit of only that service. We should donate with our own hands, and only that donation will bring benefit to us. Who knows whether money we leave in this world will give us any benefit or not? Who knows where that money will be spent?" So whatever we do with our own hands, whether it is service to the Master, or if it is donations, we get the benefit only of that.

Master Sawan Singh Ji used to say, "After donating we should not feel proud of it." He used to say, "We should be very grateful to God that He has given us the opportunity to help other people." Further He used to say, "We should donate in such a way that if we are using our right hand in donating, not even our left hand should know that we have done so."

Guru Nanak Sahib also said, "Those who visit the places of pilgrimage, who keep fasts, and give donations and who, after doing all those things, become proud of it — all the benefit which they have gained by doing those virtuous deeds will become useless, just as the bathing of an elephant is useless."

In India it is very expensive to get a daughter married, that is why, when a baby girl is born in a family, the people are not very pleased. It becomes a problem for them to find a groom and they have to spend a lot of money in getting her married. That is why, in India, if anyone helps in getting a daughter married that is considered as a very high and virtuous deed.

When I was in the army and I would go to see Baba Bishan Das, He used all the money which I was paid from the army in getting people's daughters married. He used to tell me, "You should not remember whose daughter has been married using your money." Whatever money He used to take from me He never kept that for His own expenses, for His own purposes, instead He always used that money in getting other people's daughters married.

22

What is a Holy Place?

Sant Ajaib Singh Ji

two meditation talks from Bombay, January 1991

It is the morning, the ambrosial hour, and we have just awakened, and our soul has just newly entered the body. The meditation done at this time is very successful. All Rishis, Munis and all the Masters have always said that the meditation done at this time is very beneficial. Because we have just awakened, it becomes easier for us to bring our consciousness together at the Eye Center, to withdraw from all the outer things and bring it to the Eye Center at this time. Master used to say, suppose there is a piece of silken cloth thrown over a thorny bush — if you remove it using all your force it is possible that it may tear. But if you do it slowly and gradually then you can take that piece of silk out of the thorny bush without tearing it apart. In the same way, our soul, ever since she was separated from God Almighty, is spread not only into every single cell of our body but beyond our body outside in the world, in our relatives and everywhere. If we try to withdraw our soul from all these outer things and from every single cell of our body using all our force, and if we try to do it all at once, naturally we will have pain. The best way to withdraw our attention or our consciousness from all the outer things and bring it to the Eye Center is with the Simran.

Last night I said, "No doubt there are other ways to concentrate and bring your attention to the Eye Center, but Simran is the best." Simran is the only method doing which you can bring your attention to the Eye Center, and it is the only practice which everyone can do. Even a small child can do this, and an old person can also do it. Anyone, it doesn't matter what age he is, every worldly person, every householder, can do this.

So withdrawing our attention from all the outer things, we should sit in the meditation and we should do the Simran as we have been instructed by the Master.

January 10, 1991

When you are making efforts in doing the devotion of God Almighty, when you are sitting for doing the meditation, when you have come here for that purpose only, it pleases me very much. That is why I am always very happy, I am always very delighted, to sit among you and do the devotion and sing the praises of God.

The place where we do the Satsangs and the place where we sit in the meditation becomes very holy. What is a holy place? Only that place where we do the remembrance of God, where we remember our Master, is the holy place. So we should consider this place where we are having the Satsangs or where we sit in the meditation as a holy place. And in this holy place you should not do anything which is not holy. I mean to say that you should not do any worldly thing here, you should not think of the worldly things, you should not discuss any worldly problems and things like that. You have left your home and everything behind, so when you have come here you should not involve your worldly things here; neither you should talk about your home and other things with the other people nor should you listen to other people. Here you should only be doing the Bhajan and Simran and the remembrance of the Master whether you are standing or sitting, walking or doing anything — you should always be doing the Simran, so that the cleanliness and the holiness of this place can be maintained.

January 10, 1991

23

On Satsang and Darshan

Baba Sawan Singh Ji

reprinted from the May 1984, Sant Bani*, and first published in* Sari Duniya *magazine*

You will find the gate of salvation by attending Satsangs of the Saints. No one will get comfort without Satsang. You will find this recorded in the Vedas.

Satsang is a very great wealth, but we do not value it. Even if one word of Satsang be imbibed, it will transform the whole life of an individual, what to speak of a whole discourse.

A thief, while dying, called his only son and gave him a twofold piece of advice: (1) Do not go to any temple to hear the sermon; (2) If you are caught while stealing, do not confess even if you are hanged.

Once the young man was coming back from breaking into a home, when he saw a policeman coming. There was an alley nearby, so he ran there to save his life. There he found a temple where a sermon was being given. Immediately he recollected the advice of his father and put his fingers in his ears so as not to hear any word. While doing this he heard one sentence: *The angels, gods and goddesses do not have shadows.*

At another time the young man was caught as a suspect. He was presented before a king who asked him if he had committed theft. He answered, "No sir, I did not steal." The man was then beaten, but still he would not confess. He was then put into a prison house.

One woman in the king's police force was very clever and

told the king that she would cause the man to confess. The king agreed to her plan and gave her the assignment. That night she disguised herself as a goddess.

She got two artificial arms fixed and held two burning torches in her hands. She walked with an artificial lion and made a terrible commotion. The doors of the jail where flung open, and in the darkness the light of her candles shone brilliantly. When the poor thief saw that the goddess Durga was standing in front of him, he leaped up and prostrated himself at her feet. The self-made goddess gave him her blessings and said, "Behold, son! I am Durga goddess. I have come to remove your misery. Please tell the truth, if you have committed a theft. If you tell the truth, I will help you to be released."

The thief was ready to confess, but when he saw the shadow of the fake goddess, he remembered the utterances at the temple that gods and goddesses do not have shadows. He understood immediately that it was all deception. The thief said, "Mother! I did not commit theft, and the king is punishing me unnecessarily."

The next day the clever woman told the king that the young man was not the culprit. The king ordered the man to be set free. The thief was pleased at this. He considered how wonderful it was that by hearing only one sentence from Satsang, he was released from prison — "If I could hear all the words of Satsang, it would surely transform my life." Thus, he started attending Satsangs. The result was that he left the profession of a thief and became a Mahatma.

(Great Master Baba Sawan Singh Ji gives here some specific, practical advice concerning conduct at the Satsang.)

Do not sit ahead of the entire audience. Do not talk unless the Great Master asks you to do so. Before the arrival of the Master, sit at such a place which won't cause you to move in order to have the Master's darshan clearly. When taking a seat, whether the Great Master is on the stage or not, please be amiable before the audience — consider that all initiates are brothers and sisters and that you are their servant. Do not be contemptuous toward a poor man.

Secrets Not Revealed Before:

Remember the Satguru so much so that at every breath a pang of separation from Him troubles the heart. This condition will only come when you drive away all other thoughts.

When you meet the Great Master, as a result of good fortune, then have Master's darshan as if you were a man tormented by acute hunger, or like an infant who yearns for the protective mother, the only source of nourishment; if anyone interferes between him and his mother, he cries painfully and falls into desperation —

Like a rainbird who drinks only the water of the rain,
when finally the skies burst into showers —
Like a fish separated from water, when it goes back
to the soothing water —

Like this, one should get elated on seeing the Satguru, so much so that on having darshan, the devotee should forget the consciousness of his body and have no thought or consideration of rain, sunshine, or shadow.

Look minutely into the middle of Master's two luminous eyes, riveting your attention. Don't blink your eyes, as far as possible. Hear the recitation and utterances of the Great Master with your ears and have darshan with your eyes.

The gaze should be so confined that you see only the holy face of the Satguru and do not see the face of anyone else. Silently, imbibe the utterances of the Satguru. Do not pay any attention to any noise, such as knocking at the door or what anyone else says. If individuals come in and say hello, shake hands or say good morning or evening to the Great Master, don't pay attention to them. If you do it means disrespect to the Master. It is a great loss for one to leave the Master's precious darshan and look toward others. Be so much absorbed that your attention doesn't divert toward the person who might interrupt.

Do not laugh in the Satsang. Even if the Master laughs, you need not do it.

Value of Darshan:

If my Satguru, Great Master Baba Jaimal Singh, would come and give me darshan even for a minute, I would gladly give away everything I have.

At the time of distribution of parshad, generally there is noise and disturbance. This is a great mistake. You need not pay attention to parshad, as to whether you get any or not. Do not leave the most precious darshan of the Satguru to lose yourself in the thought of parshad. Parshad may be taken, but do not sacrifice the darshan.

Do not get bored when listening to the discourse. It is a sin to do so. When the Master gets up from the Satsang, having finished His discourse, consider yourselves as unfortunate that this most valuable time went out of your hands.

Duties of a Satsangi after the Satsang:

After hearing the discourse, one should not speak with anyone. Put emphasis on Simran. Escape from the company of those talking and socializing. Rest assured that the Satguru has filled the pipe of our heart with His darshan. If you start talking with anyone, the heart will keep on emptying of the darshan. It is the duty of a Satsangi not to squander the boon given by the Satguru. He is, rather, to increase Master's gift. It will increase if a devotee engages in Simran for three to six hours after Satsang. Also, he should recall the utterances made by the Satguru in the Satsang. He should ask himself what shortcomings he has. From that day on, he should try to eliminate those faults. If those faults are not overcome, then he should pray before the Great Master, "O True Emperor, I am feeble and a sinner. Please forgive me." When the disciple will devote more time to Bhajan and Simran, the attributes of the Satguru will start coming into the devotee, and his shortcomings will begin to depart. This is the benefit of hearing the Satsang.

Therefore, a satsangi should try to follow and act upon the

commandments, after listening to the Satsang of a perfect Master. He should leave off lust, anger, criticism, back-biting and bad company. One should eat morsels gained only from hard-earned and honest money. A satsangi will not progress spiritually until he earns his living by the sweat of his brow.

If a satsangi is a guest of someone and is served food, he has to compensate the same by giving the merit of three hours of meditation. Otherwise the mirror of his heart will not be clear. Unless and until the mirror of his heart is clear, he cannot love the Satguru.

Devotion and Deep Faith:

Love and faith are the foundations of Spirituality. A house cannot be built without a foundation. Similarly, if a person devotes twenty hours daily in meditation and has no love and faith, he cannot progress spiritually even a little bit. Of course, the ego comes up that one is an aspirant on the spiritual path. Just like a bullock at an oil press who keeps on going all day long, but remains at the same place (walking in a circle) — such is the situation of the person who has not yet developed love.

It is seen generally that any work done with enthusiasm is accomplished quickly and well. The student who studies wholeheartedly gets smart in his studies. It is a principle that the teacher who teaches the students with love gets better results from his students. On the other hand, if a teacher is full of anger, then the students do not get benefit from his efforts.

Therefore, it is necessary that a Satguru be love personified and the satsangis meditate with love and devotion. When the Satguru is love personified and the satsangis love Him, they will also love to follow the Master's commandments. This way the benefit is gained very soon. One cannot bring the mind into concentration unless one has developed love and devotion for the Satguru. Unless the scattered mind gathers together, one cannot enjoy the Simran.

Without love the Simran seems to be a burden. If you do

Simran now and will forget it after a little while, you will remain forgetful for several hours. The sign of complete Simran is that the soul will gradually start leaving the body. After crossing the stars, moon and sun, it will reach the luminous form of the Satguru. To reach this point is the job of Simran. Before that, consider that the course of Simran is not yet accomplished.

24
What We Should Ask of the Master

Sant Ajaib Singh Ji

a question and answer session given January 28, 1990, at Sant Bani Ashram, Rajasthan, India

Would Sant Ji comment on which things the disciples should request from the physical form of the Master? What is the appropriate and respectful way to use the precious contact we have with His outer form, and which things are in the Will of God for the outer Master to do for the disciples? . . . and what should we do for ourselves by relying upon His constant presence within us in His Shabd Form and how can we develop and use our own discrimination and receptivity to find the answers by ourselves rather than constantly putting all our worldly questions and problems on the physical form of the Master. [question shortened for clarity]

The question is very good and it can be very helpful to many dear ones, but whenever you put a question you should try to make it brief, because the dear ones understand the answers to the brief questions in a much better way.

Most of the things which the dear one has asked in this question are answered in the Satsangs, but we people do not pay any attention to the Satsangs. It is not that everybody does not pay attention; there are some people who pay a lot of attention to the Satsang. But most of these things are always mentioned in the Satsangs: what our faults are and what we should ask from the Master and what we should not ask from the Master. These things are mentioned many times in the Satsangs.

Often I advise the dear ones that they should subscribe to *Sant Bani Magazine*. You get it once a month and you people spend a lot of money on buying the magazine, so when you get that magazine you should read it thoroughly, because most of such questions are answered in the magazine. Many Satsangs are published, and many question and answer sessions are also published. So if you would read the magazine thoroughly, you can get the answer to most of your questions.

Now I would like to explain the answer to this question to you. In order to understand the answer to this question we will have to go very deep, and we should understand this. A part of this question was asked by Baba Sawan Singh to Baba Jaimal Singh.

Master has given us the greatest gift of Naam and He always encourages us outwardly through His outer form to meditate on the Naam. He encourages us not just by talking to us, but He Himself sits in meditation, and presenting a living example to us, He encourages us to meditate. Also in His Satsangs, in His discourses, whenever He talks to us, He tells us that we have to protect ourselves from lust, anger, greed, attachment and egoism, those five dacoits who are plundering our meditations, who are plundering our souls, and who have made us spiritually bankrupt. He tells us all these things and He tells us how we have to keep our life pure, and He tells us many other things outwardly through His outer form, through His physical form — those things which we should do in order to progress in meditation.

Swami Ji Maharaj also said that the Master has two Forms: one is the outer, another is the inner. And what did He say to His Master? He said, "O my Master! You show me Your Real Form. Even though I love this outer form also, but You show me Your Inner Form also."

Master Sawan Singh and Master Kirpal Singh were the greatest of those souls who came into this world, but still, how much love They had for Their Master, and how hard They worked in order to give us the demonstration. And we know what They asked from Their Master, what questions They asked from Their Master. So thinking and remembering what They did, we need to understand a lot.

Most of the dear ones, whenever they get to see the Inner Form of the Master, they misunderstand it and they think it is a dream which they have had of the Master. But often I have said, "Dear Ones, the vision of the Master which you get is not a dream" — because we get the dreams only when our soul drops down from the Eye Center and goes into the lower organs of the body, and then, according to the thoughts of the past day, we have the dreams. But the Master is very pure and holy: He never goes below the Eye Center into the lower organs of the body, because what is there in the organs of the body? It is only filled with dirt, and the Master never goes there. What happens at that time when we have a vision of the Master, which we often misunderstand as a dream of the Master? Whenever our mind is quiet and peaceful, then Master graciously lifts our soul up through His gracious and loving sight, with the hook of His Love, and in that way He takes us into the higher planes and He blesses us with His Inner Form. But we people think that it was just like any other dream, and so we do not take advantage of it. Often you will find a lot of happiness and peace after you have had such a vision of the Master. Some dear souls who get such grace from the Master, do not misunderstand it, and for many days they often remember that Form of the Master which they have seen inside, and in that way, taking advantage of that remembrance of that Form of the Master, they progress in meditation.

Once, regarding the Inner Form of the Master, Baba Sawan Singh Ji asked Baba Jaimal Singh, "Master, sometimes Master appears within and says 'yes' to something, He answers that question, but that does not happen outwardly. Master does not shower His grace like that. What is the reason?" So Baba Jaimal Singh said, "Often it happens, when the disciple is meditating and the Master appears, that the disciple in all his excitement does not think about what he is asking from the Master, and whatever he asks, Master says, "Okay, that will be granted," or "You will have this." But when the Master sees that this will be bad for his spiritual progress, then the Master does not give what He promised to him within.

The dear ones who go within and connect themselves with the Almighty Lord every day know the Reality. They have seen the Reality and that is why the worldly things are of no use to them. So they do not present any worldly questions; they do not ask anything from the Master, because they are in constant connection with the Master within every day. But those dear ones who occasionally go within, or if Master graciously pulls them up some time, then they ask so many worldly things of the Master, and when the answers which the Master has told them do not happen outwardly, then they become confused. So the best thing would be that the dear ones would go within every day, so that if there was any confusion the next day they could clarify that with the Master. If the things do not happen according to what the Master has said, then they themselves can go within and clarify with the Master the next day.

Dear Ones, the jivas are very ignorant. They are more ignorant than a five-year old child. You know that a five-year-old child is very ignorant. He does not know that it is not good for him to put his hand in the fire. But the parents are very wise, and they know that if he puts his hand in the fire he will get burned. So that is why they always keep him away from the fire, and whenever he tries to put his hand in the fire they tell him, "No, it is not good for you," and they always stop him from doing that. But the child gets upset, because he does not know why the parents are telling him not to do that. Similarly, suppose the child has a cold, he is coughing. The parents will not give him anything which will increase his cough. But he wants to eat the sour pickle, which will increase his cough. The parents say "No, you should not eat this." He does not understand that it is only for his health that his parents are not giving him the pickle. He does not understand, and he gets upset, and throws himself on the ground, etc. But the parents are wise, and they do not give him the pickle.

The same is our condition. We people do not know. We are very ignorant ones, and we do not know what is good and what is bad for us. We see all the outer things in this physical world, all the material things in this world, and we always desire those things. We do not know what things are good and what are not good for us. Therefore, when we ask for all those things from the Master, He has to use His discrimination, and He has to decide which things will be good for us. And when we do not get the things which we desire, then we get upset. But our Master is like that wise parent who knows what is good and what is not good for us. He does not give us anything which will be harmful to us.

We do not know what the Master wants to give to us, and we do not know what He has for us. He wishes that while we are living we should go within and go back to our Real Home. He wants us to sit on that Throne which belongs to our Almighty Lord. He wants us to go back to our Real Home, but we people do not understand, and that is why we do not take any advantage of the Forms of the Master, and instead of asking for the inner grace, we always go on asking outer things from the Form of the Master.

Many times I have told this story in Satsang, and I will repeat it again. It is the story about a wood cutter. Once there was a king who had gone into the forest for hunting. He lost his way and he became very thirsty. A woodcutter was cutting wood in that forest. He had some water with him. So the king, who was very thirsty, came there looking for water, and the woodcutter gave him some water to drink. You know how much a thirsty man appreciates it when he is given water, because he thinks that the one who has given him the water has saved his life. So the king was very pleased with that woodcutter, and he said, "I am a king, and since you have saved my life,

I will give you something very valuable. I will give you a sandalwood garden, so that you may live your life very comfortably."

Now that woodcutter did not have any appreciation for sandalwood; he did not know how valuable sandalwood is. He thought that sandalwood was like any other wood. So he began cutting down all the sandalwood trees. He would burn it and make it into charcoal and then sell it in the market; and in that way he continued earning his living as he had been doing before.

After some time the king needed some sandalwood, so he thought of sending his people to that woodcutter, thinking that he might have a lot of sandalwood and he might be living his life very comfortably, because sandalwood was very expensive. But when his people went there, they were surprised to see that there was not a single sandalwood tree left. Everything had been turned into charcoal. So they asked him if he had any piece of sandalwood. He said, "No, I don't have anything. You can see that I have cut down the whole garden of sandalwood trees, and I have made it into charcoal and sold it. I don't have anything."

But they wanted some piece of sandalwood, so they asked, "Isn't there anything left?" He said, "Well, there is this small piece, which I have made into the handle of my axe." So they bought that small piece of sandalwood from him, and in return they gave him a lot of money. When he realized that the small piece of sandalwood was worth that much, he felt terrible; and then he realized that he had not appreciated the sandalwood which he had been given. He had not even appreciated the fragrance of the sandalwood, but had cut down all the sandalwood trees. And he felt so depressed and sad about what he had done, he left his body right there, in that state of depression.

This is just a story. In reality, what is the sandalwood which God Almighty has given to us? Master has given us the greatest gift of Naam, which is the sandalwood garden, but we people do not appreciate the fragrance of the sandalwood. What is the fragrance of the sandalwood? The presence of the Living Master is the fragrance of the sandalwood which inspires us to go within and see that reality which God Almighty has placed within us. But we people do not appreciate the fragrance. We people do not appreciate the gift of God, the Naam which God Almighty has given to us. And so we go on wasting the gift of Naam, we go on wasting this precious birth which God Almighty has given us, in doing all the worldly things. We always go on indulging in the worldly things, and in the end what happens? Like that woodcutter, we leave this body, we leave this world, without gaining anything.

But the Master Who has given us Initiation is not careless. He always looks after our soul, even if He leaves the physical body and goes back to His Real Home, Sach Khand. He always thinks about our welfare, our betterment, and He always tries to think of one way or another through which He can help us. So in many ways He again encourages us. He inspires us to meditate on Naam, and somehow He makes us meditate on the Naam. Afterwards, when we leave the body and our Master takes us up and makes us sit on that throne which is in Sach Khand, and when He rewards us for that little bit of meditation which we may have done, then we come to realize that if the meditation was so valuable, why didn't we do it with our every single breath. Then our condition becomes like that of the woodcutter. We feel depressed and disappointed, and we regret that we didn't take advantage of the precious time which God Almighty had given to us, and we didn't meditate.

But the Master Who has given us Initiation is never careless. Whatever meditation we do, He always rewards us for that. But if we had appreciated Him earlier, we would have spent all our time doing the meditation and going within, and we would not have wasted any time asking Him the outer questions.

What should we ask from the outer form of the Master, and what are the things about which we should rely on the outer form of the Master? It is true that God Almighty has given us this faculty of discrimination, and there are many things which we have to decide ourselves, and the Masters also tell us to use our discrimination and make decisions ourselves. But the ways of the Master are very unique. You know that through the Satsangs, They touch upon almost all the things which happen in our life, and They answer almost all the questions. Many times They go into very deep detail in answering our worldly questions, and also, since the Masters do not interfere in our worldly lives, They leave many things for us to determine, and many decisions for us to make.

Dear Ones, the mission of any perfect Master is not dependent on any Vedas or Shastras, or upon any holy Scriptures. The mission of the perfect Saints is dependent only upon the Naam — upon God Almighty and upon the Master Who has given Them this work of giving the Naam Initiation.

Even then, the Masters quote from the writings of the past Mahatmas, past Masters, only to make us understand that They are not telling us anything new — so that we may not feel that the Masters are saying anything different from what the other Masters have said. They tell us, "We are not saying anything new to you; all these things have been said previously by the past Masters."

Often I have said that Master Sawan Singh Ji used to tell the dear ones in the sangat that those who go to the Masters expecting the Master to cure them of their illness, or to help them win some lawsuit, or sort out the problems in their home — those who go to the Master expecting all these worldly things — they should not bother going to the Satsang, because what can such people gain from Sant Mat?

Many people who used to go within in the time of Baba Sawan Singh know very well how many years earlier Master Sawan Singh had to leave this world only because He was burdened with all the problems of the dear ones. Similarly those who used to go within also know how many years earlier Master Kirpal Singh left the body and how much He had to suffer physically. He also had to undergo an operation and many other difficulties, and He also left earlier. We people do not understand this, and still we go on burdening the physical form of the Master with all our problems and outer things.

This does not mean that if we are not opening up our heart in front of the Master, if we are not telling Him about our pains and problems, He will not help us. It is not like that. If we are doing our Bhajan and Simran, whatever amount is feasible, He helps us in that way, and wherever we need the help of the Master, He extends all feasible help to us.

If a bad person goes to prison because of doing something bad, and if he continues to be a bad person and also creates troubles in the prison, then what would the authorities there do? They would make his imprisonment even stronger, they would put him in a stronger room; and also, he would be looked upon as a troublemaker, and it is possible that his sentence might be increased. But another person who is not a bad person but somehow had to go to prison because something went wrong, if he lives according to the rules and regulations of the prison and does not create any problems there, then the authorities have mercy upon him and they may reduce the sentence which he has to suffer there.

Is the One in Whose remembrance we are sitting not looking at us? Whenever we are sitting in His remembrance, He is always looking at us. But we people, because we are involved in our ego, that is why whenever anything good happens we say that we have done it, and whenever anything goes badly we always blame it on the Master. But the Master Who is sitting within us, in Whose remembrance we are sitting, knows everything about us and He is constantly watching us.

Guru Nanak Sahib says, "Even without your asking, He knows everything about you. To whom are you making the prayers?"

Regarding those who go within, Guru Nanak Sahib says that such people say, "O Lord, to ask anything from You except You is like asking for more sufferings. Kindly give us Naam, which would give us more contentment, so that the hunger of our mind would go away."

In his *Vars*, Bhai Gurdas has written that even the tree under which the Master sits becomes so pleased and so blessed that it gets liberation from that body of a tree. And even if a ghost has the darshan of the Master in his astral form, he becomes free from that body. And even the stones get liberation. What is difficult for one who goes into the refuge of the Master to get liberation? But only if we have faith, if we have constant faith and love for the Master, can we get liberation.

The jiva does not know whether the worldly things which he is asking from the Master are good for him or bad for him. The Saints come into this world to liberate us. We are the ones who are involved in the worldly things, and They have come into the world to liberate us. If we are asking Them for worldly things again, then?

Guru Nanak Sahib asked only for Naam from His Master. He said, "O Master, give me the Naam, which will give me contentment, so that the hunger of my mind may go away." He said, "O Lord, if You want to give me anything, give me Naam."

You know that Master Kirpal had the gift of being all-conscious right from His childhood, but He never used that. And when He went to His Master, what did He ask from Him? He said, "Master, give me only respectful love for You." Because He knew that Baba Sawan Singh was a great Power, He was God, and He knew what to ask from God, what to ask from the perfect Master. That is why He asked only for respectful love for the Master. Those who go in the higher planes and have seen the glory of the Master within, they are the only ones who have real love and appreciation for the Master, and only they know what they should ask from the Master.

Master Kirpal Singh Ji used to say that at Master Sawan Singh's end time when people were making all the prayers, at that time Master Sawan Singh said, "If you want to give me more opportunity to do the seva, if you want me to remain here and do more seva for you, then kindly do not write me letters with worldly problems. If you want, you can write me letters about Bhajan and Simran, about meditation, but do not burden me with all your worldly problems, because you have already burdened me a lot. Now you know that I have become old, so before putting any more burden on me, at least you should consider that I have become older."

Hazrat Bahu said that the heart of the lover of God is as soft as wax, and the hearts of the worldly lovers are black. He said, "You know that whenever we ask for anything from the Master, whenever we tell Him about our pains and problems, His heart is like wax and it melts easily and He is affected." Master Kirpal Singh Ji used to say that most of the things that we ask of the Master are those things which, if we got them, we could never progress on the Spiritual Path. All the worldly things which we ask from the Master will not help us, in fact they will become obstacles on our Spiritual Path, that is why Master does not give them to us. Master does only those things which He should be doing.

Master Kirpal Singh Ji used to say that if the perfect Masters went on granting the wishes and desires of the disciples, even if They came millions of times into this world and even if They gave millions of human births to the disciples, still They could not take them inside. They could not take the disciples back to the Real Home because the desires and wishes of the disciples would never stop. So that is why He always grants only that wish of the disciple which is helpful for his spiritual growth. But most of the things that we ask of the worldly nature are such which will not help us but will create an obstacle in our Spiritual Path.

Master used to say that at the time of Initiation, the perfect Masters make an arrangement within the disciples so that on one side they go on paying off the karmas which they have to pay, and on the other side they also go on progressing spiritually.

We should take advantage of the precious time which we get with the Master in the interviews. Not everybody is like that. There are many dear ones who understand the value of that precious time; they do not waste it in asking the worldly questions. But most of the dear ones, when they come in the interview, they always talk about their worldly things.

Master Sawan Singh was very strict. He said, "I will not answer any questions, any letter, which has worldly problems in it. I will only answer questions regarding Bhajan and Simran." Master Kirpal Singh Ji also did the same thing, and I also made this request in front of all the dear ones in the sangat, that they should write me questions only about Bhajan and Simran. If they will ask me anything of the worldly nature, I will not answer their letters.

If you want to write letters to the Master, it should be only about spiritual matters. You should not write any worldly problems in it; you should only ask about Bhajan and Simran and the spiritual matters. In the same way, if you are coming for an interview, you should take advantage of that precious time. It will be beneficial for you if you will not ask any worldly things in your interview.

Saints do not interfere in the worldly lives of Their disciples, and They do not impose any of Their ideas on Their disciples as far as worldly matters go. They have left the disciple free. Whatever they want, they can do it. But They do tell us that if you do the Bhajan and Simran your soul will get strength, and whatever you have to face according to the karmas of the past, if you are doing Bhajan and Simran your soul will get strength, and you will get the strength to bear the consequences, to suffer the consequences of what you have done in the past. And They always tell us that we should try to avoid creating more karmas, and whatever we have to pay off from the past, we should do it happily.

Well, if I want I could go on talking on this subject for many days and still it would not be enough. Since the time is up I hope that whatever little I have said you will understand this and you will live up to it.

If the Satsangis would do their Bhajan and Simran, the mind would not create any questions in them. What happens? Our mind creates questions because we do not do the meditation and we want our Master to answer those questions.

Are we doing the devotion of the mind? Or are we doing the devotion of the Master? Why not do the meditation so that we may become free from all these thoughts, these questions, and fantasies created by the mind which are bothering us.

Dear Ones, we have made our mind our owner, our everything, and instead of obeying the commandments of the Master, we ask our Master to obey us.

Master gives us the great gift of Naam, and He has taken our responsibility on His shoulders. He takes us to our Real Home and makes us speak in front of Almighty Lord, and whatever mistakes we have made in the past, He forgives us for that, and He always takes care of our soul. There is no doubt about this fact. Even now, many people who were initiated by Master say how the Masters came and took care of their souls. Even after going back to Sach Khand, His Real Home, our beloved Master is still looking after our soul and He is always protecting us.

25

Shot By the Bullet of Love

Sant Ajaib Singh Ji

from a talk given, November 2, 1983, Rajasthan

Could Master talk about when we come and spend these ten days with Him? Could He talk about the effect on our souls? I've heard that it . . . [is] like when you're initiated and He takes away all your sins.

This is a matter of great understanding. Kabir Sahib has said, "One moment of Lord Indra is worth more than twelve years of sitting by a well; in the same way one moment spent in the company of the living Master is worth more than doing Simran for fifty years sitting in your home." If a well supplies water for twelve years it cannot give as much water as Lord Indra, the Lord of Rain, can do in one moment. In the same way, the benefit which we get by just one moment's company of the living Master is more than the benefit we would get of doing Simran sitting in our homes for fifty years.

Further Kabir Sahib has said, "When you go to see a Sadhu, don't take anyone along with you. Don't worry about what is going to happen next, and don't worry about anything which has happened in the past." Once you have started going towards the Master, towards the Saint, you should go on doing it.

At another place Kabir Sahib has said we should not give up the company of the Saint and we should try to follow His Path, because, as soon as He looks at us, He makes us pure and, when we spend time in His company, He makes us meditate on Naam.

Those who have been benefited by the company of the living

Master, what do they say? Kabir Sahib says, "Whatever I have achieved is not because of my reading, writing, or doing outer practices. I have achieved all these things because of the Satsang, because of the company of the living Master." Kabir Sahib had a lot of knowledge. He knew all the four Vedas, but still He says, "I did not achieve all that I have accomplished by reading or writing. Everything which I have achieved is because of the Satsang."

One moment, even half a moment, or even half of a half moment, whatever time you spend in the company of the Sadhu, Kabir says that it will cut millions of your sins.

Guru Nanak Sahib says that living without the company of the Sadhu is useless.

We pay off a lot of our karmas, a lot of our sins, just by having the darshan of the Sadhu. When we sit in front of Him, whatever He speaks from His mouth, whatever sweet words He speaks are good for us; they are like advice. We come to know about the benefit of all these things only when we go back to the Real Home. But then we repent and say, "If we had known that the company of the living Master was so valuable, we would have done it always."

Master Sawan Singh Ji used to say that God is not unjust. If we spend money in a bad cause or if we spend time in a bad cause it is counted as our bad karma, bad deed. In the same way if we have spent money for a good cause or time in a good cause, it will be counted as our good deed.

I say this to every dear one: You have got this opportunity of making this holy trip because of a lot of grace of Almighty God and you should never forget this holy trip; because in this holy trip you come to see a person who has real sympathy for you.

Yesterday also I talked about the company of the living Master, about the Satsang, the company of good people, and today also I said a lot about spending time in the company of the Living Master. As we need food, and as the Naam is the food and water of our life, in the same way the Satsang also serves as the water of our life. If we do not spend time in the

Satsang, if we do not have Satsang in our life, we cannot get the inspiration to do the meditation and we can never do the meditation of Shabd Naam. Satsang is like the fence to protect our meditation. If we do not go to the Satsang, if we do not spend time in the company of the Living Master, we can never know whether we are doing right or wrong.

Guru Nanak Sahib says, "Brother, listen to me. I will sing the praise and the qualities of the company of the Sadhu. By going in the company of the Sadhu you become free from all kinds of dirt and become pure."

Once in Sant Bani Ashram I commented on Kabir Sahib's hymn in which He started from one minute without the company of the Master and went on increasing up to one year, and then finally He said that if one does not have the darshan of the Master at least once a year the connection between him and the Master is cut off. Guru Nanak Sahib has said, "I do not get satisfied even after seeing the body of my Master always. The body where Almighty Lord is manifested, the glory of it cannot be described in any words." Guru Nanak Sahib says, "He by seeing whom we get liberated, how can one sing His praise?"

So I always say that you should never forget this holy trip. You should always go on praying to Almighty Lord, to the Master, that He may give you another opportunity to come here.

Those who get the interest from having the darshan of the Master, they cannot be stopped by anyone. Master Sawan Singh used to say that those who are shot by the bullet of love, they do not remain useful for their homes, for their families. They throw away all the account books and they will not deal with any business.

The entire talk is printed in the January, 1984, Sant Bani Magazine.

26

You Have Made a Long Journey

Sant Ajaib Singh Ji

a talk given September 24, 1978, at Village 77 RB, Rajasthan, India

As you can see it is very hot. From the letters of the dear ones who have come here, we know that in America, they have the problem of snow. The records of many years were broken. In the same way, here also the records are broken. But not of snow; here it is sand and heat.

But we are grateful to Almighty Hazur Kirpal, Who has showered His grace both in snow and in sand. And none of His dear ones had any serious problems with the snow or the sand. And still He is showering His grace in this heat.

The cold and heat which we experience on this physical plane is much easier to bear than the cold and heat which the soul feels when she goes into the womb after death. As Master Kirpal used to say, "That cold and heat is unbearable, because in that cold and heat our bones — our bodies — come into existence, and that is unbearable." In this physical plane, we can find some means of removing cold or we can have a fan to remove the heat. But we cannot do anything in the womb.

So we are very grateful that on this physical plane we are not having that cold and heat. In the womb of the mother, when the bone comes into existence, the soul is heated for ninety days. So for ninety days continuously it has to experience that heat and the soul is helpless there. If there is any support there, it is only the support of Naam. So if we take refuge in that Naam in the physical plane, then we won't have to go in the womb of the mother again, and suffer that heat and cold.

Saints know the power and strength of that Naam. They always emphasize to meditate on Naam. But while the souls cannot see the Naam as it really is, they can see the Satguru. Satguru is one who has seen and manifested that Naam. So those who obey the commandments of the Satguru and who catch His worth, they can get everything, including Naam. Only Master manifests that Naam. And Naam is the cause of all creation.

You have made a long journey to come here. And you know why you have come here . . . only to give comfort to your soul. You can give comfort to your souls only if you will always remember the purpose of your visit here. The purpose of your visit here is to be in the remembrance of God. So if you will spend every single minute in the remembrance of the Master, that will be very beneficial for you. Nobody should go back carrying any question in his mind. Everyone will be given a lot of time to talk with me in private at eleven each morning. [EDITOR'S NOTE: *See Chapters 1 and 24 for more recent comments on asking questions.*]

This period of ten or eleven days is kept for you. In this time I don't bother about my external comfort. I am bothering much about your convenience; so please don't hesitate in asking me anything you wish. During the private interview time, those who are not scheduled for interviews should keep doing their meditation in their room. And they should not gossip and talk about the various things in their own private interviews.

I receive many letters from the dear ones who have come here. And while they are here, they don't appreciate the time, but use their time in talking among themselves or in praising the sevadars. This is only because of their mind. When they go back to their homes, then they realize their mistake and they repent. But this is of no use. This is why you are requested not to talk and not to waste your time in praising any sevadars. If you want to praise anyone, you should praise only your Master. You see, I do not praise anyone except my Master. Whatever He told me, I did that. So here also, if you will devote your time completely to the will of the Master, do your meditation and do whatever He says, that will be very good for you.

Whenever you breathe, your every single breath should contain Simran. You should be doing Simran always, because this period of ten or eleven days is very important for you people. And if you will devote all your time to Simran and Bhajan, then you will realize one day that this was a very valuable experience for you.

Guru Nanak says, "O my mind, remember the Master, always remember the Master; don't remember anybody else." So Guru Nanak says, "For every single moment, O my mind, go on remembering the Master; when you are sitting, when you are sleeping, always keep this remembrance of the Master in your heart."

We will talk more when you come for private interviews. Nobody should feel that I don't know them or that I don't recognize them. I recognize everybody.

Truly my Master Kirpal was very strong because He pulled me out from my condition and He brought me to Sant Bani Ashram. This is the same place where I first met Russell Perkins. At that time we didn't have this roof. And here I told [Russell] that I was planning to spend all my life in meditation. When I came back from America, I put a roof on this place because I wanted people to meditate here more and more, because this is the place where I was planning to spend the rest of my life in meditation.

27
Simran
Sant Kirpal Singh Ji

excerpts from the 1954 Birthday Message

Dear Brothers and Sisters: Mr. Khanna has asked me to give some message on my birth anniversary. The day of my physical birth fell on the 6th of February, 1894. The true date of my birth is the day when I sat physically at the holy feet of my Master Sawan Singh in February 1924. Still the truer date is when I was reborn anew into the beyond and met my Master in all His glory in 1917, i.e., seven years before my meeting with Him physically. I respect all holy scriptures of all the Saints who came in the past as they all were given by inspiration of God. I had the good fortune to sit at the feet of my Master. That which I have received of my Master is what I deliver unto you. I find it parallel with what all the past Saints have said. The difference is in the language or the way of expression, but the subject matter is the same. They all talk as to how to liberate our souls from mind and matter and know ourselves and know God. At the time of Initiation the Satguru resides with the devotee. He is with you always even unto the end of the world and will be extending all feasible help. He will never leave thee, nor forsake thee. Whosoever's mind is stayed on Him with full faith, He will keep him in perfect peace. There is hope for everybody. Master Power comes into the world to save sinners and to put them on the way back to God. It is for you to remain devoted to Him, and keep His commandments. The rest is for Him to do. God is love, You are also love. Love is the potent factor in meeting God. "He that loveth not, knoweth not

God." Therefore, "thou shalt love the Lord thy God with all thy heart and with all thy soul and with all thy mind." I wish you to be the doers of the Word and not hearers only, for an ounce of practice is worth more than tons of theories. Reformers are badly needed, not of others, but of themselves. You shall have Godhead as salary. I wish you all Godspeed in your efforts to tread the way back to God, which lies within you. My love and best wishes are always with you and will remain with you. The mystery of life is solved in the company of those who have solved that for themselves. How to find such a man? One who has solved this mystery can help in finding the same Truth.

* * *

The Master teaches us how to withdraw from the body and contact the Sound Current — the Word within. There are so many ways to withdraw from the body, but the one devised by the Saints is the most natural and quickest, and that is achieved through *Simran* or repetition of the names of God. So I would like to just give in detail something about this subject which is very important and is the first step toward going up. . . .

Everyone in the world is doing simran of one kind or another. In fact none can do without it. A housewife, for instance, is thinking all the while of the kitchen requirements like flour, pulses, spices and pepper, lest any of these things run short.

She is thinking of recipes for new dishes and delicacies. Similarly, a farmer is always thinking of plowing the land, furrowing the fields, sowing the seeds and harvesting and the like, besides his cattle and fodder. A shopkeeper is preoccupied with his stock-in-trade and keenly alive to rise and fall in the prices of commodities he deals in, and how he can make huge profits in his business. A school-master likewise dreams of his school, classes, pupils and lessons, on all of which his attention is closely riveted. Again, a contractor is engrossed in problems of labor, material, and various building processes.

Thus every one of us is constantly dwelling on one thing or another. This close association leaves an imprint in the human mind which, in course of time, becomes indelible enough and leads to complete identification of the subject with the object — and hence it is said, "As you think so you become," or "Where the mind is, there you are also," no matter where the physical self is. This being the case, Saints take hold of a person from the line of least resistance.

As no one can do without Simran, the Saints try to set one type of Simran for another type. They substitute for Simran of the world and worldly relations and objects, a Simran of God's Name, or "Word." As the former leads to distraction of the mind, the latter pulls heavenward, leading to peace of mind and liberation of the soul. Three to four hours in a day has been enjoined as the minimum for Simran, and it may be gradually increased. The Mahatmas are never without Simran even for a single moment. As it is altogether a mental process — for it is to be done by the tongue of thought — no amount of physical and manual labor can interfere with it. In course of time, like the tick of a clock, it becomes automatic and ceaseless for all the twenty-four hours. While the hands are engaged in work, the mind rests in the Lord. . . .

The Seat of Simran

Now we have to see where the repetition of Simran is to be done.

The Divine Ground on which Simran should be done is the center between the two eyebrows, called variously as Third Eye, *Tisra Til, Shiv-Netra* or *Nukta-i-Sweda*. It is the gateway leading to the subtle planes. In the state of wakefulness it is the seat of the spirit or psyche and it is located above the six physical ganglions. We have to transcend both the astral and causal planes above the physical plane. The Yogis cross over the six physical centers step by step until they finally and completely traverse and go over the physical plane. Instead of descending down into the lower ganglions and then going up by piercing them through in the upward journey, it would be easier and better by far if one were to commence the journey right ahead from the seat of the soul in the wakeful state, which is at the back of the two eyes. The easiest way to withdraw the spirit from the body to its own seat is by means of some mental Simran, as may be enjoined by the Master-soul .

The Basic Names of God

Let us now see what Simran is and what the relation is between the Name and named.

For Simran there are two kinds of Names, original and derivative. Generally people engage in Simran or one or another of the derivative or attributive Names of God, as may have an appeal to the individual concerned. This may be good and useful to a certain extent, but it cannot work as an "Open Sesame" to the higher and spiritual planes within.

Master-souls always do and recommend Simran of the highest type, to wit, of the Original or *Basic Names of God*; for these open up charmed casements and bring to view vistas leading to spiritual realms within the body. Such Names are charged with and electrified by the thought transference that usually accompanies them when communicated to an aspirant by a Master-soul. As these are magnetized, they have the power to attract and pull the spirit up to the planes to which they relate. The engrafted words charged with the Divine Spirit of the Master very soon bear fruit. Christ in this connection says, "I am the vine, ye are the branches, and as branches cannot do without the vine, ye cannot do without me . . . Let you abide in me and my words abide in you."

Again, these charmed words of the Master — Basic Names of God — have the power to dispel the forces of darkness that may meet and assail a Spirit on its onward journey. Simran of these Names helps the soul both in the physical plane and supraphysical planes, one after the other. Hence it is imperative that Simran be done of such Names as the Master-soul enjoins, for they are charged with a tremendous spiritual power which negative powers can hardly put up with and from which they flee as from an enchanter driven. Immortal and everlasting as these words of the Master are, they bestow life everlasting to the soul in which they sink and take root. Death cannot come near such a soul. This is why it is said, "Take not God's name in vain."

Every name has its own significance, influence, energy and power. If one thinks of ice, he is reminded of the bleak cold and the shivers it brings; the thought of fire brings to mind its attributes of heat and warmth. The word "lawyer" is suggestive of courts and cases, and "doctor" at once conjures up pictures of hospitals, patients and medicine chests, etc. It is a common saying, "As you think, so you become." Thought is said to be the keynote to success. There is always a strong link between a name and the named, and much greater and stronger is this link between God and His Names. It may be said that God Himself resides and dwells in His own Names (basic and original, and not derivative or attributive).

Simran of the Basic Names of God has an inevitable influence on the mind. It leads to dhyan, making the spirit forgetful of the world and worldly objects. In meditation nothing but concentrated Simran remains and from the great and deep silence of the heart (*Hriday Kamal* of the Saints, i.e., the Divine Ground behind the eyebrows) there issues forth a ceaseless Sound Current, which helps in pulling the spirit up, leading to the withdrawal from the body (without of course breaking the silver cord) and guides the spirit in its onward journey into various spirit realms. The luminous form of the Master always remains with the spirit, helping and guiding it at every step. *This Sound Principle is the link between God and man,* and in this way an indissoluble bond and relationship is established between the Creator and His creation. . . .

How to do Simran

For Simran one has to adopt some convenient posture and then fix his attention on the Divine Ground between the eyebrows. Simran is entirely a mental process and is to be done mentally with the tongue of thought, while the gazing faculty is to be fixed at the spot behind the two eyebrows as said above.

The Words as given by the Master may slowly be repeated mentally or with the tongue of thought. It should be done without causing any strain or pressure on the forehead. The practice may be started with a half hour or so as many be convenient; but in course of time it should be developed to two or three hours a day or even longer. Simran of the Divine Names introverts the mind and weans it from worldly thoughts and mundane matters, until it gets stilled and equipoised.

Some do Simran with closed eyes and others with open eyes. The first in some cases sinks into drowsiness leading to what may be called *Yog Nidra*, and the second in some cases keeps the mind engaged on environments. One has therefore to guard against both pitfalls. Simran with closed eyes is preferable provided one retains full consciousness. It must be done regularly every day at a fixed time. Hafiz, Sufi poet of Persia, says "The only job is to pray, unmindful of whether it is accepted or not." This means you have to remember the Lord internally without any clutching to receive one thing or the other. We have to leave everything to Lord or Master working overhead. Just as we need food for the body, so do we need food for the soul. We are very careful in giving food to the horse of the body, but starve the rider — the spirit — the life-giving fountainhead that enlivens the body and without which it has no value. We must provide food to spirit more regularly than we do for the body; no matter where we are, whether at home or abroad, and no matter what the circumstances may be, this should be our first and foremost concern.

The Simran of Naam or Word is an elixir of life and in fact a panacea (healing) for all ills, physical, mental, accidental or ordained. It is a food for the spirit, and when the spirit is strong and healthy it will charge the body with vital currents of life and light, dispelling all darkness from head to foot. It is the bread of life spoken of by Christ when he declared you cannot live on bread alone. *But you can live on the Name of God alone.*

Simran and Dhyan (meditation) flood the spirit with the waters of life. Spirit comes to its own, rises in its latent Godhood, and like a tumultuous mountain stream rushes headlong toward the ocean of life which is its perennial source and merges therein, losing its separate identity.

There are no limitations as to time and place for Simran. It may be done at any time and at any place, sitting or standing, walking, or in bed, but it must be done in a state of conscious wakefulness. Early morning hours (*Amrit Vela*) is the best time for Simran. A light and frugal night meal, consisting of milk and fruits, and morning ablutions are aids in the right direction. Purity of thoughts, words and deeds goes a long way to make success of the Sadhan (spiritual discipline), for ethical life precedes spiritual life and is in fact the very ground on which the spiritual structure has to be raised. For a householder, it is very necessary to observe strict discipline in life, in matters of diet, drink and speech. Simran must be done slowly and the Words are to be repeated or thought out with clarity. The whole process is to be carried out with love, devotion, and single-minded attention to ensure quick results. When properly done for some time, a state of divine intoxication comes upon the spirit and blessed calmness is experienced. All worldly thoughts vanish like thin air and the spirit feels freed from the bodily tenements and is irresistibly drawn upward by the Unseen Power of the Master. When it thus withdraws from the sensual planes, it gets concentrated at its own seat, the inner light dawns, and one by one Spiritual experiences like the starry welkin, the moon and the sun unfold themselves. One comes across frequent references to these things in all the scriptures both ancient and modern, like the Vedas, the Upanishads, the Holy Koran, the Gurbani, the Gospel, etc. The Prophets Mohammed and Moses speak of the various inner lights. In the Bible there are repeated references to the thunder and lightning in connection with the Voice of God as it spoke to the prophets.

As the spirit crosses over these initial stages and lands in the subtle plane, the luminous form of the Master appears, takes charge of the soul, and leads it on the onward spiritual journey from plane to plane. With the advent of the Master the work of Simran is completed, and the aspirant's soul lies wholly in the hands of the Master-soul.

Guru Arjan, the fifth Guru of the Sikhs, has given a glowing account of the results which one can have by doing the sweet remembrance of the Word. He impresses on us to remember Him all the time in the words as used by the Saints in the past. There are so many names of the One Reality and our aim and goal is common. *We have to start from the name and contact with the Named.* Unless you contact the Named you cannot derive full benefit of the words repeated by you. For instance, you say "water" in English, *aqua* in Latin, *pani* and *aab* in Urdu and Persian, *jal* and *nir* in Hindi, but by repetition of these names alone your thirst cannot be satisfied. It is only by drinking the particular fluid which is called by so many names that your thirst is appeased. By doing Simran of the world and its environments, they have so much taken possession of us that we have become the world and its environments. We have to use the same methods so as to eliminate all the worldly thoughts from within by remembering sweetly of the Lord in the words devised by the Saints so far. So there are two uses of Simran, one use is to withdraw from the body by Simran of the electrified words given by a competent Master, and the second is to drive out the world and its thoughts from within us by the constant remembrance of the Lord in so many ways as prescribed, the description of which has been given above in detail.

Kabir on Simran

I have given a digest of the whole subject matter in connection with Simran. It will not be out of place to put before you the Sayings of the different Saints on this subject. I now put before you the statements made by Saint Kabir on the subject. He says:

> *Comforting is God's Name. All ills it cures.*
> *Remembrance of God's Name leads to Him besides.*

Further, Kabir says:

Among high and low, among rich and poor,
Great is he who prays, and greater still he that motiveless does so.

Pelf and power hardly make a man. Poverty and riches are both transitory. A man of Simran stands far above all mankind. He is much more blessed than the rest. Most people crave for worldly things. Some are desirous of having children, others hanker after wealth, and still others after name and fame. The kind Father, of course, grants prayers of all. But a man of Simran, on the other hand, asks for nothing. He seeks God for God's sake and hence is the crowning glory to Him.

Once Akbar, the great Moghul Emperor, while riding, lost his way and felt thirsty. He asked a farmer standing near a well for water. The peasant tied the Emperor's horse to a nearby tree and gave water and food to him, little knowing who he was. The King was pleased with his hospitality and told him who he was, and bade the farmer to see him, should he ever stand in need of anything. After some time the farmer had an opportunity to visit the metropolis. He went to see the King as he had been bidden to do. On going to the royal palace, he found that the King was busy praying and at the end he requested God for the peace and prosperity of his kingdom. Seeing this, the farmer felt humiliated for having come to beg from a beggar; for he too could appeal directly to the Great God, who listens alike to the prayers of both rich and poor.

Guru Nanak has said, "Why should we ask for worldly things from God?" All those who love the body and bodily relations go the way of hell, but one who does Simran motiveless is truly great. We generally pray for the fulfillment of our wishes and desires. So long as a man or woman is full of these, the human body, far from being a temple of God, is an abode of Satan. So Kabir says that God loves those who love God alone: for no other purpose but for the love of God. The same is in the Sikh

Scriptures: "What should I ask for? There is nothing lasting in all the world over. I see the whole world passing away."

Kabir says,

In pain we pray to God, in pleasure we forget,
Could we in pleasure pray, then pain would not come up.

We remember God only when we are hard pressed from every side. It is affliction and not affluence that turns us Godward. If one were not to forget God in prosperity, adversity would never come near him. Hard times only come as a result of sins committed when forgetful of the Lord. Simran (or constant remembrance of God) is a tonic for the soul. It makes the will grow stronger from day to day. Troubles and trials, however severe, cannot cow him down. With a smiling face he pulls through the storms of fate or destiny unscathed. Simran is a panacea for all the ills of the world. It is a potent remedy and works wonders to remove worry where all human efforts fail. A man of Simran never has any worry or anxiety.

Simran to be very effective must be constant and ceaseless. Once Moses, the Prophet of the Hebrews, felt that he was the most devoted of God's creatures. In an egoistic frame of mind, he questioned God if there was in the world a greater devotee than himself. The Great God told Moses that among His devotees were included many birds and animals besides human beings. Pointing to a solitary bird in the jungle, God directed Moses to meet the said bird, if he wanted to know the great depths of devotion. As Moses did not know the language of the birds, God endowed him with an understanding so that he could talk with him. Moses approached the bird and inquired as to how he was. The bird replied that engaged as he was in constant remembrance (Simran) he could ill afford any time for a useless conversation except for the Beloved's sake who had sent him. Next the prophet asked the bird if he had any trouble in which he could be of any help to him. The bird replied that he had no trouble whatsoever, but if the prophet wished to do him a favor, he asked him to bring nearer to him the spring of water that lay at a distance, as a flight to quench his thirst interfered in his Simran. This incident humbled the pride of Moses.

Guru Nanak also speaks in this wise: "If I forget You, O God, even for a fraction of a minute, this amounts to me more than fifty years." Again He Says, "He who is in constant remembrance of God, only he is alive, O Nanak; all others are dead."

Simran must be done at all costs. Constant remembrance of God is life-giving to the devotee. Guru Nanak says, "If I remember Thee I live. When I forget Thee that means death to me." . . .

[*The article which is excerpted here can be found in its entirety in the book,* The Way of the Saints.]

PART III

Meditation on the Naam of the Lord

Nothing is equal to the Naam of the Lord.
Nanak says, By meditating on the Naam given by the Gurumukh one reaches his destination.

GURU ARJAN DEV

There is nothing in this world which we can say is equal to the meditation of Naam. Only those who meditate on Naam get high status, and only those who merge themselves into Naam get liberation.

SANT JI

28

To Change the Mind's Habits

Sant Kirpal Singh Ji

The fourth of a series of Circular Letters on the subject of Receptivity, dated February 20, 1971 — The Way of the Saints *contains the other four parts, which are also published in booklet form.*

Over the past year, I have observed from the spiritual diaries sent in by the dear ones, that they report little or no inner progress, some even mentioning that they have made no headway since the time of their holy Initiation. Because there appears to be a lack of right understanding as to why steady progress has not been made, I should like to clarify the process by which such progress can be achieved.

If the dear ones were to do their spiritual practices correctly, with due regard to self-introspection, they would, as sure as two and two make four, rise above body consciousness and transcend into the Beyond, where the Inner Master is patiently waiting to greet His children at the threshold of the astral plane. But because they are unable to do this, even for a short while, they erroneously believe their meditations to be barren of all concrete results.

If you were able to follow the Master's instructions accurately, you would be sure to agree with St. Paul, who tells us in the Bible: "I die daily." Therefore, what is it that prevents you from following the Master's instructions? It is your own mind, which you have not yet been able to coax away from the outer attachments of the world to the bliss that awaits it inside.

What the Master tells you to do is not really difficult if you could but comprehend the simplicity of it. He tells you to sit in a position most comfortable to you, one in which you can sit the longest without moving; that while sitting in this position, you are to remain wide awake with your attention directed at the seat of the soul behind and between the two eyebrows; that you are to look sweetly and serenely into the middle of the darkness in front of you, repeating the Simran of five charged names slowly and at intervals.

Some succeed in performing their spiritual disciplines in the prescribed manner in a short period, others do not for want of the conscious control of the mind and the outgoing faculties. This is why it has always been stressed to weed out all undesirable traits and habits, and to replace them by the opposite ennobling virtues; and for this, the maintenance of the monthly self-introspection diary is mandatory. The more you progress in man-making, the more your mind and senses will come under your conscious control. This has already been dealt with very thoroughly, as well as other aspects of spiritual development, in my previous Circular Letters which together with *Morning Talks* constitute the yardsticks which you may apply to measure how far you have succeeded in your disciplines, both outer and inner.

So what is meant by not doing the practices properly is simply another way of saying that the one-pointed concentration preluding complete withdrawal to the eye focus has not yet been achieved by the dear ones.

You are the indweller of your own body, but are not yet its Master. Your servants, the mind and five senses, have usurped the throne on which your soul should sit. Until they are dispossessed and placed in their rightful place as servants, they will not allow you to withdraw and go in. The Master within, like any loving father, is eagerly awaiting the day when you have set your house in order. He only requires one opportunity to snatch you from the prisonhouse of the body, and like an expert angler, once He has successfully hooked His fish, He will not allow it to escape until He has it safely in His basket.

Man is so constituted that he cannot for long remain at one level. He either progresses or slips back. You may judge for yourselves which way you are going by seeing how far your mind and senses are coming under your conscious control.

This is achieved not only by ethical living, but also by the inner help and strength you get every time you sit for your meditations. So, if no apparent inner headway is achieved, know it for sure that the ground is being watered. Every time you sit, you are creating a habit which one day the mind will accept as in its best interest, as opposed to its present habit of seeking enjoyment in outside things. Habit strengthens into nature, and this is the reason for the present difficulties experienced by the dear ones in their routine meditations. The habit of the mind in running after outside enjoyments has become natural to it. Therefore, it resents sitting in the quiet. By creating a new habit, you will, in time, change the nature of the mind from one seeking pleasure in things external to one thirsting for the bliss and sweetness to be had from things internal.

> *"Thy restless mind continually goes astray; how can it ever be brought to heel? Only by giving the heart and soul to the Word or Name of God; no other way has ever been found or ever will be found."* — Swami Ji

So I wish for you to tread the Path having full faith and confidence in the Master, and above all, be grateful that you have been accepted for Initiation in this difficult age we are living in. Persevere, persevere, and persevere again. Perseverance combined with full faith in the gracious Master Power working overhead will one day remove all obstacles, and your cherished goal will be achieved.

With all love and best wishes,
Yours affectionately,

KIRPAL SINGH

29

The Glory of the Disciple

Sant Ajaib Singh Ji

An excerpt from chapter five of The Two Ways, *a book of commentaries on the Gauri Vars of Guru Ramdas, given at Sant Bani Ashram, N.H., July 8, 1980.*

He who is called a disciple of the Master rises up early and meditates on the Naam

The one who is called the disciple of the Master, what does he do? The first thing he does is to get up in the morning, sit for meditation and connect himself with Naam. The one who is called a disciple of the Master starts his day with the work of the Master.

Hazur Maharaj Kirpal used to say, "Leave one hundred urgent works to attend Satsang, and give up one thousand urgent works to meditate." He used to say that as it is necessary for us to give food to our body, in the same way, it is very important for us to give food to our soul — because our soul has been hungry from ages and ages and it needs the food of meditation and Shabd.

He makes efforts early in the morning; he bathes in the pool of Nectar.

First of all we have this physical cover. Inside this physical cover is the astral cover, and within that is the causal cover. The one who is called the disciple of the Master, he should remove all these three covers from his soul and rise above *raja guna*, *tamo guna*, and *sata guna*. He should enter into the Amritsar or pool of nectar, and bathe there.

There is no Amritsar or pool of nectar outside which can remove the dirt of our sins. The real Pool of Nectar is within our body, within our own existence.

The town of Amritsar, which is now in Punjab in India, was started by Guru Ramdas and completed by Guru Arjan Dev, the fifth Guru. It is a copy of the real Amritsar of Pool of Nectar in Daswan Dwar. The architect who was told to make the copy of Amritsar said that he had not seen the lotus of Daswan Dwar, so how could he make it? Guru Sahib gave him special attention and graciously took him up to Daswan Dwar. That dear one requested the Master to allow him to stay there forever, but the Master said, "No, you have to come out, because you have to make the copy of it outside; then I will take you back." So the pool in Amritsar is the copy of the lotus of Daswan Dwar. This outer Amritsar was begun by Guru Ramdas and completed by Guru Arjan Dev, and there was no such place when Guru Amardas was alive. But still Guru Amardas has written that we should bathe in Amritsar the real Amritsar within the body in which Truth and the true Nectar resides.

So Guru Ramdas Ji says that it is the duty of the disciple to give up laziness and sleep in the morning and get up, and by making efforts, reach this Amritsar and bathe there.

> *According to the instructions of the Master he remembers the Lord,*
> *By which all his sins and faults go away.*

Such a disciple of the Master should read the teachings of the Master daily, and he should reach Amritsar: because by bathing in this Pool of Nectar, all sins and bad habits are removed. By bathing in this Amritsar, one attains the status of Sadh.

> *Again when the day starts, he sings the Gurubani (words of Master)*

Whether sitting or standing he meditates on the Naam of the Lord.

When the day starts he should not waste time. He should go to the Satsang, and at Satsang also he should go on doing His Simran. While he is going to the place of Satsang, he should do Simran. While he is attending Satsang, he should do Simran. And while he is returning from the Satsang, then also he should do Simran. He should go on doing Simran with every single breath and should not waste any time.

He who meditates on my Lord at every breath and morsel,
Such a disciple of Master is liked by the Master.

The disciple who does Simran with his every single breath is liked by the Master.

Often I have said that when we sit for meditation, we are sitting at the door of our Master. If the door is not open to us, it means that we are not yet ready to enter His Home. But we should not put any condition to the Master. We should not say that we will sit for meditation only if the door is open to us. We should develop the quality of beggars. It is the work of the beggars to arouse people in the Name of the Lord and it is the work of the householders to give to them. It is our work to sit for meditation, and it is up to the Master, if He wishes, to open the door for us. If He doesn't wish to, He will not.

To whom my Lord is Merciful, such a disciple of the Master makes others hear the teachings of the Master.

Those on whom the Lord is gracious and those with whom He is pleased, only such people have the yearning and longing to go to the Master. Only such people like the teachings of the Master.

Nanak asks for the dust of such a disciple of the Master,
Who himself meditates and makes others meditate on Naam.

Now Guru Ramdas Ji says, "I ask for the dust of the feet of such a disciple, because the title of Sadh is not a small title. It is a very great title." And He says, "I long for the dust of the feet of such disciples, such Sadhs, who themselves do the meditation of Naam, and who make other people meditate on Naam."

Only those who have experienced the pain of separation know what this pain is like. Only the lovers can tell us how to love. The message of lovers is only for lovers.

I have the pain of love and I am telling this to lovers. I will get healed only by lovers. Without the lovers, the story of the lover cannot be completed. If you think that this is not true, you can fall in love and see.

Lovers do not argue with clever people; they would rather remain quiet than to argue with the wise.

Everybody talks of their own pains. But to whom can Ajaib Singh talk about His pains? He has the pain of love.

The reality is that such a disciple has only love for his Master, and the pain of the love of his Master. By all means and in every way, he sings of the love of his Master. Such a disciple understands all moments and breaths as illegal which he spends without the love and remembrance of the Master.

30

A Broom to Clean Our Soul

Sant Ajaib Singh Ji

a meditation talk given March 30, 1985

Make the mind quiet as only a quiet mind can meditate. Don't understand the meditation as a burden, do it lovingly. During the meditation, don't pay any attention to the outer sounds or disturbances. Don't allow your mind to wander outside, concentrate it at the Eye Center.

Satsangis should make the habit of keeping their attention concentrated at the Eye Center, even when they are not meditating, even when they are walking and doing other things of the world, because when we allow our attention to drop down from the Eye Center, it means that we are wasting a lot of our spiritual energy.

There is a great importance in these Five Sacred Names which we go on repeating again and again. Behind these Five Names the charging of the Master works. Saints go within and They have contact with the owners of the five planes which our soul has to cross in order to get to the Real Home. These Five Names are the names of the owners of those five great planes. We can concentrate our attention and rise above the body consciousness only with the help of doing the Simran, and our soul can cross these planes only by climbing on the Shabd.

The satsangis who want to make their thoughts pure and holy need to do Simran as much as possible, because our thoughts will only be purified by doing the Simran. Simran works like a broom to clean our soul, and the mirror of our soul also gets purified only by doing the Simran. When our soul becomes clean then the Shabd pulls her up.

No matter how close you bring the rusted iron in contact with a magnet, still it will not attract the iron towards it. Unless you clean that iron, unless you remove the rust from that iron, that magnet will not pull it towards itself. In the same way, if our soul is not purified, if our soul has the dirt of the organs of the worldly pleasures and the worldly things, then that Shabd will not pull our soul up. What happens now? The Shabd is sounding in our within and it is very close to our soul. We are hearing it, we are even enjoying it, but because our soul is not purified, that Shabd is not pulling our soul up. So that is why we need to do a lot of Simran, because when our soul will be purified it will take no time for the Shabd to pull her up.

31
Make the Mind Quiet
Sant Ajaib Singh Ji

a meditation talk given April 4, 1985

Make the mind quiet as only a quiet mind can meditate. Don't understand meditation as a burden, do it lovingly. Don't pay any attention to the outer sounds during the meditation; concentrate at the Eye Center.

The dear ones who have difficulty in finding the Third Eye should know that when they close their eyes, whatever they see within — it is their Third Eye which is seeing all those things. When you have to focus your attention, you should be looking exactly in the center of your two eyebrows, you should not take your attention upwards or downwards or on the left or right side, it should be right in the middle of what you see.

Some dear ones have this complaint, that the Light sometimes comes and sometimes goes; sometimes it becomes very brilliant. They should know that it is not the Light which comes and goes. When our mind is still, when our mind does not run a lot, then we find the Light still there, but when our mind is not there, when it is running all around, then we feel that the Light has gone away. Light is at one place; it is always our mind which comes and goes.

You know that the reflection of the trees or things on the shore of the sea can be seen clearly only when the water of the sea is still. If the water is moving, if there are many waves in that sea, we cannot see the reflection of the things on the shore. It does not mean that the trees or other things have gone somewhere else, they are still there, but it is only because the water is not still, all the waves are moving it, that is why we cannot see the reflection of those things very clearly. We see them only when the water is still; in the same way, as long as our mind is still we see our reflection, we see the things very clearly. But our mind is also like a very big ocean, in this ocean there are many waves of lust, anger, greed and all the things, many thoughts are also coming up, and they are always moving around our mind, and that is why we are not able to see our own image, our own reflection very clearly. We have to still our mind with the Shabd, with the Naam, with the Simran, and only then can we see our image and the inner things very clearly.

Often I have talked about the training which I got in the army when they were teaching us how to shoot. They would teach us that first of all you should keep your body, the gun, and the target all in one line, and then you should keep the crosshairs of the two sights in one line, and it should be in line with the target. And you should hold your breath, and you should not look here or there, and very slowly, very lightly you should just pull the trigger. Those who shot according to the training, keeping all the things in one line and doing it very gently and smoothly, would always become successful. But some people who did not keep their body, the gun, and the target in one line, who would move, those who would not hold their breath, those who would not do it correctly, they would never become successful.

The same thing applies in the practice of Sant Mat also. If our body is still and our mind is still, what is the target we have to hit? The target is the Eye Center, and after hitting the target we have to go further, we have to go to Sach Khand. So if our body is still, our mind is still, and if we are concentrating correctly at the Eye Center, then only after a few sittings you will know that you have progressed a lot.

Those who used to change their aim at the target again and again would not become successful. This is my personal experience; we had to shoot five bullets, placing them in an area of one inch. And I myself have done that only by keeping one target all the time, only by trying to hit the same place again and again. And the same thing helped me a lot in the Sant Mat, because my Master taught me, "Dear Son, if you will go on changing your contemplation, if you will go on changing the place where you have to concentrate, you will not become successful. You have to go on looking at the same place, you have to concentrate at the same place if you want to become successful."

You should try to understand this: when our thoughts are stilled, then the Light also gets manifested within us and it also remains still there. And when such a thing happens then the Sound of the Shabd also starts coming within us. Only in the beginning do you need to close your ears, later on when the Light is manifested the Sound starts coming from within that Light, and even if you have not closed your ears still you will hear the Sound of the bells or of the conch or some kind of Sound. And whatever Sound you are hearing you should always try to listen to that, you should not go on changing the Sounds. Whatever sound you have caught, you should continue with that same sound and concentrate on it, because even if it is a smaller sound, or a little sound, still it has the connection, it has the contact with the higher Sound.

When the soul sees the Light and hears the Sound of the bell, then all the impurities, all the dirt of the soul is removed, and then the mirror of the soul becomes very clean, very reflecting, and after that, all the forces of the mind which were pulling the soul downwards, all the chains are broken one by one, and after that whenever we sit for meditation, just in a moment our attention goes straight to the Eye Center.

I hope that you will sit in the meditation according to what I have tried to explain to you. You should meditate here as well as when you go back to your home, because those who will meditate according to these instructions, they will definitely get success and it will be very helpful.

32

"Knock at the Door and it Shall be Opened"

Sant Ajaib Singh Ji

four meditation talks given at Shamaz Meditation Retreat, Potter Valley, California, May 1985

At the time of the Initiation we are told that we should make our mind quiet and meditate because only with a quiet mind can we do our meditation. We have to withdraw our attention from all the outer things, from the outer surroundings. We should not pay any attention to the outer sounds or disturbances. We should concentrate at the Eye Center because God Almighty, the Master Who has given us the Initiation, is sitting within us. He will not open His door until we become pure, and until we go to the place where the door is. The Eye Center, the *Tisra Til*, is the place where our journey begins and it is the door of our home. It will be opened only when we reach there and we sit there lovingly, doing the Simran.

Christ has said, "Knock at the door and it shall be opened." God Almighty, the Master Who has given us the Initiation, is sitting there in the Form of the Shabd. Ever since He gave us the Initiation, He has been sitting there in the Form of the Shabd; and when we reach there by doing the Simran, and when we knock on that door, He will know that His child needs something and He will open the door. So we should withdraw from all the outer surroundings, from all the outer things. We should not allow our mind to wander outside. We should sit at this door and we should do the Simran lovingly, because when we will reach there by doing the Simran and knock on the door it will be opened. Daily Simran that we do is like knocking at the door and it will be opened when we reach there. So we should make our mind quiet and concentrate our mind at the Eye Center. We should not let him wander here and there outside in the world.

May 3, 1985

With the grace of God we have received this human body, and we can do God Realization only in the human body. Having more grace on us, God has brought us in contact with the Sant Satguru. The Satgurus have graciously given us the Shabd Naam; They have connected us with the Real Naam. And Satguru Himself is sitting at the *Tisra Til* or the Eye Center. He is sitting there because He wants to help us in our struggle with the mind. So, as He has graciously given us the Shabd Naam, and is sitting there to help us in our struggle, we should also make our mind quiet; and lovingly, faithfully, and devotedly we should do our meditation, because He is sitting at the Eye Center to help us.

For God Realization the dear one has to fulfill some conditions. He has to bear the taunts and criticism of society. He has to face the criticism and hatred of family members. He has to be very strong when dealing with his friends and relatives. Criticism, slander and hatred by other people work like a guard because they always protect the dear one. When the dear one becomes successful in accepting the criticism, slander and hatred of other people he becomes free from all the burden. Because those who criticize him or comment on him take away the burden from his head and he becomes free and becomes successful in going back home.

Beloveds of God are the real people, the real dear ones of God. They come and tell us, "God, for Whom you are searching, is nowhere outside, He is within you. The distance of east and west is not an obstacle in the way of realizing God. He cannot be obtained by any amount of power or wealth; He is within you and you can realize Him only after going within."

So make the mind quiet as only a quiet mind can meditate. Don't understand meditation as a burden, do it lovingly. Don't allow your mind to wander outside during meditation. Don't pay any attention to the outer sounds or disturbances; concentrate your mind at the Eye Center.

May 4, 1985

The human body is the best of all animals and birds. It is the best in the eighty-four lakhs different kinds of creatures. With a lot of grace of God we have been given this human body and God has showered even more grace on us by giving us the opportunity to do the devotion of Naam. He has brought us in the company of the Master and graciously Master has given us the Naam Initiation. In the Form of the Shabd He is sitting in our *Tisra Til*, our Eye Center. So we should also reach the Eye Center and, diving into the Ocean of Satguru, we should also bring out the pearl of precious Naam.

Make the mind quiet as only quiet mind can meditate. Don't understand meditation as a burden, do it lovingly. While meditating don't pay any attention to the outer sounds or disturbances. Concentrate your mind at the Eye Center; don't allow your mind to wander outside.

May 5,1985

Saints and Mahatmas do not come for any particular community, for any particular religion, or for any particular country. They understand this whole world as Their own home and They love people from all different religions and communities.

Mahatmas come to tell us about the relationship of the soul with Almighty God. They tell us how great the soul is and how she has been suffering ever since she got separated from Almighty God. She has fallen into the clutches of the mind and the organs of senses and that is why she is suffering a lot. Saints and Mahatmas come into this world to make the soul meet Almighty God.

They tell us that we do not need to change our country; we do not need to change our profession or our religion. Living in your own religion and in your own country, whether you are sick or healthy, and doing all the things which you are doing in the world, still you can do the devotion of the Lord. The Lord is within you and you can go there and do the meditation and meet Him.

Mahatmas ask us, "Have we ever gone inside this human body and seen how many beautiful things God has put in the human body and how many treasures God has manifested in our within?" Every day we spend a lot of time beautifying our body and we are afraid of when we will lose this body or lose the beauty of the body. But have we ever paid any attention to that Power with Whose Presence we have the body and the beauty of this body? We never pay any attention to and we never think of meeting that Power. Christ has said, "In my Father's home there are many palaces." Have we ever tried to go and see those palaces? Kabir Sahib says that this body is not only made of skin, bones and flesh. In this body there are millions of suns, stars, moons and there are so many gardens and so many beautiful things. And the Creator, the Gardener of the gardens, the Creator of this creation, He Who has created the suns, stars and moons — Almighty God is also sitting within your body.

Is it not surprising that God Almighty, for Whom we are searching, is within us, and that ever since our body was created He has been sitting within us? But we have never gone in our within and seen Him.

This is the only thing which the Master's tell us; They tell us, "Go in the within and hear the Sound of God, because He is within you." So according to what They say, we should go within, we should spend some time in His devotion and see Him there.

May 7, 1985

33

The Stairway of Simran

Sant Ajaib Singh Ji

a meditation talk given January 28, 1986, at Sant Bani Ashram, Village 16 PS, Rajasthan, India

Make the mind quiet as only a quiet mind can meditate. Don't understand meditation as a burden, do it lovingly. While meditating, do not pay any attention to the outer sounds and disturbances and do not allow your mind to wander outside. Concentrate your mind at the Eye Center.

There are three means of achieving liberation: Simran, Bhajan and Dhyan.

We are in the habit of doing Simran in age after age. It is not very difficult to develop the Simran. Simran means remembering something again and again. When we are doing anything of the world, even at that time, our mind is thinking or doing the simran of something else.

As a crop ruined by water can be made alive only by giving more water, in the same way, Saints have the knowledge of Simran — They know that only the Simran of God can cut the simran or remembrance of the world and that is why They give us the Simran of God.

Our ears get intoxicated by hearing the outer melodies and sounds. Saints know and say that when we start listening to the Inner Divine Melody, when we start listening to the Inner Music, then our ears won't find any attraction or any intoxication in the outer sounds.

Hazur Maharaj Kirpal, as well as Master Sawan Singh Ji, used to give the example of a clerk. They used to say, "As the clerk is doing the simran of the work he has to do, he thinks about the client whom he has to deal with the next day, and the form of that person comes in front of him. Whether he is shopping in the market, or sitting in his home — whatever he is doing when he remembers the work which he is supposed to do the next day, everything comes in front of him by itself."

Just by remembering the kitchen and the things of their homes; all those things appear to the women and at once they start thinking about what has to be finished and what to buy, and when they have to get something new. Just by remembering the kitchen and their work, they see all those things with their eyes.

The farmers do the simran of their farming. They think of what seeds are good for their farm and what seeds they have to sow, and when they have to water the field. Just by remembering their work, all those things come in front of their eyes.

In the same way, judges do the simran of their work when they think of what cases they have to deal with the next day. The people whose cases they are remembering also come in front of them. They just need to remember and they visualize and see everything in front of them.

So Saints and Mahatmas say, "You have been doing the simran birth after birth. You have been in the habit of doing simran age after age, so what difficulty is it for you to do this Simran?" The Simran that the Saints and Mahatmas give us is the Simran that They Themselves have meditated upon and behind that Simran Their charging, Their meditation and Their sacrifices work.

If lovingly we do the repetition, or the Simran of those Sacred Names which the Master gives us, then the Form of the Master comes at the Eye Center by Himself and It starts remaining there by Himself.

When we do the simran, or when we remember anything, at first, by itself, our attention goes to the Eye Center. So when we do the Simran given to us by the Master, then the Form of the Master who has given us the Simran also comes there by Himself and It starts remaining there.

As we do not find it difficult to do the simran of the world and we do not have to make any efforts in remembering the world, in the same way the Simran given to us by the Master should go on happening within us. Twenty-four hours a day the simran of the world which we are doing should be replaced by the Simran of the Master, and without finding it difficult, lovingly we should do the Simran of the Master.

Our mind is always free and we can always do the Simran, only when we are using our mind for the accounts, then the mind is busy, otherwise he can do the Simran all the time.

So on the tongue of the dear ones, the Simran should go on happening all the time. Whether one is sitting, sleeping, whether one is talking to other people, traveling in a train, or whatever one is doing, he should always be doing the Simran. When he develops such a habit of doing the Simran, then he feels as if the Master is always with him. He is sleeping with him, He is sitting with him, He is doing everything with him. When we develop such a habit of doing the Simran we always feel the presence of the Master with us.

The simran of the world will always pull us back into this world. Where you are attached, there you will go. Where the Simran of the Master will take us is toward the Naam.

When we do the Simran, our soul, or our attention, withdraws from outside and it gets concentrated at the Eye Center. Then we will start rising above the mind and the sense organs. The Master Who is present at the Eye Center never goes below the Eye Center because in the sense organs is the outer dirt and He does not go into the dirty places. So whenever we have to do the Simran we should always keep our attention concentrated at the Eye Center.

Guru Nanak Sahib says, "If you want to climb a fort, you need the stairs. In the same way, if you want to climb to the Real Home, Sach Khand, you will need the stair." All the Mahatmas's have said that in our within there are the stairs, climbing which we can go from one plane to another. That stairway is of the Simran, that stairway is of our yearning.

When we climb the stairs of yearning by doing the Simran, one after another we reach the planes and finally we reach our Eternal Home.

So withdrawing our attention from outside, we have to go within; we should concentrate at the Eye Center. Without any hesitation we should try to go within because the things which we are desiring, the things which we are looking for are within us and we can find them easily if we withdraw from outside and go within.

In the beginning we have to struggle very hard. In the beginning this Path seems very dry, very long, very tiresome, and very hard, but gradually when we start stilling our mind at the Eye Center, then we find sweetness, we find a lot of love from this Path and then we do not feel like giving it up.

When the child is born, at the beginning it is difficult for the child to drink or to get the milk from the nipples of the mother. The mother tries and the child does not accept it, but as the child tastes the milk, and when he finds it very sweet and very tasty, then it doesn't matter whether the mother tries or not, whether the mother wants or not, whenever the mother carries the child in her lap, at once the child tries to get the milk.

The mind who at present is understanding the pleasures of the world as the highest of all, as the truest of all, and who does not want to do anything but enjoy the pleasures of the world, when he tastes the inner intoxication, the Inner Elixir, then he does not want to indulge in the worldly pleasures. He always helps us and he becomes our best friend, in fact he requests us, "At least for a couple of minutes, go within and let me have the Inner Bliss."

Swami Ji Maharaj says that, "Your mind will not come under your control no matter how many outer means you adopt. You just make him hear the Inner Divine Melody and he will come under your control."

34
Make a Habit of Meditating
Sant Ajaib Singh Ji

a meditation talk given in March 1986

Make the mind quiet as only a quiet mind can meditate, do not understand meditation as a burden, do it lovingly. While meditating don't pay any attention to the outer disturbances, don't allow your mind to wander outside, concentrate him at the Eye Center.

The seat of our mind and soul is between the two eyes where usually the Indian women put the *tika*, or the signs. This is the place where our journey begins; this is the door of our home.

Meditation seems difficult to us as long as we do not adopt it, as long as we do not start doing it. But when we start doing it, when we adopt it, since it is according to the laws of Nature, it becomes very easy for us to meditate and gradually, as we go on meditating, we become competent in it.

In the beginning it is very difficult for us to meditate because we have not made the habit of meditating and, since we have not made a habit of meditating, that is why sometimes we have pain in the legs, sometimes we have pain in the knees. This is only because we have not made our mind quiet. Making the mind quiet means that we should not think of anything except the work for which we are sitting. When we sit for the meditation mind creates thoughts and desires, the thoughts which he has had since ages and ages, birth after birth; when he involves us in all those kinds of thoughts and desires, then it becomes restless. That is why making the mind quiet means that we should sit here for meditation and when you are sitting here you should only do the meditation. We are sitting here for meditation but our mind is taking us outside in the market place, in the shopping places, here and there and he is not allowing us to meditate.

We can do only one thing at a time, either we can think about the world while sitting here, or we can do the meditation.

We all know that all the forms and materials of the world are in fact traps laid down by the Negative Power to trap our soul. Our soul has become weak and helpless; she sees her destruction with her own eyes but she is helpless, she is weak, she cannot do anything. When we do the meditation of Shabd Naam our soul becomes stronger and then she does not fall into the trap of the Negative Power.

Whenever we meditate we satsangis should always remember these few things: that when we are meditating we should sit only for the meditation and nothing else. The satsangis do not have any understanding of the importance of the Simran. As long as we have not crossed the limits of mind and the organs of senses we do not know the importance of the Simran. When we rise above the mind and the organs of senses then we begin to realize how important and how valuable the Simran is.

So all of you lovingly, and without understanding it as a burden, do the Simran.

35
Reach the Form of the Master
Sant Ajaib Singh Ji

a meditation talk given March 30, 1986, in Rajasthan, India

Make the mind quiet as only a quiet mind can meditate. Don't understand meditation as a burden; do it lovingly. During meditation don't pay any attention to the outer disturbances. Don't allow your mind to wander outside. Concentrate him at the Eye Center.

The more Simran we do in a much better way, the more our mind will become pure. The more our mind becomes pure, the more our thoughts will become pure, and the purity of the mind will make our soul also pure. It is just like if anyone wants to keep his courtyard clean, he uses the broom very thoroughly. He sweeps out all the dirt. In the same way, the example is also applied to us. The dear soul who will do the Simran, without allowing the mind to interfere in doing the Simran, he will clean the mirror of his soul in a much better way.

I have often said that there are three means, three practices, doing which we can achieve liberation: Simran, Dhyan, and Bhajan. By doing constant Simran we can collect our scattered thoughts, bring our attention to the Eye Center and withdraw our soul there. We can vacate the nine openings of our body and bring our soul to the Eye Center. When we reach the Eye Center with the help of doing the Simran, our soul does not stay there for a long time. Sometimes it drops down, sometimes it comes up and again it drops down. It goes on happening like that there. In that stage we need the Dhyan or contemplation.

When we reach the Eye Center by doing the Simran, we need to do contemplation or Dhyan so much so that our soul, our attention, may always remain at the Eye Center. At that time we need to remember the Form of the Master, we need to contemplate on the Form of the Master which is present there even before we get there. Regarding this, Guru Nanak said, "The Form of the Saints and Mahatmas is the Formless One." By doing the Dhyan or contemplation of the Master's Form we can stay at the Eye Center.

So when we reach the Eye Center by doing the Simran, we need the contemplation or the Dhyan. When with the help of the contemplation or Dhyan we are able to stay at the Eye Center and when our soul comes in the range of the Shabd then the Shabd Himself attracts and pulls our soul up and from there the Shabd takes the soul to her Real Home. Master Himself accompanies the soul. Taking the soul across plane after plane He takes the soul back to the Real Home. Regarding that Guru Nanak has said, "One has to forget himself, one has to give up his own self, and absorb in the Form of the Master."

So first of all it is very important for us to do the Simran. Simran can take us only up to the sun, stars, and moon, and beyond that when the Form of the Master is manifested, then it is the duty of the Master to take the disciple up. When the disciple reaches the Form of the Master, then his duty is completed, his job is completed, because after that it is the job of the Master to take the disciple up to the Real Home. In the inner world the Negative Power has created so many cells and different places where the soul can get lost. Those souls who try to go in the within without the guidance of the Master can never become successful, because in the inner world the Negative Power has created many illusory things.

That is why it is very important for an initiate to reach the Form of the Master. Without getting to the Form of the Master and without getting the guidance of the perfect Master, the initiate cannot make his journey back to the Real Home.

We know that thieves come only to the place where there is

wealth. In the same way, the soul within whom God Almighty is manifested, all the people of the world come and gather around near that person, and start giving him name and fame and they start praising him. It should not be like that. The person who has received the grace and blessings of the Masters should not get puffed up by the praises and the name and fame given to him by the worldly people, because he should know that he still has to go a long way. Master still has to take him to the final destination. He still has to take him very high. That is why he should always remain content, he should always have patience. He should not get puffed up by the praises of the people. He should not use his powers which he has acquired by doing the meditation. He should always remain patient. He should always remain content in the Will of God, exactly the way Fakir Sarmad* was. As I told you, Fakir Sarmad, even though He had everything, still he did not curse anyone. He did not think badly of anyone, because even one bad thought can bring us down from the peak of Brahm. That is why the disciple who has received the grace of the Master should always remain patient, He should always be content in the Will of God. He should always go on doing the Simran. He should always guard his mind because mind can create bad thoughts and he can pull you down from the peak of Brahm.

* See "Content in the Will of God," Chapter 10.

36
The Streams of Mind and Soul

Sant Ajaib Singh Ji

a talk given before meditation, on December 5, 1986, at Sant Bani Ashram, Village 16 PS, Rajasthan

The streams of our mind and soul come onwards into our body in the way that sunshine comes to earth. It is not an easy task to change the direction of the streams of our mind and soul. It is not an easy thing to withdraw the attention of our soul from all over the body and bring it to the Eye Center. It is not the work of a few days, a few months, or a few years. It is a work which requires our total attention and complete devotion. When we are able to change the direction of the streams of our mind and soul, and when we withdraw our attention from all over the body and take our soul to the Eye Center, then we can easily see why this Creation was created, Who has created it, and how it is being run. The Mahatma who reaches this place, and sees the world from up high, understands it as no more than a playground.

Our body is a laboratory for realizing God Almighty. We can realize God only after going within this laboratory. We cannot find Him anywhere outside. This is because whatever God has created outside, the same is within the human body, and unless we go into it we cannot realize Him. Mahatma Pipa says, "Whatever is in Brahmand, the same thing is in the Pind," the body, also. Pipa says, "God Almighty is residing within us." Those who go within with the grace and help of the Master are able to realize Him. Up until now, ever since the Creation has been created, God Almighty has sent His Saints, His Beloveds, into this world, and those who have taken advantage of Their coming, who have taken refuge at Their feet, have easily gone within the laboratory of the human body and realized God. Those who make their lives according to the instructions of such great souls, they realize God while they are living in this body and they become the liberated ones in their lifetimes.

When we know that God Almighty has created this Creation, and that He has created its astral form and it is within us, when we even know that our Creator, our Almighty Lord, is residing within us behind the veil of mind, and that if we lift this veil of mind we can see it all clearly within — then we think, what is difficult in going within and seeing them? When we know that everything is within us, why not withdraw our attention from outside, take it within, and try to see what God Almighty has manifested within us? But Mahatmas tell us that unless we have a real and true love for the Master, unless we become really and truly devoted to the Master, we cannot become able to see it all. Love for the Master is the only thing which will change the direction of the streams of our mind and soul. It is the only thing which will help us withdraw from outside and go within. So withdrawing your attention from outside, concentrate at the Eye Center.

37

Sow the Seed which is in Season

Sant Ajaib Singh Ji

a meditation talk given at Sant Bani Ashram, Village 16 PS, Rajasthan, on September 25, 1987

I thank my Satguru, Almighty Kirpal, who gave us the gift of Naam in this Iron Age; because we get the parents in all the bodies, and in all the lives. We get lust, greed, attachment and egoism in all the bodies. We get pain and happiness, comfort and good things in all the bodies. Naam is the only thing which we cannot get in any other body. We can only get it in the human birth. So we are grateful to Lord Kirpal who came into this world, in this Iron Age and gave us the Naam initiation. God Almighty always sends the Saints and Mahatmas, His beloved children, to give us the wealth of Naam.

We can get the wealth of Naam only from the Sadhus and the Saints. Our mind is such a thing that it always involves us in the unique kind of practices in order to achieve and realize God Almighty. Many times it involves us in going to the places of pilgrimage; many times it involves us in doing fasts and other rites and rituals; many times it will involve us in doing so many different kinds of outer practices. All the ages have their own way of doing the devotion of God and realizing God Almighty. In this Iron Age the devotion of Naam is the only thing which can bring us closer to God and make us realize God Almighty. In this Iron Age God Almighty has sent His Saints and Beloveds to give us the Naam and we are very grateful that we are among the fortunate ones who have been given Naam.

Saints do not reject even the worst of the sinners from Their door. They accept everyone. They even shower Their grace on the birds and animals, because They know that underneath the sinner there is a pure soul which is inclined toward God.

We cannot get to the door of the home of the Lord without doing the meditation of Shabd Naam. We cannot achieve liberation without doing the meditation of Shabd Naam. If we are doing anything other than the meditation of Shabd Naam it is just like a farmer who is trying to sow a seed out of season. Guru Arjan Dev Ji Maharaj says that the person who tries to sow the seed which is not in season, which will not grow, is wasting his time and energy, because he will not get any benefit from it.

Swami Ji Maharaj also said that in this Kali Yuga or Iron Age, Naam is the only means of liberation. Without doing its devotion there is no way to reach Home.

We can realize God Almighty, for Whom we are searching and working very hard. We are the same essence as God, and we can realize Him, we can see Him, only after going within. Masters have told us how to go within. So that is why we should withdraw our attention from all the outer things and go within. Because God, for Whom we are searching, is nowhere outside. He is only within us.

38

When We Do Simran Lovingly

Sant Ajaib Singh Ji

a talk given May 26, 1988, in New York City

Make the mind quiet as only quiet minds can meditate. Don't understand meditation as a burden. Do it lovingly. While meditating don't pay any attention to the outer sounds. Don't allow your mind to wander outside. Concentrate at the Eye Center. When we do the Simran lovingly, keeping our attention at the Eye Center, the streams of the lower forces which are pulling our soul down, become weaker and one by one those forces (you can even call them the chains of the forces of the mind), start breaking by themselves, and they free our soul.

When we do the Simran lovingly, keeping our attention at the Eye Center, we rise above the level of mind and the organs of sense and our soul becomes free from the forces of the mind. When we are doing the Simran our soul is being pulled down by all these negative forces or streams, and that is why we are not able to remain at the Eye Center. But when we make the habit of remaining at the Eye Center and when we do the Simran lovingly, then our soul also rises above and the middle of our soul brightens up — it becomes bright — and we can see a very beautiful, very bright light within. Then we can remain at the Eye Center for a longer time. Right now because we are not doing the Simran lovingly and not keeping our attention at the Eye Center, our attention drops down and the worldly thoughts bother us a lot. But when we do the Simran lovingly, keeping ourselves at the Eye Center, then one by one all the worldly thoughts go away from our within and in their place comes Simran. Now we may hear the Shabd, but that Shabd is not pulling us up, because our soul is not at the Eye Center. Our soul, our attention, is wandering here and there below in the body. And because she is being pulled down by the lower forces: lust, anger, greed, attachment and egoism, that is why she is not being pulled up even though we may hear the Shabd. Only when iron is placed in the range of a magnet will that magnet pull it towards itself. If the piece of iron is not in the range of the magnet, or if it is rusted, then what is the fault of the magnet? The magnet has the power, but since the iron is not purified and it is not placed in the range of the magnet, it is not being attracted by the magnet. In the same way, when our soul is not purified, when our soul is not in the range of the Shabd, how can the Shabd pull it up? We may hear the Shabd, but because our soul is still down in our body, the Shabd does not pull us up. So it is very important to keep ourselves at the Eye Center and do our Simran devotedly and lovingly.

Satsangis should not miss the regularity because in regularity is the prosperity. If we miss meditation even for one day it takes us three days or more to meditate and fill up that gap. Because even if we meditate for four or five hours daily, still because we think about the world a lot, the worldly portion is much more. That is why the Satsangis should make a habit of regularity in their meditation. Even if it is only a little, it doesn't matter, but they should be regular in meditation.

Satsangis should be very careful with their mind. They should live their life differently than the lives of worldly people. You should know that this is the last chance; this is the last time that you have come into this suffering world, and with the grace of the Master, you have to go back to your real Home. That is why Satsangis should always be very careful with, and always keep a strong guard against their mind. Master Kirpal graciously gave us the diary to fill up. It is the best way to keep a strong guard against the mind and to introspect ourselves.

So you have to do your Simran lovingly. Don't bring any worldly thoughts in front of you while doing the Simran.

39
The Master Loves His Satsangi Children

Sant Ajaib Singh Ji

a meditation talk given December 23, 1988, at Sant Bani Ashram, Rajasthan

Every day I will be saying the Simran, but please do not record it.

I feel great happiness sitting in meditation with all of you dear ones, because you know that Saints and Mahatmas are full of love. They are the Form of Love and in fact They have come into this world carrying a lot of love from God Almighty only to distribute that love amongst us.

The worldly family of the Masters can become the heir to the worldly property or the worldly things the Masters own, whether they are the children of the Master or those who live around the Master, they can only become the heir to the worldly belongings of the Master. But the devoted Satsangis have to become the heir spiritually, of the spiritual wealth of the Masters, and that is why the Master loves His Satsangi children more than He loves His own life.

We do not know the Power of the Simran until we go within. Behind the Simran we do, the great Power of the Master is hidden. The renunciation, the hard work which the Master has done, is contained in the Simran we do.

Our progress in this Path mainly depends upon our concentration in the meditation. The more we concentrate, the speedier our progress in this Path will be. When, after concentrating at the Eye Center, we get the habit of remaining there for some time, then the inner path or the inner way becomes open to us very clearly; it is even clearer than a clear mirror. And then we can see everything with our own eyes.

Dear Ones, at present, it is very difficult for us to give up the bad thoughts because we have become like a form of the bad thoughts. Whatever thoughts we have are bad; they all have to do with the worldly things. That is why it is very difficult for us to get rid of those thoughts, and only because of that we are not able to concentrate. But gradually, when we do the Simran and start concentrating and remaining at the Eye Center, then all these bad thoughts go away, and instead of the bad thoughts and the worldly thoughts, we get the good thoughts. After that, no matter how much we try, we cannot think of a bad thought, we cannot think of a worldly thought. We cannot even think of the passionate thoughts of the world; whatever thought we have, will only be regarding the Simran or the Path.

If there is any fortunate dear one who has had success over the bad thoughts he has done so only after going in the within.

All this meditation we are trying to do day and night and all the efforts we are making is in the direction of going within.

We can reach the plane which has the suns, moons, and stars only by doing the Simran, and only by doing the Simran can we can cross these planes and reach the Form of the Master. Our within is full of Light and before reaching the Form of the Master all our inner path is illuminated with these stars, suns, and moons. Dear Ones, our real journey starts only after going within and only after reaching the Form of the Master.

Before we start doing the meditation we should be mentally prepared for doing it. We should remove all the worldly thoughts from within us. We should know that we are sitting here for some very special work, and we are supposed to do only the Simran while we are sitting here in the meditation. You can even tell your mind, "We do not interfere in your work when you are doing the worldly things, now when we are sitting here for doing something very special you should not interfere in our work and you should not bring in the bad thoughts, or any thought, to distract our attention." And having this kind of attitude you should start doing the meditation. I have often said that you should never understand meditation as a burden, because only if you do it lovingly will you become successful. Any work you do with all your love, even in this world, you are sure to get success in that, so that is why you should never understand meditation as a burden; do it lovingly.

40

Because He Had Sympathy for Us

Sant Ajaib Singh Ji

a meditation talk given March 24, 1989, at Sant Bani Ashram, 16 PS, Rajasthan, India

No one should record the Simran, please. I will be repeating the Simran each time before we sit for the meditation, but no one should record it. This is only for those dear ones who may have any difficulty in pronouncing the Names. So you should correct your pronunciation, after hearing me repeat the Names, but do not record it in the tape recorder.

The other reason I will be repeating the Simran is that I want every Satsangi to repeat these Holy Words with their tongue at least a couple of times before they sit in meditation, so that your mind may know for what purpose you are sitting. Because many times it happens that when we sit for meditation, and we have not repeated the Words like we repeat them here, our mind makes us forget the purpose for which we are sitting. Only our body is sitting there, whereas our mind is not involved in doing any Simran, which is the purpose of sitting for meditation. So that is why I will be repeating the Simran each time before we sit for the meditation.

Since we all have come from different communities and religions — and you know that people belonging to all these different communities think that they are following the Path of the Masters — but the fact is that we do not even know what the Path of the Masters is. So now when you have become Satsangis, when you have really come on the Path of the Masters, you know what is meant by saying, "follow the Path of the

Master." You know how one can follow the Path, and how we have to become gurumukhs, and what is involved in becoming a gurumukh. So I think that now you have realized the difference. And being Satsangis, now you should put all your effort into following this Path of the Masters.

It is like this: suppose we had only heard about rock candy, that "it is sweet," and that "when you eat it, it tastes sweet in your mouth," and things like that, but we had not tasted it yet. Later when we have eaten rock candy and have enjoyed its sweetness on our tongue, then we know how sweet the rock candy actually is. In the same way, before we come to the Master and start following the Path of the Master, we have only heard about the Master and this Path. But now when we are actually put on this Path of the Master, when we have met the Master, and we have brought the Master into our experience, then we know the difference between just talking about Him and knowing about Him, and really knowing Him.

The same thing is true about the importance of Naam. Previously we did not know the importance of the Naam, nor how great the Naam is. But after we come to the Master and He puts the ray of Naam within us, which is out of His great treasure of Naam, and afterwards when we develop that capital of Naam, and really manifest that Naam within us, only then do we realize how great a gift the Master has given us. Only then do we realize that there can be no more precious donation than the donation of the Life Impulse of the Master, which is in fact in the Form of the Naam.

Guru Nanak Sahib says, "Naam is my friend; Naam is my companion; Naam is my mother; Naam is my father; Naam is everything I have; Naam is my sangat; and Naam is the only Light, and Naam is the only thing which has brought me out from the darkness. With which tongue can we go on describing the glory and importance of Naam? But I am very grateful to my beloved Lord; He has given me the Naam, and has connected me with the Naam." He says, "I sleep in Naam, I awake in Naam; I deal in Naam, I play with Naam. Wherever I go and whatever I do, it is all with the Naam."

That is why Sehjo Bhai has said, "There is no way we can pay back the Master for what He has given to us, because He has given us the precious Naam." She says, "Even if I sacrifice my everything, I still cannot pay back my Master for the Naam He has given me." In the same way Kabir Sahib also says, "It is not possible for a disciple to pay back the Master for the precious Naam which He has given to the disciple, because Naam is that Power which supports all the three worlds. He has given us that Power of Naam only because He felt gracious; only because of His Grace have we received It."

Even though India has developed a lot, still in comparison to America it is nowhere, and that is why some people who go to the United States, when they come back, they tell people that America is like heaven in comparison to India, because of all the material comforts over there. But those who go within, and those who have seen the Home of our Beloved Lord Kirpal, they say, "What to speak of the heavens, even the heavens are nothing in comparison to the Home of our Beloved Lord Kirpal." Because in the heavens also there are many difficulties, there are many problems; there is lust, anger, there is birth and death, there is darkness over there. Even in the heavens all these things exist. But in the Home of Beloved Lord Kirpal there is no trace of darkness, there is no lust, there is no anger and there are no passions. There are no difficulties, there are no pains and problems of this world. It is the plane of complete consciousness and complete light. There is no birth, there is no death, it is all happiness over there and our Beloved Lord Kirpal is there.

When the dear ones go within and see the Home of our Beloved Lord, only then do they realize how gracious our Beloved Lord was to come down into this world and assume this body which is full of hardships and difficulties. He did that because He had sympathy for us and because of His sympathy

He came and lived among us. He told us about His home and He prepared us to go back to our Real Home. So Dear Ones, how can we be grateful to our Beloved Lord, and how can we ever try to pay back for all the things He has given to us? Because He left His home which is full of comfort and convenience and He came down into this world which you know is full of hardship and sufferings and He did that only because He had sympathy for us. He gave us that powerful Naam, that precious Naam, which is supporting the three worlds. And Dear Ones, when He has put us on that Path of the Naam, when He has given us that Power of Naam, it becomes our responsibility also to do the devotion of Naam.

So Dear Ones, I am very happy to be able to meditate with all of you, because only those people who have the realization of the importance of Naam, know how important it is to meditate and only they appreciate the devotees of Naam. So I am very happy to be able to sit here and do the meditation with you. Kabir Sahib has said, "I am ready to sacrifice myself for those dear ones, and I would even make shoes out of the skin of my body for those dear ones who repeat the Naam even in the state of sleep." Such is the glory of the devotees and the meditators of the Naam. I hope that — since we have been given this precious opportunity to sit in the remembrance of our Beloved Lord and do the meditation which He has graciously given to us — that you will withdraw your attention from all the outer things. Forgetting all of the difficulties and problems which you might have back in your home, I hope that you will concentrate mainly and completely on the meditation of the Naam, and that while you are sitting here you will always do the Simran and that you will do the Simran lovingly, without understanding it as a burden.

41
We Need a Guide
Sant Ajaib Singh Ji

a talk given in Bangalore, India, July 1989

It is a very good time, God Almighty has given us this human birth. Human birth is the highest in all creation, man is called the leader of the creation. As he is the leader of creation, he has more responsibilities because the bigger heads have more headaches.

What is the responsibility the human has? It is the responsibility to think and to consider where he was before he came into this world and where he has to go after this world. This problem can be solved only if he does the devotion of the Lord and only if he goes in the company of someone who has solved this problem himself. Master is the one who can solve this problem for us; God Almighty Himself comes into this world in the Form of the Masters and He puts us on the Path. Guru Nanak Sahib says, "We are the forgetful ones, we are the lost ones, and the Master Himself puts us on the Path and makes us do the devotion of the Lord." You know that in this world there are many stumbling blocks, there are many pitfalls, and there are many obstacles. Even in this world we need a guide; we need someone who can help us make our journey. In the same way, in the Path of Spirituality we also need a guide. Master is the One Who helps us and Who takes us across. In this human body we have more responsibilities and we have the bigger responsibility of doing the devotion of the Lord. Guru Nanak Sahib says, "Meditate on Naam, do not forget, because this is the only benefit you can gain in the human body."

We should also do our meditation wholeheartedly, without paying any attention to the outer disturbances. You know that in this world everyone is turning to his own work. We are also sitting here for doing something very special — the work which we have been given by our Master. So we should do our meditation sincerely, without paying any attention to the outer disturbances. We should not understand the meditation as a burden, we should do it lovingly.

42

With the Help of the Master

Sant Ajaib Singh Ji

a meditation talk given July 25, 1990, at Sant Bani Ashram, Sanbornton, N.H.

I am very thankful to my Gurudev, Supreme Father Kirpal, and I am indebted to Him that, showering His limitless grace upon me and upon all of us, He has connected us with the Naam.

Ever since our soul has come down into this world, come down from the pure, holy spiritual worlds, the physical, astral, and causal covers have covered our soul and she has forgotten, she has lost her light completely.

The essence of God has completely forgotten the Path to go back to her Real Home, and she has been given this human body. Graciously God Almighty has given her the human body, and, in order to take the soul back, God Almighty also comes in the human form.

The world which is full of pains and happiness — this is the place where we are stuck, and we are stuck in this world only because we are accompanying our mind.

Usually we say, "We get what we wish for," and it is also said, "You go to the place where you are attached." When we go to the Masters and get Initiation from Them, and when we wish to return to our home, then that wish is also granted with the grace and the help of the Master; because of our wish to return to our home, we also get back to our home.

So it is a very precious time. Taking advantage of this precious time, all of you should remember the Five Sacred Names in your within, and closing your eyes and repeating these Holy Words you should start doing your meditation.

SILENCE

43
Something Worth Experiencing
Sant Ajaib Singh Ji

a meditation talk given on July 29, 1990, at Sant Bani Ashram, in Sanbornton, N.H.

It is a very precious time, Supreme Father Kirpal has showered so much grace upon us. He has given us the secret of His Real Home, He has made us hear the Shabd, the Sound Current. In the beginning anything which you try to do is difficult. The mind becomes dry. It is difficult to sit in meditation. But if we go on meditating, if we go on listening to the Sound Current, if we go on doing the Simran everyday, then we become competent in that because whatever work you do on a regular basis you become perfect in that. So when we collect our attention at the Eye Center, when we start remaining there, then we start enjoying the nectar which is dripping down from the Naam. We can taste that nectar of Naam only when we come to the Eye Center. That nectar which our soul experiences or tastes, only the soul can describe its quality. It is something worth experiencing.

Bhagat Nam Dev says, "We cannot become the exalted one, the highest one, by any worldly name and fame. We cannot be the highest one by any rule or any power. We cannot get any high position by doing anything of this world. If there is any way to become the highest of all that is by the meditation of Naam. Lovingly He says, "By repeating the name Gobind, Gobind, by repeating the name of the Lord, my mind was imbued in the love of God. I was worth nothing but because I was doing the meditation of the Lord I became precious."

Kabir Sahib was born in a poor family, a low caste family, and He was working as a weaver. Because of His devotion to God, He gave up His job as a weaver and He became a very serious devotee of the Lord.

Sain the Barber was the one who was rejected and looked upon as a bad person by everyone in every home. They used to talk against him, but because of his devotion to the Lord he became worth worshiping and became the Beloved of God.

History tells us that when Bhagat Nam Dev was doing his devotion he was bothered a lot by the Mogul Emperor of that time. The rulers of that time often forced other people to join their religion, and the Mogul Emperor Sikander Lodi bothered Bhagat Nam Dev a lot. You know that no one takes care of those forts and palaces where Sikander Lodi used to live, and there is no one there to remember his name. But because Bhagat Nam Dev did the devotion of the Lord, He has so many disciples. Millions of people get up in the morning and they lovingly remember the name of Bhagat Nam Dev and they do the devotion of the Lord. They feel honored doing that because He was the Beloved of God who made contact with God Almighty and did the devotion of the Lord. That is why lovingly people remember Him, whereas nobody remembers or takes care of the places where Sikander Lodi lived. They have become ruins. Guru Nanak Sahib says, "The low one who is not known by anyone, if he does the meditation of Naam, he becomes known in all the four directions."

The Naam has so many good qualities in it, and by meditating on such a Naam we gain so much — so why not do the meditation of such a Naam which gives us eternal peace and happiness? Catching hold of that Naam we can go back to our Real Home. Why not do the meditation of that Naam? We should especially take advantage of this precious Ambrosial Hour and we should devote ourselves to the meditation of Naam.

It is a very pleasing thing that anyone can do the devotion of Naam. It doesn't matter whether one is old or young or whether one is man or woman. It doesn't matter to which country or to which state we belong, people belonging to all different countries and states, and all different religions can do the devotion of the Lord and they can meet Him within. So taking advantage of this precious time we should all sit in meditation, closing our eyes.

44

The Ambrosial Hour

Sant Ajaib Singh Ji

three meditation talks from Idaho

Well, it is the morning ambrosial hour. Our beloved Lords, Sawan and Kirpal, have showered so much grace upon us. They have done such a favor to us. They have given us this opportunity to do Their devotion, to sit in Their remembrance. They have given us the Naam which is Their life impulse. When the Master gives us the Initiation, He gives us His own life impulse. So He has given us such a gift that we cannot thank Him enough. There is no way we can pay Him back for all He has done for us. So that is why millions of times I salute the Feet of my Beloved Lords Sawan and Kirpal.

Guru Arjan Dev Ji Maharaj said, “Do not spend all your night in sleeping. Sleep as much as it is required for maintaining good health, but don’t spend all your night in sleep. Wake up early in the morning and do the meditation.” He says that for those who wake up in the morning and do the meditation, the Negative Power does not play mischief with them. And one who meditates on Naam becomes free from the tricks of the Negative Power. You know that there are so many tricks of the Negative Power with which he is always bothering us, like lust, anger, greed, attachment and egoism. So Guru Arjan Dev Ji Maharaj says, “Those who get up in the morning and do the meditation of Naam, and take advantage of this precious time, they are not bothered by the tricks of the Negative Power. They become free of It.”

Before we sit for the meditation, it doesn't matter if you are sitting here, back in your home or anywhere, anytime before you sit in the meditation, make sure that you remember the Five Sacred Names. And when you have memorized them, when you remember those Five Sacred Names, then with your eyes closed and without understanding meditation as a burden, you should lovingly sit for meditation.

June 12, 1992

It is the morning ambrosial hour; salutations unto the Holy Feet of our Beloved Gurudevs, Sawan and Kirpal, who gave us that donation of Naam, Who gave us this opportunity to sit in Their remembrance. This is a reality, all the Saints have said this aloud, that there is one God, there is one Giver, and He can forgive whomever He wants to. Wherever He wants He can shower the Naam, wherever He wants He can cause the prosperity to shower.

Humilty is the sign of greatness. In Punjab there is a very famous saying that the branch of the tree which bears more fruit lowers itself down. So humilty is the ornament of the Masters and the Saints. It is the sign that they are great.

Naam is all-pervading, Naam is within us, and only from our within can we unite ourselves with the Naam. So with all our strength, withdrawing our attention from the outside we should sit within and we should do our Simran.

June 13, 1992

It is the ambrosial hour, human birth also is an ambrosial hour. God Almighty has given us an opportunity, a chance, to meet Him and do His devotion.

Before you start doing the meditation, here or at your home — it doesn't matter where you are meditating — but whenever you have to start doing your meditation, first of all think about this precious hour which you are going to devote to the meditation. Make sure that you do not have to do anything in the middle of this hour. If there is anything which you must do or which you must attend to during the hour, you should finish it before starting the meditation. And after that, do the meditation lovingly, don't understand it as a burden. Also before starting the meditation make sure that you remember the Five Sacred Names.

I am very thankful to my Beloved Gurudevs, Lords Sawan and Kirpal, Who have given us this opportunity to sit in Their remembrance. So all of you please close your eyes and start doing the meditation.

June 14, 1992

45

God Almighty Hears our Plea

Sant Ajaib Singh Ji

a meditation talk given January 6, 1994, in Bombay, India

I bow down at the Feet of Lords Sawan and Kirpal, Who showering limitless grace upon us, have given us this opportunity to sit together in Their remembrance. It is only because of Their grace that we are sitting here and are practicing to connect ourselves with Them.

Before sitting in the meditation, whether it is here or at your homes, tell your mind that now you are going to sit for a very important work and he should not bother you. Then you should repeat the Five Holy Words of the Simran, slowly with your tongue. When you do not find any difficulty in repeating the words with your tongue, then do it mentally. Tell your mind that this is a very important work and he should not disturb you. To struggle with the mind is meditation.

Never understand meditation as a burden. Do it lovingly. The work which we do lovingly we become successful in it.

I am very pleased to be sitting with you in the meditation every day. I never go away after making you sit in the meditation. I feel the same happiness sitting with you in the meditation which I got on the very first day, when I became a receptacle of the grace, when Master Kirpal first made me sit in the meditation.

So it is the ambrosial hour. Guru Nanak Sahib has said that when the rainbird is looking for the *swanti* drop [pure rain], he calls for that drop and the Almighty Lord, God Almighty orders

Lord Indra, the god of rain, to shower rain on the earth. So when God Almighty hears the plea, hears the cry of the rainbird, He orders Lord Indra and in that way that papiha, that rainbird, satisfies his thirst, he gets that swanti drop. In the same way, the meditation which we do here, the Simran which we do here, is like calling, just like making the plea at the Court of the Lord.

So just as God Almighty listens to and responds to the call and the prayer of the rainbird, He also listens to our call, He also responds to our call. But since we do not reach the place where He is responding to our call, where He is responding to our Simran, that is why we do not have the knowledge of how He is showering grace upon us. The Saints and Mahatmas, those Who go within after doing the meditation and Who reach that place, they know how God Almighty is listening to our every single word and how He is responding and how He is showering grace upon us.

So all of you start doing your meditation, closing your eyes. Don't open your eyes until you are asked to open them. Some dear ones think that their friends have left while they are still sitting here. No Dear Ones, it is not this way. You will be told to open your eyes and we will also sing a bhajan. So until you are asked to leave off, continue doing your meditation.

46

Carrying the Basket of Grace

Sant Ajaib Singh Ji

a meditation talk given in Ahmedabad, India, on September 16, 1994

Salutations unto the Feet of Lords Sawan and Kirpal Who have given us the opportunity to do Their devotion; we the forgetful and the wandering ones, and He Who has given us the strength to do Their remembrance. I have always been telling you, whether you were sitting here in the meditation for the last eight days or back in your homes, I have always said, "Never understand meditation as a burden, always do it lovingly."

When I was coming back from South Africa to Bombay, at the airport, I saw some dear ones from Arabia, some sheiks, and when the time came for offering their prayers, the *namaz*, not all of them, but some of them, those who had maintained the regularity in performing the namaz, offering the prayers, even though the airport was very crowded but still at that time they spread out their mat, they spread out their piece of cloth and they started offering their prayers. Now they did not have the grace of the living Master. They don't have the perfect Masters over their head, but whatever practices they were doing, even though the name which they are repeating is not the True Naam, but still they did not miss it, they maintained their regularity. We satsangis are always told that we have to be regular in our meditations. We should never miss the meditation. Master Kirpal Singh Ji used to say that you should not feed your body until you have fed your soul with the food of meditation.

Usually in the houses or around the houses there are small

gardens and trees and in the morning hours the birds come there. Very early in the morning they remember God Almighty in their own language.

Farid Sahib says, "I sacrifice myself on those birds who live in the jungles, in the forest. They pick up their food among the pebbles on the wayside and they eat, but not even for one moment do they forget God." They only get to eat the weeds and the fruit pits and things like that because the real fruit is taken away by the owners of the field. If the birds try to eat the real fruit then the owners chase them away. But still the birds express their gratitude to God Almighty in their own ways.

We human beings try to eat the best food. We try to sleep on the best beds. But do we have at least that much yearning, which the birds have, to get up early in the morning and connect ourselves with Him?

Who gets connected with God Almighty? Only one who has done His devotion and has become His own form. Guru Arjan Dev Ji Maharaj says, "In the early morning hours before the sun rises and all the birds get up, the Saints have assumed this surprising form." "They connect themselves with Lord Almighty," says Nanak.

Mirabai fell in love with the Naam. She fell in love with Her Master and said, "O sleep, if I may find any customer of yours, I would sell you off. People may be selling you for ten kilos but I will sell you without asking for anything; I will just sell you free of charge. Go to those people who do not do the devotion. What do you have to do in the homes of the devotees."

When Guru Arjan Dev Ji fell in love with His Master Guru Ramdas; when He got in love with the Naam, what did He tell sleep? He said, "O sleep, you go on decreasing," and He said to the night, "O night you go on increasing. May the night be of six months so that I may always remain connected to my beloved."

Master Kirpal used to say that those who have made their nights they have made everything. And I often say, Dear Ones, that gold can be obtained only by digging in the mine. If you want to have the valuable pearl you have dive deep into the ocean. Not even a mother can give birth to a child without enduring the pain.

So the obstacle which is in the way of the meditator is that of sleep and laziness.

That is why Sant Mat demands hard work. The wealth which we have earned ourselves is our very own. If the student will pay attention to the talks or to the things of the teacher only then will that teacher put all his attention on that student. In the same way, the Master will shower grace upon us only if we will do our part.

Everyday the Saints tell us not to get attached to the feet because whatever They have, whatever there is, it is in the forehead and in the eyes of the Sadhu.

The hypocrites have made us have the habit of touching the feet of the Masters. Once a dear one went to Master Sawan Singh and he fell at the feet of Master Sawan Singh. He did not want to get away from the feet of Master Sawan Singh. Master Sawan Singh rebuked him. The other dear one who was there said, "Master he has so much yearning for you and it is not in his control so shower grace on him." Master Sawan Singh said, "Every morning at 3:00 a.m. I go to every person carrying the basket of grace. Rare are the fortunate ones, who at that time wake up and get the grace."

Sufi Saint Farid Sahib says, "The early morning meditation is just like the flowering of the plant. And the meditation which we do in the later part of the day is like getting the fruit." So those who remain awake in the early morning hours and meditate they get the grace of the Master. Those who sleep during that time they remain without the grace.

In the early morning hours the Master is distributing the musk, the grace to everyone. Those who get up at that time they receive it from the Master. Some dear ones get up but if they fall asleep once again they are deprived of that grace.

So that is why he says that in the early morning hours it is like the flowering of the plant and then we get the fruit. Those who will remain awake they will get the grace from the Master. In the night the Master distributes the musk. One can not get it if he is asleep. One can get it only when he is awake and if it is written in his fate. So that is why all the satsangis should put meditation as number one. Then as number two you should have sleep. And unless you have done the meditation in the early morning hours don't let the sleep bother you.

So before starting the meditation remember the Holy Simran. Close your eyes and start the Simran.

47

An Ounce of Practice

Sant Ajaib Singh Ji

a meditation talk given January 12, 1994, in Bombay, India

I bow down at the Feet of my Beloved Gurudev Lords Sawan and Kirpal Who have showered so much grace upon us and Who allowed us to do Their devotion. For the past so many days I have been sitting here meditating with you. I have been very happy to do that because an ounce of practice is worth much more than tons of knowledge. It is better to meditate than to teach others. It is much better, a million times better, to become an example than to preach to others. Our Hazur Maharaj Ji used to say that this Path of the Masters, the Sant Mat, is the Path of the brave people. It is not the Path of the cowards. Those people who are always ready to practice anything in order to conquer this fort of the body — for them only is this Path.

It is worse to surrender than to be defeated. When you sit for the meditation every satsangi should say, "No," to the mind and should tell his mind, "Now we are sitting for something very special, you should not bother me." The mind should just leave you alone so that you can do your meditation.

Before sitting in the meditation make sure you remember the Five Holy Words and if there are any important works to be attended to before the meditation, like your work of the home, or the worldly work, finish all of them before doing the meditation. When you sit in meditation do not understand it as a burden.

Everyday meditate regularly — do it with love and affection.

48
The Only True Wealth
Sant Ajaib Singh Ji

meditation talks from Bombay, January 1995

Salutations unto the Feet of God Almighty Kirpal and Sawan Who have given us this opportunity to sit in Their remembrance. It is all Their grace that we are sitting here in His remembrance — the One Who is the Form of the Shabd, Who came into this world, assumed the body, and told us about the secret of His Home.

You know that for many days which are going to come, we have to sit together in Their remembrance and collect that wealth, that capital of Naam, which will go with us when we leave this world. And also collecting that wealth of Naam we have to live our life in this world peacefully and happily.

We know that at this time of day everyone is running towards his destination, be it the birds, or animals, or the human beings. Everyone is running, they are fast progressing toward their destination. They are not stopped by any things which come in their way. So in the same way, since we are also sitting here for doing our own work, without paying any attention to the outer disturbances and noises, without feeling any obstacles on the way, without getting stopped by anything, we should do the Simran with a quiet mind, and move towards our destination.

It is the message of all the Saints that the devotion of God Almighty is the only true wealth. It is the giver of true peace and happiness and it is the remover of lust, anger, greed, attachment, and egoism — and of all the sins.

But it is a reality that we do not get this wealth of devotion of God Almighty until we go and sit at the feet of the Master Who has pleased Lord Almighty and who has manifested Him within Himself. The Saints and Mahatmas are not the equals to God but They are the beloved children of God. You know that whatever a beloved child wants, his father will do for him. Because of Their devotion and sacrifice the Masters have pleased God Almighty and even though the Masters, the Saints and Mahatmas, are not equal to God, but still because of Their love and devotion, They are far superior to God Almighty.

Guru Nanak Sahib says, "Whatever They want to get done, They get done. Once you take refuge at the feet of the Master, you do not have to come back into this world again."

Bhagat Namdev Ji says, "God Almighty says, 'Even if I tie someone up, the devotee, the *bhagat*, can untie that person.' And He also says, 'Even if I have tied anyone, the devotee, or the perfect Master can untie that person.' The Masters, or the *bhaktas*, the devotees, have controlled God Almighty; because of Their devotion, They have pleased Him."

So first of all, in these days that we will sit here, before starting the meditation, make sure that you remember the Five Sacred Names. Before sitting in the meditation you should weed out all the fantasies and all the thoughts in your mind.

Those who have not yet gotten Initiation and have come here with the intention of getting Initiation, they should not waste their time either, they should not wander here and there. They should also sit here quietly and, keeping their attention at the Eye Center, they should go on repeating, "Satguru, Satguru," until they are initiated.

All of you please close your eyes and start doing the Simran.

January 5, 1995

Salutations unto the Feet of Supreme Father, Lords Almighty Sawan and Kirpal, Who have showered so much grace on this poor soul and have given an opportunity to this poor soul to sit in Their remembrance and to do Their devotion.

Guru Arjan Dev Ji Maharaj says, "In your mind, always go on thinking about It, always go on remembering Him, and every morning rise up early and make the efforts. Take the food of the devotion of Lord Almighty, then you will have no difficulties at all."

All the Saints have laid a great emphasis on doing the Simran. The satsangis who do the Simran also know about its importance. Guru Arjan Dev Ji has said, "We have to make the efforts, we have to work harder, and also we have to do the thinking, we have to remember."

What kind of thinking or remembrance do we have to do? We have to do the Simran, which our beloved Masters have given to us. All the time, whether we are walking, talking, or doing anything, we should always be doing the Simran.

That Kirtan [or Divine Music] emanates from Sach Khand, our Real Home, the place where there is no question of one's being a Hindu or Muslim, where it doesn't matter if one is young or old, or whether one is a man or woman. That Kirtan is emitting from Sach Khand, our Real Home, and it is sounding within us. It is sounding by Itself. Our Beloved Lord, who Guru Nanak Sahib calls, "Our True Friend," or "Our Beloved Friend," He Himself is creating that Sound within us, He Himself is doing that Kirtan within us.

Guru Nanak Sahib says, "Those who do that Kirtan, those who remember Him all the time, those who are doing His Simran are able to hear that Kirtan which God Almighty Himself is creating within us all the time." That Kirtan is always going on within us and we have to listen always to that Kirtan.

When we rise above the nine openings of our body, when we rise above body consciousness, when we close these nine openings and open the tenth door inside, Guru Nanak Sahib says, "Over there the beloved Lord is creating that Sound within us."

It is very pleasant weather and you have forgotten your earlier thoughts, so the Simran done at this time, even a little bit, can be very successful. Do not think that whatever time, whatever moments you are spending, or whatever Simran you are doing, is not counted in your devotion. Guru Nanak Sahib says, "Whatever moment, whatever time, you spend in His remembrance, all that is counted in your devotion."

Those dear ones who do not have the Naam Initiation yet, they should also keep their attention at the Eye Center and go on repeating, "Satguru, Satguru." They should not open their eyes and get up. Unless you are called to leave off you should continue sitting so that the other people who are meditating may not be disturbed.

I have often said that when we sit in the meditation, at that time the mind also opens up his office, he does not want to lose any opportunity. That is why, since he is an agent of Negative Power, it is his job to keep the dear ones from doing the devotion of the Lord. So when we sit in meditation he also starts working; he starts creating such thoughts within us like: "Let me open my eyes and see if the other people are still meditating, or if they have gone?"

So I assure all of you that we will not leave you, we will first tell you to leave off; we will make you sing a bhajan, and then we will go. So nobody should open their eyes and look around to see if everyone else is still sitting or not. You should continue meditating unless you are asked to leave off.

All of you please close your eyes, and start doing your Simran.

January 6, 1995

Salutations unto the Feet of Supreme Fathers Sawan and Kirpal Who gave us the precious ideal of Their devotion and Who gave us the opportunity to do Their devotion.

The Masters have Their duties to perform and the disciples have their own to perform. Graciously the Masters have given us the capital of the devotion of Naam. Now it is for us, for the disciples, to increase the capital of that wealth of the devotion of Naam and we can do that by working hard.

Sufi Saint Farid Sahib says, "O Farid, wake up and clean your mosque. What kind of love is this? That you are sleeping while your beloved is awake?"

All the Saints have said that if there is any true temple, if there is any true mosque, or any true abode where God Almighty resides, it is our human body. Because God does not reside anywhere outside, He is residing within us. So that is why Farid says that all the bad thoughts and the other worldly things which we have in our body are like the dirt. So you should wake up in the morning and using the broom of Simran which your Master has graciously given to you, remove all the thoughts, remove all the dirt of this world from your within and make it clean. Just as we clean the temple or holy place where we worship God, in the same way, God Almighty is within us. So we must remove all the worldly thoughts, all the bad things from our within and clean it with the Simran. That Beloved Who is within you is always awake, so you should also wake up early in the morning. If you are not waking up while your Beloved is always up, that means that you are not loving Him enough. If you still claim to be the lover of God, that is a false claim, because if you really love Him, then as He is awake you will also get up.

So all the Saints have said, "Our human body is the truest temple." And They have given us the broom of Simran. Using that broom we should clean our within. And we should always remain awake, if we really love God. As He is always awake, we should also remain awake. Early in the morning we should clean our within and do our devotion.

Kabir Sahib has described this world as a blind well. He says, "We do not have any idea how deep this well is, but taking the lamp of knowledge from our beloved Master, we can remove the darkness of our ignorance." God Almighty is hidden behind a very thin wall of our mind and egoism. But when we take the lamp of knowledge from the Master we can easily remove that wall and we can easily see how, beyond the wall of our mind and egoism, that mighty Lord, Who is mightier than the biggest mountain, is residing within us.

So like every day, close your eyes and start your Simran.

January 11, 1995, Bombay

Salutations unto the Feet of Supreme Almighty Lords Sawan and Kirpal Who have given us this opportunity to sit in Their remembrance.

I often say that to struggle with the mind is meditation. Mind is a very obstinate one; he is a dog, he is a back-biter. Saints have also used so many other words, so many other ways to condemn and criticize the mind.

One who has so many bad qualities in him, if someone would obey such an enemy who is a back-biter, who is a thief, who is a dog, who has all these bad qualities, just imagine — *how can a person become successful if he will obey his enemy?*

It is the work of the mind not to allow us to do the meditation, to keep us confused all the time and, when we sit in meditation, to remind us of things which may have happened thousands of years ago.

Tulsi Sahib says, "O Tulsi, to fight in the battlefield may be the work of a moment or two, but to get up everyday and fight with the mind is meditation, and in this battle you don't have any weapons."

Whether you sit in the meditation here or when you return to your home and meditate over there, Dear Children, always before you start doing the meditation you should make sure that you remember the Five Holy Names. Do not go after the meaning of these Words, because in fact these are the Names of the Owners of those great planes through which our soul has to go. So when we go within there remains no doubt; our inner path becomes as clear as an open book to us when we meditate and go within.

For an hour or two, whatever time you have to meditate, refuse your mind and sit in the meditation. Tell your mind that now he should not create any obstacles, that he should not bother you. You just sit there and do your meditation without listening to your mind. You should tell your mind that when he does his work you do not create any troubles for him. In the same way, when you are sitting in your work then he should not create any problems for you. If he still does not understand and if he creates all the troubles within you, just ignore him, do not go after him. Often I have said that just as a crow off a ship, no matter how far it flies away, finally has to come back to the ship, in the same way, your mind has to come back to you, no matter how far he flies away. When you are sitting in the meditation just don't go after your mind. Even if your mind is taking you to America, or England, or if he is taking you around India, just don't go after him. Just sit where you are and do your meditation. If you will not go after him, if you will remain concentrated, then he will come back to you by himself.

The Simran done with love and faith, even for a few days, can become very successful. But what happens when we sit in the meditation? With many dear ones it happens that they do not remember their goal, they do not check their mind, and when they are sitting here — as soon as they close their eyes — their mind takes them away and they go all over. If they analyze the hour that they have sat in meditation here, they will find that they concentrated their mind only for a moment or so.

So I hope that you will maintain the inspiration that you have received for this last eight days. Whether you meditate here or back in your home, always do it with concentration and wholeheartedly. This was a very beautiful occasion. God Kirpal showered so much grace upon us and He gave us this opportunity to sit in His remembrance; it was all His grace. If in the future He will again allow us to do the same, whenever He will shower His grace again in any other program, at that time you should know where you were during the last program, how many faults you have removed, and how pure you have become. So when you go back to your home you should maintain the inspiration which you have received here and you should do your meditations wholeheartedly.

Okay, all of you start doing your Simran, closing your eyes.

January 12, 1995, Bombay

49

The Gift of Devotion

Sant Ajaib Singh Ji

a meditation talk given March 18, 1995

Salutations unto the Feet of Almighty Lords Sawan and Kirpal Who have given us the gift of Their devotion, Who gave us the opportunity to do Their devotion and allowed us to connect with Them.

Wherever I make the dear ones sit in the meditation I always say that before you start doing the meditation make sure that you remember the Five Sacred Names. And then weed out all the worldly fantasies, thoughts, determinations and all the anxieties which are bothering you. Remove all those thoughts and replace them with the Simran. Over there you should give the [whole] place to the Simran.

Whether you sit for meditation here or back at your home, it doesn't matter, but whenever you sit in the meditation you should be sitting with a quiet mind, without any worldly fantasies or thoughts. Your Simran should be going on constantly. Before you sit in the meditation you should make sure that you don't have any other important thing for which your mind would take you out of meditation. Because it is the habit of the mind that when anyone sits for meditation, he makes him remember things which happened hundreds of years ago, and he brings many thoughts within you. He may remind you of many different things which you are supposed to do. So that is why I say that before you sit in meditation back at your home make sure that you don't have to attend to any other work which can be used by your mind as an excuse to take you out of meditation. You should always do your meditation refusing your mind and not listening to him.

Many times the dear ones ask me this question, "Master, how do we know whether this thing has come from our mind or whether this is the Master talking to us?" I tell them that whenever any bad thought comes within you, or whenever any encouragement or inspiration to do anything bad comes to you, you should know that it is coming from your mind. And when any good thoughts, the encouraging or inspiring thoughts, or the desire for meditation comes, you should understand that it is coming from the Master. All those thoughts which have the nature of *Satogun* you should understand as coming from the Master, and you should always take advantage of those thoughts coming from the Master. When you are encouraged or inspired by the Master within, if you take advantage of that time and sit in meditation, you will definitely get a lot of grace and it will help you to go within faster.

So all of you have to do your Simran without allowing your mind to interfere. Also keep the diary. Do not spare yourself. Write in the diary exactly what you have done during the day. Improve yourself. Understand the meaning of doing the diary.

PART IV

Meditation: Questions & Answers

His qualities are limitless, His value cannot be assessed;
Nanak Says, Whomever He desires, He unites with Himself.

GURU ARJAN DEV

We cannot describe the glory of the Master, because He is limitless. He is gracious, and He can take anyone He wants to the Court of the Lord, because God has given Him permission to bring anyone He wants, and has told Him that He will accept all those who come with Him, no matter how they are. All those who go with the Master are accepted by God, and they are all forgiven.

SANT JI

50

An Interview with the Master

An excerpt from Support for the Shaken Sangat; *the questioner is A. S. Oberoi, the author.*

Before concluding this section, I asked Sant Ji a number of questions about the inner Path and am including replies given by Him to some of them in the following paragraphs, in the hope that they may help some of the dear ones.

What are the aids to spiritual progress?

Satsang, faith in the Guru and love for Him.

How can we increase and develop love for the Guru?

By His constant and continual remembrance.

What are "musts" for achievements on this Path?

Abstinence from passions and vices, inner cleanliness, fellow-feeling, spiritual discipline, sacrifice, surrender and devotion to the Guru.

What role does Simran play?

It concentrates the scattered attention at the eye focus and sweeps the soul clean. As long as the mirror of the soul is unclean, the Guru does not allow entry inside.

Where can the grace of the Guru be received?

At the eye focus, by concentration, where the Guru distributes baskets full of His Guru.

How can the progress be accelerated?

By devoting maximum time for Bhajan and Simran.

What retards the progress the most?

Criticism of others. While one has even the tiniest bit within oneself, the inner way will not open up.

What is the preeminence of the Guru?

Being the most true and helping friend and benefactor. He is always with His disciple like a shadow and protects at every step, and feels elated when he finds His disciple at peace.

How can the pleasure of the Guru be obtained?

By obedience.

What does the Guru expect His disciples to do?

To clean themselves of dross, dirt, filth and impurities, and come up to Him.

How can we increase the remembrance of the Guru?

By not allowing anyone to come in between the Guru and the disciple and by eliminating all foreign thoughts.

How can we devote maximum time to Bhajan and Simran when mind is running wild?

Mind is our only foe. We have to constantly quarrel and fight with it, so as to get over it. We have to bring the running mind repeatedly back, so that it stops running and stands still. This is bhajan.

What are "must nots" of the Path?

Non-judgment of others — instead we should judge ourselves. No ill will or ill thoughts for anyone, including one's enemies. Not causing injury to anyone by thoughts, words or deeds.

How can we increase obedience?

By taking the Guru to be All-wisdom and Almighty, and considering oneself to be nothing, so as to understand that all that He says is correct and in our own interest. In this way no sacrifice will seem too big, one will surrender before the Guru completely, and obedience to Him will increase.

What will happen to unbecoming and unmeritorious persons like me who have not meditated except for ten or fifteen minutes at a time? Is there any hope for such people?

Supreme Father Kirpal used to say that there is hope for everybody, provided one mends one's ways. Even in the worldly order, only that son attracts the eye of the father who obeys his orders. This is more true of spiritual dispensation. If we continue doing mental wrestling, the mind will betray us. We should start acting on the words of the Guru, and see how He helps us.

How does the Guru come inside every disciple at the time of Initiation, and how does He help and protect at all times?

At the time of Initiation, the perfect Master makes such an arrangement that the Word-personified Guru is always with the disciple and he keeps progressing. Perfect Masters have two Forms, one of which is inner and Word-personified, and the other is outer and physical. Physical form is necessary for giving the way to the Naam, and the Word-personified guides inside. By virtue of the body which the Guru possesses, He belongs to one world, but by the power of Shabd, He is present everywhere and always protects the disciples and others who love Him.

How does the Guru give the contact with Light and Sound at the time of Initiation?

As Naam and Shabd are manifested in the perfect Master, He is fully conversant with the inner Light and Sound and gives the contact with it by His competence and commission. It is not enough to see Light and Sound, as Kal has made full arrangements inside, and has created his own highest sound, and hidden the cords of the jivas in the Brahm. The Guru who is perfect and competent, and has become Word personified, secures the cords of His initiates from Kal by His Power and authority, and connects them in Sat Lok.

How do the perfect Masters have so much humility and meekness?

The perfect Masters manifest God Almighty within Themselves by lifelong meditation. They see the Lord face to face and realize how exalted He is and how small is the human being before Him. Just as the sea is very large and gives of itself to form rivers and brooks, similarly, the Master souls are like an ocean of humility and meekness, and smallness is their ornament and asset. The humility of the Saints is true and real, not like that of a panther who picks up its prey by bending and bowing down, nor like the bow which takes the life of others by bending; it is not deceptive.

It was seen during the days of Baba Sawan Singh Ji Maharaj and Sant Kirpal Singh Ji Maharaj that some people who were very impressed and fond of Them at first, later went away and behaved indifferently. Why does it happen?

The Path of Truth is simple and straight, and does not permit self-glorification. Mind, which is the greatest deceiver, keeps a very vigilant eye on those who are eminent in any manner, and makes a quick prey of them, by one trick or another; and in this process, inadequacy of inner access and self experience, abundance of temptations and pressures of the mind and of the material world play havoc with the jiva, with the result that faith and confidence in the perfect Master becomes the first casualty, and one starts questioning His words and ways. Saints are Masters of Their will, and act in the manner dictated by the inner power — even though They always give due recognition to what respected persons around them may say, and spare no efforts to comfort all the people who need it and put them at ease. But led by one's misfortune and bad karma, one is driven away from perfect Masters, suffering an irreparable loss. However, the Saints never allow such developments to stand in the way of Their love for those dear ones, and not only wish well for them, but actually go to their rescue and help, whenever it becomes necessary. Past events show that Hazur Maharaj Kirpal went to the hospital numerous times to see such ailing dear ones, and giving His attention, pulled their souls up, so that the dear ones would admit that the Light and Sound which had been missing for such a very long time, had been restored. The jivas may leave a Master soul, but He does not leave them.

Some people think that after a dear one is entrusted with the responsibility of doing spiritual work, he has to meditate very hard to be able to take up the karmic burden of others and liberate the initiate. What is the position?

Saints meditate throughout Their life until Their body is put on the funeral pyre, because They meditate in the first instance for manifestation of the Truth within Their own self, and later for getting its taste and joy as often as They can, because without it the world is nothing but a land of misery.

It has been seen and experienced that after Hazur Maharaj Ji left the body, many dear ones stopped hearing the Satsang, the confidence of many in this Path was shattered and there were many more who changed over to some other path and way. Why did it happen?

The going away of a perfect Master from the world is the greatest catastrophe which can befall the disciples and admirers. When violent thunderstorms and hurricanes blow, even the heaviest trees are sometimes uprooted. As the event is most extraordinary, and exposes the dear ones to very grueling and testing times, many become casualties of the mind. While there are a lot of pressures at those times, it is the lack of meditation and involvement with the Path which plays hell, and either dampens our inclination or takes us away from the Path. The remedy for all this is devotion to the Great Guru, and the utilization of every breath in His holy remembrance.

How can we secure the grace and protection of the Guru?

By reposing in the Guru lovingly, with confidence and devotion, and eliminating everything from the mind other than the Guru in a mood of utter helplessness.

When do we get some taste of Guru's wealth?

When we are lost in His remembrance and forget everything, including the body.

51
The Different Kinds of Simran

Sant Ajaib Singh Ji

a question and answer session given December 29, 1985, at Sant Bani Ashram, Village 16 PS, Rajasthan, India

Master, when doing meditation, is it better to concentrate on the Simran and listen to yourself doing Simran in the mind's eye until it is perfect, or to keep the Simran more as a background to concentrating on the Light?

Often I have said that satsangis should not do any thinking or any fantasizing of the world while doing Simran. There are three means of achieving liberation: Simran, Dhyan and Bhajan All these three practices can happen within our body. By doing Simran we vacate the nine openings, and after crossing the stars, sun, and moon we reach the Form of the Master. Simran takes us only up to the Form of the Master.

When we manifest the Form of the Master within us, that Form is very clear: It is as clear as we are sitting here in front of each other. He will answer all our questions. When the Form of the Master is manifested, we need Dhyan to keep Him there. Usually when the Form of the Master comes within the disciple, sometimes he feels that the Form has gone, sometimes he feels that it has come; but that does not happen. It is not the Form of the Master which comes and goes. It is because the disciple has not attained enough concentration; he has not had much Dhyan or contemplation on the Form of the Master, and that is why he feels that the Form sometimes comes and sometimes goes. If at that time the disciple would contemplate so much on the Form of the Master that he would forget his own self, so that he would only remember the Form of the Master, then that Form would remain there forever and the happiness which the disciple would receive cannot be described.

Many times when we do meditation, if we are aware of our mind then, when we get a little bit of concentration and if suddenly the Light is manifested within us, since we are not fully concentrating and since our mind is also working, then we become afraid and don't know what to do. Many dear ones stop doing meditation when they have such an experience. Many times it so happens that when the disciple is meditating, and if his mind is also working at that time, then if graciously Master manifests His Form there, that disciple does not understand whose Form has come there, because his mind is pulling his soul down while the Master is trying to pull him up. So he becomes afraid and gives up doing meditation. So it is very important that when you do Simran, you should not be aware of your doing Simran.

There are a couple of things which I always say before we sit for meditation. I say them to all the dear ones in all the groups. The purpose of saying them is, that you should always remember those things whether you sit for meditation here or back in your home. If you remember them, you will be able to do the meditation correctly. I always say that you should make the mind quiet, that you should not understand meditation as a burden, and you should not pay attention to the outer disturbances. You should not allow your mind to wander outside.

This is a reality: it has come in my own experience that when the Form of the Master is manifested within you, He remains with you all the time; He accompanies you like a shadow. Not even for one moment does He go away from you. But the thing is that you should first manifest the Form of the Master, and you can do that only when you are meditating correctly, when you are not allowing your mind to play tricks on you.

When the Form of the Master is manifested, other people

who have eyes, they can also see that that Form is accompanying you and that He is always with you. Once when I was going to Punjab on the Rupur canal, at a village called Dyali, I saw a sadhu sitting and many other people were listening to him. That sadhu had performed austerities, and I felt like paying homage to him. You know, before meeting the Masters, I also had done rites and rituals, and performed austerities. So I always had appreciation for those sadhus who had really done austerities. Even though I did not get anything from that, still I appreciate them, because it is very hard work.

So when I went there, he was sitting with some other people of the village. He was sitting on a rope bed, and as soon as he saw me, he got up from that bed and welcomed me. I was trying to sit on the ground, but he said, "No, don't sit on the ground, come and sit with me on the rope bed. Because I see Someone with you." I told him, "No, I am like your servant, and I have come to have your darshan; let me sit on the ground." But he did not let me sit on the ground. When he insisted, I sat on the gunny sack which was there for the people. While I was sitting there he would talk to the other people, and after talking to a couple of people he would again tell me that he was seeing Somebody with me dressed in white with a very great personality. When he told me repeatedly, I told him, "Yes" — since I knew that it was that God Almighty Kirpal Who is pervading everywhere, and it was all His grace that the sadhu saw His presence and could tell that the Master was accompanying me.

So when you are in meditation, when you attain that high position where the Form of the Master is manifested within you, the people who do a little bit of meditation and go up a little bit, even they can also see that the Form of the Master is with you. They can very well see that.

But when you attain such a position you should be very careful; you should not talk about that to other people, because other people will become jealous of you; they will start thinking, "He is an initiate like us — how come he has progressed so much and we have not? And why is Master so gracious on Him and not on us?" Their jealousy may spoil their meditations. So I always say that when you attain such a position you should protect it and not talk about it to anyone except the Master. You should protect it the way a woman protects her body. Because this is the grace of the Master, and when you have had it you should not show it off to the other people.

Sometimes when I do my Simran it sits in my throat and I can be concentrated at my forehead, but sometimes with Your grace the Simran is just in my thoughts. I find that I say it to myself a lot like I am speaking to myself, like speaking from inside, and that's why it is just stuck in my throat. And I wondered if, with time, does it move up from the throat? By doing a lot of Simran, will it move up to the Third Eye?

I have often said that the work which we do every day, if we do it regularly, we become competent in that. If you continue doing Simran in your throat, gradually it will move up and it will start happening with the tongue of your mind.

Do you think that the thoughts which you are having twenty-four hours a day, all the thoughts which are bothering you, that you have not practiced those thoughts, that you have not repeated those thoughts? Now you don't need to work to have those thoughts or fantasies come in your mind; they come by themselves. Do you think that you have not practiced for that? Ever since we got separated from the Almighty Lord, no matter in which body we went, whether it was the body of a bird or animal or any body, we always had the thoughts of that body. We always create a desire for the worldly things and materials and because of all those desires we have developed, we have practiced those thoughts, and it is those thoughts which are bothering us now. It is those fantasies which come in our mind without our making any effort.

Saints have the knowledge of that [condition] and They know what it is that keeps the souls in this world, and They tell us that at the time of death there is no one in this world whose tasks have all been accomplished. If anyone is able to fulfill ten things, five or ten other things remain unfulfilled; and at the time of death those unfulfilled tasks and the thoughts of those tasks go with that soul and in the next lifetime it is those thoughts and fantasies that bother him. So, just as you do not have to make any effort in having those worldly thoughts and fantasies because you have practiced them a lot in your previous birth — you don't know how many ages, how many births, you have practiced them but you don't have to make any efforts in thinking those thoughts now—in the same way, if you practice the Simran with the same amount of strength and energy, the time will come when you will not have to make any effort in doing Simran; it will happen by itself.

These thoughts and desires which we have at the time of death, our intellect for the next lifetime is determined or decided by them. Our thoughts and desires of the time when we leave the body have a direct effect on our intellect. Because of those thoughts of the previous lifetime our fate, our intellect, and our thoughts of the next lifetime are determined. When I was commenting on Tulsi Sahib's *Ratan Sagar* in Colombia, in one of the Satsangs I told a story that Master Sawan Singh used to tell, of a potter. Once he was taking his donkeys loaded with clay to the palace, and he was saying, "Come mothers, come sisters, come friends" — like that. He was calling the donkeys "mothers" and "sisters" and "friends." So someone asked him, "Why are you doing that? They are just donkeys!" He said, "I am practicing, because I am a potter and I am in the habit of speaking very loosely, so I don't want to speak any bad word in the palace; if I speak any bad word in the palace, the king might put me to death. So I am practicing now so that I may speak politely in the palace."

So why do the Saints always emphasize doing Simran? Why do They make us do Simran? They make us do the practice of Simran so that at the time of our death either we should be doing Simran or we may have the Form of the Master within us. If we are doing Simran, or if we are remembering the Form of the Master, we will go directly to Him.

Saints have the knowledge of how, because of the simran of the world, we come into and we go back from this world; again and again we take birth in this world because of the simran of the world. They know the weakness of our mind and how we are stuck in this world, and They also know that the crop which is destroyed by water can be healed or made whole only with other water.

They give us the Simran which They have earned Themselves; and behind that Simran given by the Masters, Their renunciation, Their hard work, Their Charging, is working — and They know that only by doing the Simran of the Master can we cut the simran or remembrance of the world. That is why They tell us to do Simran. And as you know, when we do something without making any effort to have the image or the form of that thing in front of us, that form or that image comes in front of us — if we do the Simran given by the Master, without our making any effort of having the Form of the Master in front of us, we can have it.

In that Satsang I had talked about the personal experience of Master Sawan Singh, Who used to say that there was a judge who all his life long gave out decisions and worked as a judge. At the time of his death, on one side he was about to leave the body, but on the other side he said, "Objection overruled." Whatever simran he was doing all his life long, at the time of his death he spoke the words according to that.

I also spoke about my own experience, that once there was a business man in Padampur who never got married. He always had the desire of getting married, but somehow he never did it. But he always used to think about it. When he was about to die I went to see him, because at that time I was practicing Ayurvedic medicine. When I went there and held his arm to feel his pulse, he thought I was tying a wedding band on his wrist — because in those days in India there was a tradition that people tied a piece of thread to the wrist when they are about to get married. When I held his arm he felt that I was doing that, so he at once said, "Are you tying the wedding band?" I thought in my mind, "Brother, you are preparing for the journey to the beyond; how can we get you married now?" So whatever simran he was doing throughout his life, he remembered that at the time of his death and he spoke out from that. So whatever simran, whatever remembrance, you do throughout your life, you will remember it at the time of death.

Bhagat Trilochan, whose bani is included in Guru Granth Sahib, has written that those who at the time of death do the simran or remembrance of women, are born into the body of a prostitute where they have to indulge with so many men. Nature is not a useless thing. According to our thoughts, we get those desires in our next lifetime, in our next birth. So those who remember women at the time of death, they become prostitutes and their death desire is fulfilled; but in that body they make many more new desires and in order to fulfill those new desires they have to come back into this world again.

Bhagat Trilochan says that at the time of death those who do simran of their homes, they become ghosts and come and live there. Those who do the simran of, or remember, wealth, they come back as snakes.

I have seen many married people who do not have any children. Whenever they give any donations, or do any good thing, they always have this desire: that they will be rewarded with a child. So He says that those who die doing the simran of children, they come back in the body of a pig; you know that pigs have a lot of children, and the sow is always bothered by children because she gives birth to so many children at one time.

Finally Bhagat Trilochan Ji says that those who do the Simran of God, those who love God Almighty, God manifests in their heart, and they are the ones who get liberation. So we should always do constant Simran, because only by doing Simran can we vacate the nine openings and open the tenth door. Beyond that we do not need Simran, beyond that we cross the planes only by climbing on the Shabd.

52
The Pearls of Spirituality
Sant Ajaib Singh Ji

a question and answer talk given February 23, 1986, at Sant Bani Ashram, Village 16PS, India

When children are raised on the Path and they start meditating and going to Satsang, and then they become teenagers and they don't want to meditate and they don't want to go to Satsang anymore, where is the balance of love and discipline?

Often I have said that it is the first duty of the parents to mold the lives of their children, You should tell them of the goodness of going to the Satsang and sitting for meditation, and the benefits of attending Satsangs and doing meditation. And also what good it does to get a good education. You should tell them about the disadvantage of using drugs and doing the bad things which most of the young people in the West do. You should tell them about the disadvantages and all the bad things which may happen if they do not attend Satsang and if they do not meditate. You should tell them all these things *lovingly*. If you teach them *lovingly* it will make all the difference. But the pity is, what happens when the parents are teaching all these things to the children? Either they are angry, having spoiled their own peace when they are explaining things to the children; or when they are trying to explain things to the children they are not doing it in a good way. Most of the time the parents explain these things to the children only after they have fallen into the bad habits. It is much better, and it is advised, that *before* the children fall into the bad habits the parents should explain these things to the children in a loving way — not getting upset, not with a tone of anger, but peacefully and lovingly.

I will tell you a story which Master Sawan Singh used to tell very often in Satsang. I have also told this story very often in Satsang. Once upon a time there was a prince, and he fell in love with the princess of another state. They wanted to get married, but their parents did not agree. They decided that they would run away from home and get married and live happily afterwards, in some other state. So one night, as they had planned, the princess brought a she-camel and she took the prince with her. When they were running away from home they had to cross a small river. As the she-camel came near that water, the princess said, "Pull the rein, otherwise she will sit in the water." And she added that the camel's mother also had that habit of sitting in the water.

Now when the prince, who was a very wise person, heard that the camel's mother had that habit and as a result the she-camel also had the habit, he realized that if even in the birds and animals the children take on the impressions and habits of their parents, then what about the human beings? He thought about the future. He thought, "Today this girl is going away with me and, we'll get married and have children. What if my child, be it a boy or a girl, if he or she were to run away from home and go and get married with someone whom I would not like and to whom I would not agree? What will happen to me? People will criticize me and say, 'His son or daughter has run away and has gotten married,' and at that time it will be very difficult, because whatever we are doing our children will also do the same thing."

Since he was wise and got that realization, right then he changed his heart and did not want to run away with that princess. So he said, "I have forgotten one very important thing in my palace; let us go back and get that. We still have a long night and we can make our journey after we go and get it." The princess did not know that the heart of the prince had changed, so she agreed and they went back. When they got back to his palace the prince folded his hands to her and said, "Thanks to God that we have been saved from doing a sin, because if we had gone away and produced children it would have been possible, that like this animal, they would have become like us, and then people would have criticized us. So it is better that you should go to your home and I should remain in my home and we should not do anything like this."

The purpose of telling this story is that as the birds and animals have the impression and habits of their parents, the human beings also have the habits and impression of their parents. That is why Master Sawan Singh Ji used to say, "If you want to make your children good, first of all you should yourselves become good; because the children learn a lot from their parents." So if you want to teach or explain anything to a child, first you should become perfect in that.

Master Sawan Singh Ji used to talk about His neighbor whose son would steal things from others, and when he would come bringing things from other people, his parents would always appreciate that and say that he was a good boy. Master Sawan Singh Ji used to say, "What can you say to such parents who encourage their child in bad things?"

When a child falls into bad habits he spoils his life, and you know that sooner or later the child definitely gets this thought: "My parents did not do anything good for me, and whatever I have become today, it is only because of my parents." I meet many children in the interviews who have had bad impressions from their parents, and they tell me how much it affected them when their parents were not getting along with each other. Some children who have had very good impressions from their parents because their parents are very good, they also say that they are very grateful to their parents because they have learned a great deal of good from their parents.

Those children who wander away from home and who fall into bad habits, finally when they do bad things and are put into jail, they suffer a great deal of bad karma. They suffer a lot in this world. So those children who make such bad karmas, their parents are also responsible for those karmas, because it was their duty to make the lives of their children, but they did not attend to their responsibilities. That is why whatever karmas the children are making after wandering away from home, the parents are also responsible for that. Kabir Sahib says, "Even the dog of a devotee of the Lord is much better than the mother of a worldly person, because the dog of a devotee, even though she cannot do the devotion, at least she earns the praises of God, whereas the mother of a worldly person or bad person always encourages and inspires the child to do bad things."

It is my personal experience that those parents who have good character, who do meditation, who go to Satsang and who have a very good life, they do not need to explain or tell anything to their children, because children learn by themselves. They go to the Satsang, they sit by themselves, nobody needs to tell them anything.

In the month of October I went somewhere to hold Satsang. They had set up a tent there and the dear ones had made all the arrangements for the Satsang as we do here. After I returned from that Satsang, the dear ones told me that for two months the children went on imitating how we do Satsang. The children did not have any tents to set up; they would gather some rags and used clothes and things like that and make a small tent-like thing and some children would become as the sangat and someone would become as the Baba or the Master and they would pretend they were holding Satsang. They had also made a small underground room-like thing where they would say that the Baba was meditating there. So I mean to say that whatever they had seen, for two months continuously they went on imitating that, doing the things which they had seen.

When Pappu's nephew used to live with them, Pappu's mother told him, "Whenever you go to school you should always bow down to the Master." So whenever he used to go to school he used to come and bow down to me and then go to school. But when he did not have to go to school, when he had a day off, even though I would be standing near him he would not bow down to me. If he had been told that he should bow down to the Master every day, he would have done that. But since he had been told only to bow down when he went to school, that is when he would do it.

So Dear Ones, the parents should take good care of their children. You know that they are innocent souls and they have come into this snare of mind and maya, They also have been given the opportunity to progress spiritually in this world. If their parents are good, the children can not only make their worldly life good, but they can also progress in spiritual life.

You should be very patient when dealing with children. The Masters always behave as a child of forty-days-old in front of their Master and they always get the grace of the Master. Guru Nanak Dev Ji Maharaj says that even if the child makes so many mistakes, the mother does not get upset at him; she always showers grace and she is very kind. The child may do anything wrong and he may make mistakes, but the mother always extends her gracious hand and she is always kind towards the child, because she has to make his life.

Further He says, "O Lord, I am your child; why don't you forgive me and forget all my sins?"

It seems that ever since I was a small child I have been taught to make judgments and to think critically. And up to a point this has been very productive, but having done this all my life the mind now judges automatically, and I find that the judgment extends to people's behavior. I do not wish to do this and I was wondering if there is any way or any kind of secret that one could find to stop this judging of other people's behavior.

The first thing is that it is very difficult to give up a habit. But the only way to give up this habit is meditation; other than that there is no other way by which you can give up this habit. You may have to struggle for the first few days and you may find it very difficult. Whenever your mind inspires you to fall into this habit, you should start doing Simran. He will pull you towards the habit of judging others, criticizing others, but if you are strong and keep doing Simran, gradually by doing Simran and doing meditation this habit will go away.

In the Satsangs Saints always explain these things to us, because Satsang is the only cure for all these things. Always when we sit in the Satsang we should sit with our mind and brain attentive and we should be very attentive to the Satsang. We should sit empty and we should be very attentive to the words of the Master. We should sit wholly, physically and mentally, in the Satsang so that we can understand what the Master is saying. In the Satsang Masters always tell us that you should try to look at the good qualities of other people, you should not pay attention to the bad qualities which they may have.

Once there was a Muslim Fakir who went to a market place where he saw that they were selling *julabies*. Julabies are a kind of sweet, and his mind told him he wanted to eat julabies. The Fakir thought, "Today the mind is asking for julabies, and tomorrow he will ask for a woman, and then he will ask for something else. So I will spend my life fulfilling the desires of my mind and it is not a good practice, so I should teach a lesson to the mind." Since the mind had created the desire of eating those sweets, the Fakir said, "Okay, but in order to buy the sweets you need money and you don't have any money. Let us go to the forest and pick up some wood and after selling the wood and getting some money, then I'll buy the julabies." So he went to the forest, and in the forest his mind told him, "Here is a good spot to pick up the wood and that should be enough to buy the sweets." But since the Fakir wanted to teach a lesson to his mind, he said, "No, let me go a little further and I'll get better wood and get more money." So in that way he gave punishment to his mind. He went very deep into the forest and collected a lot of wood. Instead of carrying one load of wood, he carried two loads. The mind told him that it was too much for him to carry, but he said, "No, if I carry more wood I'll get more money, and I'll get more julabies."

When he came to the city he sold the wood and bought the julabies. The Fakir then told his mind, "Let us go outside the city and then we will eat there." He went outside the city and ate some julabies. After eating some his mind said, "That is enough." But the Fakir said, "No, you wanted julabies, so you should eat all this." When he ate all that he vomited. Then the Fakir told his mind, "This is not a good thing, you should eat this vomited stuff also." So he made his mind eat the vomited stuff also. Then his mind said, "No, that is too much, I cannot do anything more." Whatever julabies were left the Fakir gave to the people who were passing by that place, and then the Fakir told his mind, "This was a punishment for you. Today you asked for the julabies and I have given you that, but now you have realized what good it has done for you. Now this is your punishment: for one year you will not get anything except warm water. And where you were meditating for one hour everyday, now you will have to meditate for two hours."

So the meaning of this is that whenever the perfect soul's mind encourages him or tells him to do anything bad, which takes him away from the Path, he always gives punishment to the mind. The perfect souls do not give in to the desires of the mind. They do not fulfill the desires of the mind, because they know that if one desire is fulfilled mind will create many others.

The Negative Power has imprisoned the soul, and to the soul he has attached the mind, and mind has many types of snares and baits to attract the soul and capture her in the snare. When anyone wants to capture a bird, they spread out some food and they also have a cage in which they catch the bird; in the same way the mind has spread so many kinds of snares to trap our soul. To whatever food the soul is attracted and in whatever way the soul could be captured and imprisoned, mind always uses those means, and the soul is helpless and cannot do anything even though she sees that she is being trapped. She cannot do anything because she is under the influence of the mind. That is why Saints always tell us that we should keep a strong guard against our mind and we should not let our mind have any influence on our soul; and the only way of doing that is by doing Simran. Only by doing Simran can we save our soul from the traps laid down by the mind.

I have read that if we can reach the point where we can keep those tears within the eyes and not let them drop out, they become Pearls of Spirituality. Would you comment on that, please?

When we reach the stage which you are talking about, we get a lot of patience, a lot of contentment, and after that we develop such a state that cannot be described in words. Bikhan Shah has tried to describe that state in His writings. He says, "In both of my eyes I have got the real contentment. Wherever I look I see only Him; whether it is inside or out, I see Him with both my contented eyes." When a soul reaches that state which you have just mentioned, that soul gets patience and contentment and real inner bliss. After that she does not weep and show the tears outside to the people; she does not weep inside, because she is seeing the Almighty Master everywhere. Outside she sees the Master, made up of the physical form which has five elements, who is none other than the Almighty Lord, and that form of the Master tells the disciple to go within. And when such a soul goes within she sees that the same Master is there. When the soul reaches such a state, then she does not need to weep or shed any tears. Even if she wants to do that, she cannot do that. If she wants to become happy she cannot do that — because she has become content, she has attained inner bliss, inner happiness. So things like shedding tears have no meaning for such a soul, because she has achieved that for which she was looking.

If you make a plan or design for making a house, the builders or masons can make the house according to the plan you have made, but a plan is different from the actual construction of the house. If just by having the plan or design of the house, you say that the cement will also come here or you will get the masons and things like that, you cannot get the idea of how all these people are going to work and how you are going to get the house constructed. Only when the house is constructed according to the design are you convinced that it is real. What you had earlier was not the real thing, it was just the design.

In the same way, to talk about the state which you are talking about, when tears become the Pearls of Spirituality, you cannot get the idea about what that stage is, just by talking about it. When the Mahatmas write about all those things in books it is different, but that point or that stage is worth experiencing for the disciple. The intoxication and happiness which the soul gets when she reaches that point is so great that it cannot be described in words. It is just like what you have said. It is just like the design: to go and live in the house is different from seeing the design. In the same way, to experience that stage where your tears become the Pearls of Spirituality, is different from talking about it.

It is pleasing to have the cold sighs, and it is worth having the cold sighs, only when the Beloved for Whom you have the cold sighs is in front of you. It is worth shedding tears, if the Beloved for Whom you shed the tears is right in front of you and He is there with the handkerchief to wipe off the tears. Because He knows that the tears which you are shedding in His remembrance, the tears which you are having for Him, are not ordinary tears, they are pearls, and He does not want to waste any of those, and that is why He has the handkerchief there. He is there to wipe off the tears Himself and to share your pain. Such dear ones who have reached this stage which you have mentioned, when they have cold sighs, or when they weep tears in the remembrance of the Master, are so full of the effect that they can even make the birds of the forest cry, just by their weeping. Their cold sighs are so effective that even the poisonous snakes would not dare to come out of their homes and stand in front of the person who is having cold sighs for the Master. Because they know that the person who is having the remembrance of the Master is so effective, he or she can do anything. So the point which you have made is worth experiencing.

They are the most fortunate people in the world, they are the best people in the world, who have this kind of crying and who can shed this kind of tears. Master Kirpal Himself told me that when Master Jaimal Singh left the body, when Baba Sawan Singh went to visit the body in Baba Jaimal Singh's home village, over there Baba Sawan Singh wept very much. He wept so much that the sangat who was accompanying Him could not resist and they started weeping. When the dear ones said to Baba Sawan Singh, "If you are weeping in your condition, then what is the hope for others; what will be the condition for us, the sangat?" Baba Sawan Singh replied, "O Dear Ones, if my beloved Master Baba Jaimal Singh would come in front of me in His physical form of five elements, even for a moment, I am ready to sacrifice everything just for that one glimpse of His physical form."

I had many opportunities to sing bhajans in front of Master Kirpal. I did not prepare for singing the bhajans. It was not that I would write a bhajan and then sing it to my Master. It would come instantly. In fact it was He Himself who would make me say the words of praise of Him. So whenever in my words of poetry, in my bhajans, I would sing the name of Master Sawan Singh Ji, at once the tears would start rolling down His cheeks and He would start weeping. And those fortunate souls are the best people, those who shed tears in the remembrance of their Master.

When Supreme Father Kirpal left the body of five elements — He came in the Will of God and He left in the Will of God; but when He left His physical body this poor Ajaib wept very much in His remembrance. When I was weeping, one person came to me and said, "You have always said that you should never cry or weep when anyone leaves the body, because just by weeping or crying for someone you cannot bring that person back. You have always said that, but now you yourself are crying. You are a wise person; why are you crying?" At that time I was in deep pain, I could not talk very properly, but still I told him this story.

There was once a king who decided to go on a tour to some other states, to some other kingdoms. He told his queen that he was going on the tour. When he left he did not really go on the tour; after some time he just came back, canceling his tour. But the queen was in love with another man, and when the king had left for the tour she had already made arrangements with this man she loved, saying, "The king has now gone on tour and he will not come for some days, so you come and we will enjoy." When the king came back, at that time the queen and the other man were enjoying and sleeping together. The king was surprised to see that another man was with the queen and he was also surprised because that was the palace. How could another man come into the palace? But when he saw that the other man was with his wife and they both were sleeping naked, he did not get upset. He did not show that he was there and they did not know that the king had come back. The king simply took off his shawl and covered them with it, and he went into the other room.

Now when both of them woke up, the queen was terrified to see the king's shawl over them, and she thought that the king would give her punishment because the king had seen all that they had done, because this was the shawl of the king and nobody else would have come and covered them with the shawl except him. So when the queen thought of that she became very afraid. But the king did not mention anything about that to the queen; even though they met many times after that and lived together for many years, the king never mentioned anything about that to the queen.

After some years, when the king's end time came, he called his sons and gave the successorship to the sons, and then he told his sons that they should respect their mother and obey her. "Take good care of her, she is a good woman; do what whatever she tells you." And then he transferred some property and things for the expenses of the queen also. But when the king was telling his sons to care of their mother, the queen started weeping and went on weeping very bitterly.

The king asked her, "Why are you weeping now? I have transferred so much property to your name and you will be comfortable when I die. What else do you want, why are you weeping?" She said, "I am not weeping for any wealth. I am crying because now, when you are leaving, who will come and throw the shawl over me? Who will hide my faults?"

So I told the dear one that that was why I was weeping. I told him that when the Beloved Master was in the physical form He used to hide my faults, He used to forgive me for my faults. Even now when He has gone back to Sach Khand, in His Radiant Form He is showering grace on me, and He is forgiving me and hiding my faults. But when you have the physical form of the Master in front of you, you can express what is in your heart, you can go and weep at His feet.

Just by having the darshan of the physical form of the Master you can get rid of so many bad sins and bad karmas that you have done, which you cannot do very easily when the Master is not there in His physical form. So that is why those who go within and see the glory of the Master within, and who know how the darshan of the Master works, they weep in the remembrance of the Master, because they know that now the Master is not going to come back in His physical form and hide their faults: He is not going to come and throw the shawl over their faults.

53

The Meditation of the Saints

Sant Ajaib Singh Ji

a talk given October 29, 1986

How do the perfect Masters meditate? How do You meditate now?

This question is very interesting. All the satsangis should listen to it carefully and live up to it.

No doubt such great souls come into this world being sent by Almighty God. They go on searching for Almighty God Who is All-pervading, and the perfect Master, the human pole where the power of God is working, until They meet Him. They are sent into this world by God Himself for the benefit of other people, and right from Their childhood They know about Their mission, They know for what purpose They have been sent into this world. Their meeting with the perfect Master, or that human pole on which the power of God Almighty is working, is also predetermined. And at the appropriate time They meet the Master. Before that appropriate time which is determined for Them, They search for the power of God. They have the effect of maya before that time, but They do not get misled by maya; because right from Their childhood They know about Their mission and They always yearn for the perfect Master. They always keep a distance from the imperfect or false masters. And when the appropriate time comes, They meet the perfect Master and get initiation from Him.

You know that if your vessel is not ready you cannot put something right into it. In the same way if the land is not prepared beforehand you cannot sow the seeds in it. If a person wants to put something in a vessel and the vessel is not ready, he will take some time to clear it and then he can put the thing into it. In the same way if you want to sow some seeds in a field, first you will have to prepare it. If it is not prepared, then it will take some time to prepare it. So such great souls who are sent into this world by Almighty Lord, prepare Themselves and make Their vessel ready before They meet the perfect Master. And when They meet the perfect Master, for Them it is not difficult to put the thing given by the Master into Their vessel.

Right from the early stages the *riddhis* and *siddhis*, the supernatural powers, stand in front of Them holding out their hands, offering themselves to such souls. But They are not interested in those supernatural powers. Right from Their childhood They have a unique kind of consciousness.

You can read the history of Baba Sawan Singh Ji and you can also read the history of all the perfect Saints who came into this world in the Will of God. You can read the history very well and confirm this.

You know about Master Kirpal Singh when He was a child in school. Once He asked for leave from His teacher, saying that His grandmother was dying and He should go home. But the teacher did not believe Him; he thought that maybe He was making a joke or some false excuse. So he said, "You go and sit in the class. How do you know about all this?" A few minutes later somebody came from His home saying, "Please send Pal home because His grandmother is leaving the body and she is remembering Him." After this incident that teacher always respected Master Kirpal Singh.

In the same way there is a story from my childhood which I have not told anyone up until now. I was about eight years old and we had some neighbors who were Muslim people. They were good people. Once I had an experience that my neighbor Ajudeem was taken by the police after being handcuffed. In the morning, about eight o'clock, when I would come out of my house he also would come out and we used to make jokes with each other. So that morning I told him, "Ajudeem, today you will be taken by the police; they will handcuff you." He laughed and said, "Did you have a dream about me?" I told him, "I don't know anything about a dream, but this is what I have felt and I am telling you." He did not believe me. But in the Will of God, at about ten o'clock the police came and they handcuffed Ajudeem and took him into police custody. After a few days they released him because they could not find any evidence against him. Somebody had just complained about him but he did not have any fault.

In the home of my father there were many facilities, many conveniences, and my father was a good person. I could easily get whatever I wanted. Once somebody asked me if I had ever seen hell. I said, "Yes, our home is like hell." So I mean to say that such souls, when they are born into this world, are not affected by poverty or by riches.

All the Mahatmas have taught that we should protect ourselves from the effects of maya. They have said that it is easier for an elephant to pass through the eye of a needle, than for a rich person to do the devotion of the Lord.

When I was with Baba Bishan Das, who laid the foundation of this poor Ajaib, I used to take all my earnings, whatever I used to get in my share of the farming, or whatever I would get as pay from the service — and offer it to Baba Bishan Das. It is very easy to give away your earnings as a donation if the Master thanks you and accepts it with love. But with Baba Bishan Das it was exactly the opposite. He would accept what I would take to him and also he would slap me. It is very difficult to suffer beating after you have given away all that you have earned. But in my case I did not feel like that. I would think, "There is some Reality and I have to look for it."

In the state of Punjab I had many facilities, because right from the beginning the state of Punjab was a very developed state, because the canals came there before they came to other states. I left that state about thirty-five or thirty-six years ago and came to Rajasthan. At present you see green trees and all kinds of things growing here, but in those days it was nothing like that. There was no water in this area. People used to go twenty miles to bring water for drinking. It was difficult for someone who had all the facilities of Punjab to leave that place and come to Rajasthan. But Baba Bishan Das told me to go to Rajasthan. This area is called the area of Bikanir and it is called a religious land. The people in this area did not kill goats or cows; they did not hunt animals for eating. They were very righteous, very religious minded. They did not drink wine, and we never used to have any doors in our houses. This was because the king of this area was also a very righteous person. He was very devoted and he had done a lot of austerities. And he used to understand the people of this state as his children and he used to protect them. This area was considered to be the most religious area, and that is why Baba Bishan Das told me to come to this area and live here. And he told me that the person or the Mahatma who would give me further knowledge would come to me by Himself. I came here after getting Initiation into the first Two Words from Baba Bishan Das, and for eighteen years I did the meditation of those Two Words. I did not waste even one minute of my time in worldly pursuits; I only meditated during that time. Because I was sitting in the remembrance of the Master who was going to come here and give me further knowledge, I did not get involved in worldly pursuits, I did not do anything else other than meditation in that time.

Kabir Sahib said that if someone is thirsty he will drink the water with much yearning, with much love and appreciation, and he will also thank the person who has given him the water. He will say, "You are very great because you have saved my life."

Baba Sawan Singh Ji used to give the example of Tan Sen, the great musician, who was one of the nine jewels in the court of Emperor Akbar. Akbar was a very good king, and he had nine "jewels" or people in his court who would give him good advice to rule over the people in a good way. He was called

Akbar the Great. So Baba Sawan Singh Ji used to say that someone who wanted to learn music would go and wipe off the shoes of Tan Sen, but someone who was not interested in learning music — even if Tan Sen came and wiped his shoes, he would say, "Okay, I'll think about it."

Baba Sawan Singh Ji used to say, "I searched for twenty-two years. I searched in every society, in every religious organization, and I went to every so-called mahatma of Spirituality in India at that time. But when I heard the Satsang of Baba Jaimal Singh, every single word pierced through my heart and removed every doubt that I had had for the last twenty-two years."

When I met the Lord of my soul, Master Kirpal, I did not ask Him which caste He was from, whether He was married or not, whether He had children or not. I did not go into any kind of details like that; because the thing for which I was searching, I got that and I was content with that.

The purpose of giving all these examples and telling you all these things is that I want you to understand the answer to your question very clearly. Now I will answer your question. The question was, "How does the Master meditate, and how do the Masters get the Naam?"

First of all They have a unique kind of yearning in Them. So whatever Their Master tells Them, They accept every single word, understanding His words as the words coming from Almighty God.

It depends upon the Mahatma of the time, whether He wants to explain the theory to the sangat or whether He wants to give the Initiation without explaining the theory. If He wishes He can give His attention and take all the souls back home without making them understand the theory, or without making them do the meditation, because He has no karmas of His own to suffer. But He makes us do the meditation just to give us a demonstration and to create this desire within us, and just to make us understand that He also has done a lot of meditation, He also has worked hard. Such pure and holy souls are very few to be found in life.

As I have said, I had been meditating on Two Words for the eighteen years since my Path had been opened to me, so when I met Master Kirpal He did not feel the necessity to explain the theory to me. He took me into His room and with His grace He took my soul up, and for whatever time He felt appropriate, He kept my soul there. And afterwards He told me to go to 16 PS and meditate, because He said that by meditating every day one becomes more competent.

I had the habit of closing my eyes and sitting on the ground, on a mat-like thing, right from my childhood. And later on when I was a young man I would make underground rooms and sit there for meditation.

Even though Hazur Himself used to stand in the waters of the River Ravi to do His meditation, and even though it was very difficult to sit in the rooms here for doing meditation, because the hot wind blows here in the summer, He Himself instructed me to make the underground room here, and with His grace the underground room was made here. He Himself put His hands on my eyes and closed them from outside, and He told me to meditate; and He also told me, "Whenever I feel it appropriate I will come to see you myself."

The faith and love was such that when He took me out of meditation . . . at that time He was giving Initiation to the dear ones. He had already explained the theory to them and He told me to make them learn the Simran. I said, "Master, what is the Simran? What is the theory? Why don't You show them the Real Form of Yours which You have shown me today — so that all the fighting may come to an end? The pundits should not say that only by putting on the saffron color sign they can do the devotion of Lord; the priests should not say that just by blowing the conch they can realize God. Why don't You show them Your Real Form which You have shown me, so that everyone in all the homes may love You, and the people may not fight over the issues of temples and mosques, and all the people may know that their God resides in a Man?"

After hearing all this, Hazur said to me, "Don't make the people tear my clothes."

So when such great souls meet such perfect Masters, whatever the Masters tell Them to do They do that wholeheartedly. They do not waste any of Their time, nor are They affected by hunger and thirst. If They wish They sit for weeks in the remembrance of the Master, and They have no problem with sleep.

I advise the dear ones here, that those who have not had the practice of getting up early in the morning in their homes, those who have not meditated enough in their homes, they should stick to the schedule and get up only when the bell rings at three o'clock. Those who try to get up before the bell rings, looking at the other people, since they have not had the practice of spending so much time in meditation, it affects their health.

If you don't believe this you can ask Pappu who is the witness. On the tours whenever he has become sick it is only because of lack of sleep. Once in Nanaimo he did not sleep enough and he got sick. Yagya Sharma, who is here, helped in doing the Satsang; you can ask him. About three or four doctors tried to help him, but when I came back after the Satsang I folded my hands to them and told them, "Now all of you should go. You have done a good job, but now let me treat him." I told him, "Now you quietly go to sleep; don't talk, just sleep, and you will be all right." So when he slept he became all right; the fever went away. In the same way, when we were coming back to India after the first tour, he got sick in the airplane. Gurbhag Singh who was accompanying us got very worried and went for some medicine. I told him, "What medicine? Why don't you go and see if there are any empty seats so that he could lie down?" So when he lay down and slept he became all right. So I mean to say that if you have not had enough sleep, only then you become sick. Not everyone can bear the lack of sleep. If the satsangis did not have the difficulty with sleep, lust, and appetite, then it would be very easy for them to meditate.

Yesterday I had said that it is the highest tradition of God Almighty that once He opens His door to any soul He does not forsake that soul.

You can read all the writings of the Mahatmas and you will find that Kabir Sahib had said, "Now I neither close my eyes nor plug my ears, because with my open eyes and open ears I see the beautiful Form of my Master."

Such a Master's work — whether it is the work of farming, or of the home, or of the sangat — all the work which such a perfect Master does is counted as His devotion, because all of His work is holy.

What to talk about criticizing others, such a Mahatma cannot even think of criticizing others. Such a Mahatma Himself is a pure being, and gradually after making the sangat understand the realities, He makes them also pure.

I get the opportunity of seeing the dear ones in the interviews, and in the interviews they tell me about their condition. Some people come here after becoming spiritually bankrupt. God Kirpal showered grace on them in one way or another. Some people get the grace of the Master in this way or the other way. Some people are purified by the Masters, and for some people the Masters suffer for their karmas. In one way or another He always purifies the souls who come in His contact. The Master wants to purify all the souls who come in contact with Him in His lifetime, and somehow make the stream of Shabd flow in them.

54

The Karmas are Revealed Within

Sant Ajaib Singh Ji

a question and answer talk given March 29, 1987, at Sant Bani Ashram, Village 16 PS, Rajasthan, India

Yesterday, Sant Ji said that when we are initiated all the accounts of our stored karmas, the sanchit *karmas, are torn up by the Master and the debt is wiped out. I thought there was some kind of karma which we had to eliminate by meditating later as we progressed in the higher planes. Aren't those the stored karmas? Also I was curious about what the Master has to do to wipe out that karmic account. There is a story that King Janak liberated all the souls in hell with three rounds of Simran. Is it like that, or does the Master have a greater price to pay?*

[*Sant Ji laughs heartily*] I am very glad that you have asked such a deep question, because this is something which is worth paying attention to. It is possible that many other dear ones may also have the same kind of question. It is good that you have asked this question.

First of all I would like to tell you that those dear ones who go within know how all these things work. Often I have quoted Master Sawan Singh Ji; He used to say, "Unless we go within we do not know who is doing all the things. Until we go within we may think that we are going to the Satsang or that we have come to the Master to receive the Initiation, or that we are making the efforts in following the Path of the Masters. But once we go within, once we contact our beloved Master in our within, then we realize that it was not because of our effort that we were coming to the Satsang, and it was not because of our own effort that we got the Initiation, it was in fact the grace of the Master who brought us to the Satsang and Who made it possible for us to receive the Initiation." In the same way, after receiving the Initiation when we progress in meditation, until we have gone within and seen the beloved Master with our own eyes, we may say that we are meditating, that we are making the effort to progress. But when we go within, then we realize that our efforts were of no use, it was only the grace of the Master which made it possible for us to do the meditation. In fact, He Himself woke us up for the meditation, He Himself gave us the inspiration and the courage to sit in the meditation, and He Himself pulled us up and made it possible for us to achieve progress in meditation.

Often I have said that at the time of the Initiation Sant Satgurus make such a unique arrangement within us that we pay off the consequences of the karmas which we are supposed to suffer, our *pralabdha* or fate karmas. Side by side, along with paying off those karmas, we also go on progressing in meditation. When we meditate it is like preparing our soul for that time when we will have to face the consequences of our fate karmas, or deal with the sufferings which are going to come according to our fate karmas, and that is why Masters always say that we should meditate. Because when we meditate we are preparing our soul to face that difficult moment.

Often I have said that when a storm comes even the strong trees get uprooted, what to talk about the small plants or the weak trees. In the same way, when the wave of karmas comes in our life, then many of the dear ones lose their faith; their faith is shaken and they may even leave the Path. But those who meditate, those who go within, they know why that pain and suffering has come. They are also aware of the help which they are receiving from their beloved Master. They know how from one side, while they are getting the pain and suffering, from the other side they are also getting help from the Master.

Those dear ones who go within and meditate also feel the pain and sufferings when the wave of karmas comes, but they do not complain. They always remain happy in the Will of the Master, because they know how much their Master has done for them and what kind of karmas they are suffering in that moment. The other dear ones who do not meditate, who have not gone within, who have not realized what Master has done for them, whenever they have to face such a condition or situation, they at once become dry, they leave the Master, or their faith is shaken and is gone.

Swami Ji Maharaj has said, describing the condition of the dear ones who go within, "They always understand the moment of pain as a blessing from the Master, because in the moment of pain we can remember our Master in a much better way than we can remember Him in the moment of happiness." Not all the satsangis have the same kind of attitude. Only those who go within know the truth about what kind of karmas are finished by the Master and what kind of karmas they are suffering now. Those who have got that realization and that awareness of the karmas do not have any complaint and they always accept, happily, whatever comes in the Will of the Master.

We can get this understanding of how the Master showers grace on us, how He cuts our karma, and how He is showering His grace and helping us, only after going within. Outwardly, by hearing the words of the Master, we may get a little bit of belief, we may get a little bit of faith in Him, but Masters always lay a lot of emphasis on going within, because only after going within can we understand and accept the reality, the truth. That is why Masters always say, "Go within and see everything with your own eyes."

Baba Bishan Das had the knowledge of the first Two Charged Words, and He was practically successful in those Two Words. He gave me the knowledge of the Two Words of the two lower planes. With His grace He also made me succeed in that practice. He Himself made me realize my previous birth, where I was born and who my parents were. He also gave me the signs about my previous birth. Only with His grace was I able to know what my connection and my give and take was with my present parents, the parents who brought me up. He Himself made me realize my give and take with the other people in the world. And with His grace I was able to finish the give and take with them. Only because of His grace was I able to tell my parents how long I was going to be with them. Many years before I left my home I had told them that I would be leaving my home at that time. So you see that it was all the grace of Baba Bishan Das by which I was able to know everything.

When a Mahatma Who had the knowledge of only Two Words could tell so many things, could have so much knowledge, you can very well imagine how much more knowledge you could have, because you are on the Complete Path; you have the complete knowledge. You can very well imagine if you would practice, how much knowledge, realization, and awareness you could achieve.

The satsangis who go very high in meditation, and the Saints and Satgurus who know everything, have so much patience and endurance in Them, that They do not perform any miracles. Even though They may know that just by walking a few steps They are going to meet with an accident, still They will not try to stop that, because They do not do anything against the will of nature. They do not perform any miracles; and even though They know everything, if it is according to nature and the Will of God, They will not try to change that Will.

There was an initiate of Baba Sawan Singh Ji who was from a low caste. He was a very good meditator but his wife had a very bad temper, she would always rebuke him and she would always go on fighting with him and sometimes would even give him a beating. He was very upset at that. He was a very nice man, a very devoted dear one. Once he went to Master Sawan Singh Ji and told Him about his sufferings.

If we do the meditation and, after doing the work which the Master has told us to do, if we go to the Master and tell Him about our sufferings and pains, sometimes the Masters do give us the hints. They shower a special grace on us and let us know why we are going through that suffering, and what is the cause of that pain.

So when he went to Master Sawan Singh Ji and told Him about his wife's nature and how it was very difficult for him to live with her, Baba Sawan Singh Ji, in His full glory and in His Will, told that dear one, "Do you know who you were in your past life? You were a crow. Your wife was a female donkey, and she was owned by a washerman. Whenever that washerman brought that donkey near the place where you lived, you used to go and sit on her. She had a wound on her back and you used to pick at that wound with your beak and in that way you tortured her. Also whenever you wanted to clean your beak you would do that in that wound. So you have tortured her a lot, and you have given her so much pain. And because your give and take with her was not good in the past life, that is why in this lifetime she became your wife and you have become her husband, and now it is her turn to give you the same kind of torture. All the Masters have said that whatever you have done in your past lifetime, you have to suffer the consequences of that. So now it is your karma. It is better for you if you would finish that karma in this lifetime, so that you may not have to come back into this world again and again."

Since that dear one used to go within, he knew how the laws of karma work, and since he had the realization that it was his own karma, he lived with that karma and he suffered whatever came in the Will of God and he never complained.

About fifteen years ago, I went to a town called Sangria. I saw a man and woman who were moving from that town. I was very surprised to see how his wife was treating him. She would give him a beating and he would just patiently suffer whatever was coming. She would beat him with sticks and finally she put a big stick in his mouth and he did not say even a word. He patiently suffered and bore all that. I was very surprised and I could not understand how on earth there could be a person who had so much patience and endurance. I thought, "I should find out about this person." So I waited there and after they finished packing their stuff, when they started moving, I followed them about a mile. When they realized that I was following them, they asked me, "Man of God, why are you following us? What do you want to know from us?" I said to that man, "I have never seen a person like you. I do not know what is wrong between you and your wife, but I am surprised to see how much patience you have. Can you tell me how you can do this?"

He told me the whole story. He said, "About forty years ago I was initiated by Baba Sawan Singh Ji. Once I told Him that it was very difficult for me to live with her, and He told me why my wife was like this. Now I know that it is my karma, and that is why I am bearing and suffering all this. I have no regrets, because I know that if I will not pay my own karma, in this lifetime, I may have to come back into this world again, because whatever I have done in the past, I have to suffer the consequences. This incident which You have seen today is nothing in comparison to what I have gone through in the past. This happens every day; if not every day, then at least once every two or three days I get a similar kind of beating. Sometimes it is even worse. But I do not have any complaints. I know that I have done even worse to her than what she is doing in this lifetime."

So those dear ones who go within and who have complete faith in the Master know which of their karmas Master has finished and what karmas they have to suffer. That is why they do not have any complaints, they do not have any regrets. They lovingly and happily suffer the consequences of the karmas which they have done in their past lifetimes, even though Master helps them a lot in understanding and paying off those karmas.

Master Sawan Singh Ji used to say, "All the family members which we have now — all our friends, brothers, sisters and relatives which are connected to us in this lifetime — they are connected as the result of our past connections with those souls. And the souls with whom our give and take, our dealings, were good in the past lifetime, we have smooth and normal relations with them in this lifetime. But those souls with whom our connection and dealings were not good in the past, in this lifetime also we have difficulties with them." You know that in the family you have good relations with some members and with some others you do not get along. So that is why Master Sawan Singh Ji always used to say, "When we meditate and go within, only then can we know what kind of karmas we are paying and what Master has done in removing our karmas."

In Mr. Oberoi's book, *Support for the Shaken Sangat*, the story of Sunder Das is written. You know that Sunder Das was a very devoted initiate of Baba Sawan Singh Ji and he lived with me for many years. He was a very good meditator. It was Baba Sawan Singh Ji Who once in His Will had told Sunder Das about what was going to happen in his future. Baba Sawan Singh had told Sunder Das that his wife would get killed, and his son and daughter would also get killed. He said, "That will upset your mind; you will go crazy and in that madness you will kill somebody. As a result you will be taken to prison. There you should confess what you have done, even though people will try to help you. Still you should not accept anyone's help, and you should go through the trial and accept the punishment. You will be sentenced to jail for twenty years, but don't worry; have faith in the Master, since you will stay in the prison for only six years and then you will be released."

It is a very interesting thing that when Baba Sawan Singh Ji told Sunder Das what would happen in his future, at that time, Sunder Das was not even married. But since he used to do a lot of meditation and he went within, he was very close and devoted to Baba Sawan Singh. He took everything that Master Sawan Singh said as true because he had a lot of faith in his Master. When he learned about his future, he thought, "Well, I will not get married. When I don't get married, then I won't have children. And all these things will not happen."

But the circumstances in his life were such that he had to get married. When his family members were telling him to get married, since he knew all about his future, and he didn't want all that to happen, he said, "I don't want to get married." But they said, "Either you get married, or all of us will jump into the well and commit suicide." There were five people in his family and they all wanted to commit suicide if Sunder Das had not agreed to get married. So that is why he gave in to them and he got married. After that everything happened as Baba Sawan Singh had said it would. He had a daughter and a son; first his wife left the body and then his son was killed in the prime of his youth, and his daughter was also killed. This upset his mind, it made him crazy, and in that craziness he killed someone.

When he was brought to the judge, the King of Faridkot, who was a very good friend of Sunder Das, knew that at the time he committed that murder he was not in his senses. He was trying to help Sunder Das so he told the magistrate, "This old man was not in his senses when he did this. He should be forgiven." But because Baba Sawan Singh had said that Sunder Das should not accept anyone's help, he said, "No, I am not crazy. When I have done this murder, why don't you give me the punishment." So according to that, since he had confessed, he was sentenced to twenty years in prison, but in 1947 when India and Pakistan were formed, the prisoners in the jails were released. And Sunder Das was one of them. When he got released from the jail he had been in the jail exactly for six years.

After that he came and lived with me. He was so much devoted to the Master, he always remained faithful to the Master even though so much happened in his life. All the things which happened in his life even made him crazy. Still he did not lose his faith in the Master, because he used to meditate and go within. He knew that all that was happening in his life was according to his own karmas and that he himself had to pay them. And he knew how much Master Sawan Singh was helping him.

Often I have told you how he used to sit with me for meditation. We used to sit for eight hours at a stretch. Once when we were sitting for meditation his leg got burned and he was not even aware of it. When he got up from that meditation with his leg burned he said, "Today I have got such an intoxication in meditation which I have not gotten in my whole life." He was not aware of his burned leg. You also know, if you have read that book, that in the interview which he had with Master Kirpal Singh Ji, Master took him inside and he was made to tell people the things which he had seen within.

So I mean to say that those who meditate, those who go within, they always remain devoted to the Master. Their faith never gets shaken off; they never lose their faith in the Master, because they know how the grace of the Master works. They know how the Master works as far as the payment of our karmas is concerned.

I always inspire the dear ones to read *Sant Bani Magazine* because a lot of Satsangs and short talks and question-and-answer talks like this have been published in the magazine. Many subjects are touched upon, and you can find out a lot of things by reading the magazine.

Last time I went to America I gave many talks regarding the inner planes and I tried to explain how things work in the inner planes. I gave brief talks about that. I also said, "At the time of Initiation Master finishes off those karmas which can be an impediment or an obstacle for us in going within." When we bring our attention to the Eye Center, we see that our Master Who has given us the Initiation is present there even before we get there. We see how He helps us to go within. As we go on progressing in meditation, we see how He, along with our progress in meditation, helps us to pay off our karmas.

I even said that when we progress in our meditation and go to *Trikuti*, the place where our *sanchit* karmas are stored, at that place also we are made to meditate a lot, if we are not purified enough. Because the effect which our soul has from the bad karmas can be removed only after doing a lot of meditation. Only by becoming completely pure can our soul go to the causal plane which is beyond Trikuti.

We do not know anything about the inner planes. Master is always with us every single step we take in our inner journey. We cannot take even one step without the help and guidance of the Master. He is always with us in our within. As we go on progressing in meditation, as we go from the astral to the causal plane, as we go on progressing in meditation, we realize how great the help of the Master is and how much the Master is doing for us. Master takes us from plane to plane and He takes us to Sach Khand, our Real Home. Even after reaching Sach Khand, He does not leave us. He makes us stand in front of Almighty God and He requests on our behalf, "He is Your child, and he had forgotten Your Home; now he has come back asking forgiveness from You, and You should forgive him." So I mean to say that Masters always help the disciple in the inner planes, in the inner journey. When we go within, even before we reach there They are already there to help us. They take us and guide us on every single step we take in the inner journey.

Swami Ji Maharaj said, "If you want to see everything while you are living, if you want to practice all the things which you are taught, it is your courage and your efforts; you are great if you have the desire to do all that. *But the most important and first thing you need in order to go within, is to understand and accept the grace of the Master*."

Now in the sangat you know that we all have faith in the Master according to the meditation which we have done. Those who have done more meditation and who go within have more faith in the Master. Those who have not done a lot of meditation, do not have enough faith in the Master. Those who have a lot of faith, those who do the meditation, do not find faults in the Master even after reaching Sach Khand. In fact, they become indebted to the Master after reaching Sach Khand. But those who have not done a lot of meditation easily find fault with the Master if anything goes wrong.

Dear Ones, I mean to say only this — as all the Mahatmas have said, "This world is the land of karmas; this is the place where we have to pay off our karmas." We have been given this human body only to enjoy the rewards of the good karmas and to suffer the consequences of the bad karmas. Only in this lifetime, in this birth, can we square off our karmas.

In the Bhagavad Gita, Lord Krishna told Arjuna that neither our good karmas nor our bad karmas help us in getting liberation from this body. He said, "Good karmas are like gold chains, and the bad karmas are like the iron chains. Neither our good nor our bad karmas can help us get liberation. Liberation is only in the meditation of Naam."

Guru Nanak said, "O Brother, do not blame anyone for the sufferings you are getting. Whatever I have done I suffer the consequences of that. I am the one who is to be blamed."

So we should also lovingly do our meditation according to the instructions of the Master. We should go within so that we may become free from this imprisonment of the karmas, and may gain the pleasure of the Master.

55

On Forgiving Others

Sant Ajaib Singh Ji

a question and answer talk given March 26, 1989, at Sant Bani Ashram, Village 16 PS, Rajasthan

When someone has done something to hurt me deeply, I may feel that I want to forgive them, and I may say that I forgive them, but I don't know how to truly forgive and forget, in my heart. Please help me understand how to do this.

This question should be understood by all the Satsangis, because in the Path of the Masters forgiveness is a very important element. When you have forgiven somebody you should completely forget about it, because if you go on remembering that you have forgiven some person, or if you think in terms of how that person has accepted your forgiveness and how he has taken advantage of your forgiveness — if you will remember all these things — then it is possible that your mind may bother you and you may get more ego. Also it is possible that your mind may give you more trouble, and in fact you have not really forgiven that person. So not even in the state of dreams should you remember that you have forgiven that person. After you have forgiven anyone for their faults you should completely forget about them.

The most important thing is that when you are in a position, or situation, where you have to forgive someone you should remember the Form of the Master, and having the Form of the Master in front of you, only with that kind of feeling you should forgive that person. You should say that it is not you who are forgiving that person but it is the Master who is forgiving that person. If you will take the credit for forgiving the other person, it is possible that ego may haunt you and bother you, but if you will give the credit to the Master and say, "It is the Master Who is within me who has forgiven you," then you will not have any difficulty with the ego.

You know that we jivas are not worth anything and we do not have the capacity to forgive anyone. Instead of taking the credit on our own selves, that we have forgiven the person, we should pass it on to our Master. And we should instead do our meditation and sit at the Feet of the Master and pray to Him, "O Beloved Lord, you should forgive me as you have forgiven that person through me."

On this subject I once commented on the bani of Swami Ji Maharaj; it is possible that many of the dear ones may have had the opportunity to read that talk. In that talk I said that if anyone has made any mistake, knowingly or unknowingly, once he realizes that he has made the mistake, he should confess his mistake and ask for forgiveness. He should apologize to the person whom he has hurt; and the one who was hurt also has a responsibility of acknowledging that apology — he should also forgive that person in the Name of the Master.

Our soul never makes any mistakes because she is innocent and she is of the same essence as that of God Almighty. God Almighty never makes any mistakes; He is free from all kinds of faults. In the same way our soul is also free of all kinds of faults; she never makes any mistakes. We find faults in God Almighty only when we go away from Him. As long as we are connected to Him we never find any faults in Him, because He does not have any faults. When we are looking at Him as a soul, we do not find any faults in Him; but when we go away from Him, when we get disconnected with Him, only then we start finding faults in Him. So the meaning of this is that the soul does not have any faults, the soul does not make any mistakes, because she is the same essence as that of God Almighty; it is our mind who makes the mistakes. And mind does not have the capacity, the strength, to forgive anyone, because God has not given that capacity or that power to forgive others to our mind. So mind cannot forgive anyone because mind does not have the power of forgiving anyone. It is the soul — or the power of the Shabd Naam which our Beloved Master has put within our soul — who forgives and who asks for the forgiveness.

So you know that whenever anyone makes any mistake it is his mind who is making him do the mistake; but his mind does not want to confess — it does not want to admit — he has made the mistake. And it is the soul, his inner heart, who is confessing, who is admitting, his faults; and it is the Master who is asking for forgiveness. And on the other side also, it is the Master, that power of the Shabd Naam, Who is granting that forgiveness. *So when it is the Master who is asking for the forgiveness, and when it is the Master who is giving the forgiveness, then where is the problem? Whenever anyone asks for our forgiveness we should always be willing to forgive them.*

I am not much acquainted with the Holy Bible but you have read it many times and you know a lot about it. It is said in the Bible that only he can be called a true Christian who forgives others and who does not hurt anyone. You know that when Christ was being crucified, how much torture He was given. He was made to wear the crown of thorns and He was taken to the cross. You know how painful that would be. The soul trembles just to think of all that torture He was given, and you can very well imagine what he went through. But still He said, "O Lord, forgive them, because they do not know what they are doing; whatever they are doing is in their innocence and you should forgive them."

We are the disciples of those great Masters Whose writings we read every day and from Whom we have learned that They were the Form of Forgiveness and They forgave even the worst sinners. I will tell you something from the history of Guru Arjan Dev Ji Maharaj. You know how much He was tortured and how He was made to sit on hot coals and how hot sand was thrown on His head. He was tortured so much by the government of that time and toward His end time, the officer in charge, whose name was Chandu Savai, tried to poison His son. His house and family were destroyed right in front of Him but still He didn't say any word against them, He always forgave them. Even though all these things happened still Guru Arjan Dev was full of forgiveness for all the people. But some time after Guru Arjan Dev left the body, Chandu Savai left his post — because people who are in government do not remain in their posts forever; the time comes when the people who once ruled over the country become ordinary people. And when they fall into the hands of the people who they had tortured, those people take their revenge.

When Guru Har Gobind started working, His Glory started spreading all over, and the government of that time told Guru Har Gobind to do His work wherever he wanted. He was also asked if he wanted to give punishment to Chandu Savai, because Chandu Savai was the main person behind all of the torture that Guru Arjan Dev had received, but Guru Har Gobind said, "No, I do not want to put him to trial. I do not want to give him any punishment, because in the court of my beloved Lord there is no place for punishment, that is the place of forgiveness. And I do not want to give any punishment, because whatever he did, he was supposed to do that. Masters always forgive even the worst sinners, so I do not want to give him any punishment."

Such was the heart of Guru Har Gobind, but you know that the disciples are very emotional, and they do not have such a heart like the Masters. So when Chandu Savai came into the hands of the disciples of Guru Arjan and when they remembered all the torture which Chandu Savai had given to Guru Arjan Dev, they could not control themselves. They put a chain around the neck of Chandu Savai and made him walk on the streets of Lahore like a dog. When they came to the shop where Chandu Savai had gotten the hot sand to put on Guru Arjan Dev's head, that shopkeeper became very angry and he said,

"Well this is the same Chandu Savai who in the intoxication of his power made me throw the hot sand on that great Guru Arjan Dev." So he also put hot sand on Chandu Savai's head and when he did that he hit him with a big stone. Chandu Savai almost died and he called for the help of Guru Har Gobind, saying, "O Guru Har Gobind, now I am in Your refuge and You protect me!"

So by the grace of the beloved Master and because of the forgiveness which the Masters have, Chandu Savai was liberated right then, because he requested Guru Har Gobind for His help. So you see how much forgiveness and grace the Masters have; They forgive even those people who have done so many bad things to Their Master.

In the time of Guru Gobind Singh there was a very devoted disciple, Bhai Daya Singh, who used to meditate a lot and go within. One day when he was all alone with Guru Gobind Singh, he asked Him, "Master, I have read about so many great sinners who tortured our past Masters, and how they were bothering the other dear ones — are they in hell now because of all the bad things they did?" He particularly mentioned Chandu Savai who had tortured Guru Arjan Dev. But Guru Gobind Singh Ji replied, "No Dear One, Chandu Savai was liberated right then because he had the darshan of two great Masters. First he had the darshan of Guru Arjan Dev and then he had the darshan of Guru Har Gobind. And also when he was dragged by the disciples of Guru Arjan Dev through the streets of Lahore, at that time he was always remembering the form of Guru Har Gobind because he knew that Guru Har Gobind was the only One Who could forgive him and could protect him. So he had been contemplating on the form of Guru Har Gobind and he was remembering Him so much so that at the time of his death Guru Har Gobind had to come and liberate him."

So you see, Dear Ones, that we are the disciples of those great Masters Who forgive even the worst sinners. So whenever we are in that kind of situation when we have to forgive anyone we should always remember the Form of the Masters, and in the Name of our Beloved Master we should always forgive them. And after forgiving the people who hurt us, or who have done any mistake, we should never remember them and we should never even make them realize that we have forgiven them. Once we have forgiven them in the Name of our beloved Master we should forget all about what happened.

Often I have said that we should not give up this element of forgiveness even in our household, even in our married life. Why do we have all these conflicts and problems in our married life? — only because the husband and wife do not have this element of forgiveness in them. If both of them would have the element of forgiveness and if they would forgive and forget each others' faults they could easily make their home life like a heaven on earth.

Do you think that we have been brought to the Master because of our good deeds only? Those who go within know that we have not come to the Master because of our good deeds. It was because of the grace and forgiveness of the Master that we were brought to Him; we were already so full of faults that unless He had forgiven us we would never have been able to come to Him. When we come to the Master it is only because of His forgiveness. He forgives our past faults and He tells us not to make any more mistakes in the future; and He always tells us that whatever we have done in the past, we have been forgiven. And even after giving us so much forgiveness the Master never tells us, "I have done this favor for you and I have forgiven you." He always remains very humble. Even if the disciple stands in front of other people and says, "Master, You have forgiven me for this — " or "You have done this seva for me — " He always says, "No Dear One, it is not me who has forgiven you, it is the grace of my Beloved Master Who has forgiven you."

Matraput was a great scholar of Sanskrit in his time; he had done a lot of research, and he had searched a long time for a Master. Finally when he came to Guru Ram Das, he became His disciple, and was so devoted that his writings are included in the Guru Granth Sahib also. There he says, "I do not have any good qualities in me, I am full of bad qualities. Giving up the nectarful Naam, I went for the poison of this world, I attached myself to the sons, daughters, and all the family members and everything of this world, but finally after searching all over the world for You, I have come to Your door. This is one request which the Prakriti* makes to You, 'O Guru Ram Das, always keep me in Your refuge.' "

Those who have children know that children go on making mistakes all day long, but the mother has forgiveness and the mother has been given attachment to the children. That is why she does not remember any of the mistakes which the children are making. And even though they go on making mistakes again and again, she always goes on forgiving them. In the same way, the Masters also behave like a forty-day-old child in front of Their Lord, and They always say, "O Lord, as the mother does not remember the mistakes the child makes, in the same way, don't You remember the mistakes we make. O my beloved Mother, I am Your child and why don't You forget and forgive me for all the mistakes I make?"

I hope that you have understood lovingly what I told you about the subject of forgiveness; there is a lot more which I could say on this subject.

* Roughly speaking, *prakriti* is a collective term for all the forms of matter as quickened with the spirit of the Creator. See *Crown of Life*, pp. 12-13.

56

The Master Becomes Happy

Sant Ajaib Singh Ji

a question and answer talk given in Ahmedabad, India, on September 12, 1994

Dear Sant Ji, while doing Simran is it best to remember the Master, also is it appropriate to hold a motive for doing Simran?

It is a very good question I hope that everyone will write the answer to this question on your heart because mind usually brings such kind of illusions, such kind of thoughts within all the satsangis.

First of all the satsangi should have a very strong heart. Always I have said that we can do the meditation only if we have made our heart like iron.

We have to struggle harder in the astral plane than we have to struggle in the physical plane. So unless we have a strong heart, we cannot struggle over there, because there are many powers whom we have to encounter in the astral plane. They come and they tempt us and intimidate us. Kabir Sahib says, "Over there, there are the intimidators, there are the ones who tempt you, so unless the meditator has a strong heart he won't be able to progress over there."

One Indian dear one came in the darshan this morning and he told me when he wakes up at three o'clock in the morning for meditation he feels afraid. I asked him, "If you have to go to your job at that time do you still feel afraid?" He said, "No." Then I asked him, "If you have to watch television at that time, or if you have to sleep at that time do you still feel afraid?"

He said, "No, I only feel afraid when I sit in meditation." So I told him, "This is only because you are not strong-hearted and you do not have enough faith and confidence, that the fear is bothering you."

The only motive that you should hold on to or that you should have is that you have to go within, manifest the Master, and talk to the Master.

If you will not remember the Master, if you are not sitting to manifest the Master, Dear Ones, whose devotion are you doing?

This is why we should always go on remembering the Master. Guru Arjan Dev says, "Master, Master, always go on repeating the Master, because I am nothing without Him."

If we will not remember Him then how are we doing His devotion? We should always remember Him, whether we are travelling on a bus, or sitting in the toilet, or bathing, or doing anything — we should always remember Him. The Simran which we are doing has been given to us by the Master. We should always remember His Form in front of us.

If you will sit with the worldly thoughts, you will not get anything from your within as far as the worldly thought or the worldly thing is concerned. Nor will you be able to go within, and you won't be doing the meditation at that time, so you are wasting your time.

I have told you about this before: in the village where I used to live there was a dear one who once needed some money, so he sat in meditation with this worldly desire or thought of getting the money. Over there he saw his trunk full of all the currency notes. So at once he told his daughter to open the trunk and see if the trunk was all full of those notes. He also said that if he would open his eyes they would disappear. When she opened the trunk there were no notes there, because it was just in his mind that he was seeing the notes. When you think about the worldly things you do not get anything.

So he came to me and he told me that this is what happened to him, that he was sitting in the meditation with this thought and he saw that his trunk was full of the money, but that it was not real. I told him, "Dear One, if in a state of dreams you eat sweets and other goodies, you don't feel satisfied, you don't remove your hunger. So it is like that — even if you see all these worldly things inside, still you are not getting them."

The meditation is only done, Dear Ones, to remove the worldly thoughts from our within. The meditation is done only to empty our within which is filled with the worldly thoughts, so that our Beloved can come and reside there.

All the satsangis should always remember those couple of things which I always remind you before we sit in the meditation. The first thing is that you should not understand meditation as a burden, you should always do it lovingly. The other thing is that before you sit in meditation, all the anxieties, worries, and desires of the world which are coming within you just like the waves in the ocean, you should first cool them down, quiet them down, and then do the Simran. If you will do the Simran after forgetting all the worldly wishes and desires, then as Guru Nanak says, "If you do the Simran like that, after quieting down your mind and all the desires of the world, just one moment of the Simran will be enough for you."

I have told you about this incident previously. Once there was an initiate of Baba Sawan Singh in a place called Muksar. She came to me saying that she had come for doing the meditation and she would leave only after her inner veil was lifted up, only when the inner door was opened.

I became very pleased and I said, "Thanks be to you, that you have come for doing the meditation."

Since she was an elderly lady I told the girls who were there doing the seva, "You should take care of her; you should serve her."

So those girls would serve her very much and they would even wash her clothes and do all the things for her. Then that elderly woman, whose name was Bhagwanti, asked us to call another woman who used to live about two miles from our place. I knew that lady, and I also knew that Bhagwanti was very talkative, and the other lady whom she wanted to invite was also very talkative. So I told her, "Just you alone are not able to control yourself, and if you invite this other person who is as talkative as you, how are both of you going to manage doing the meditation?"

She meditated for a few more days, and then she said to me that she wanted to go back to Muksar and that I should arrange for her to go back to her place. I asked her, "Why do you want to go back to your home? Your sons came and they dropped you here, now it is very difficult for us to make arrangements to take you back to your home. But why do you want to go back? You came here to do the meditation."

She told me when she sat in meditation she was seeing her sons in front of her, also she saw all the work to be done at her home, and the worldly things, and that was bothering her very much and so she wanted to back to her home.

So Dear Ones, if she had remembered Master Sawan Singh, if she had this motive of manifesting Master Sawan Singh within her, then she would have become successful in that. But what happened when she sat in the meditation? First it was her mind that encouraged her to come to me and do the meditation and that is why she came. But when she started doing the meditation she started remembering her family. Because she was remembering them and thinking about them, the balance or the weight of the worldly things was more, that is why she gave in to that attachment and she did not fulfill the wish that she had had of manifesting Baba Sawan Singh.

So I told her, "Dear one, if you had sat with the motive of manifesting Master Sawan Singh He would have come to you, He would have manifested Himself within you. But since you were remembering and you were attached to your family members, that is why your sons and your worldly work came in front of you."

Both Master Sawan Singh and Master Kirpal Singh were very gracious ones and many times when any true seeker would come to Them, They would at once agree to give them the

Initiation and they would initiate them right there. They were very gracious ones.

Once it so happened that — I have narrated this incident to you previously also — when Master Kirpal was visiting in my home, a dear one came and asked Master Kirpal Singh for the Initiation. Master Kirpal was so gracious that He readily accepted him and He told me to convey the Initiation to that dear one. Master was resting in one room and I took that dear one into another room and I made him sit in the meditation and I also sat with him, closing my eyes. It didn't take him more than a few moments to get up from that place and run away. I did not know that he had already left that place; I was sitting there to convey the Initiation to this dear one and after a while I realized that the person whom I was initiating was not sitting there and I was sitting there all by myself. When I realized that, I came out and ran after him. He had already travelled two kilometers along the road which went past my house. So when I caught up with him I asked him what had happened.

He said, "Well, I don't know what happened. I came from my home and family; I was so absorbed in my work and family. And I came to the Master, He was very gracious, and He accepted me to get the Initiation and you were giving it to me and I don't know what happened. Once again my mind played a trick on me. Master was very gracious, but my mind did not let me take advantage of that grace, and he put me on this road back to my home."

So Dear Ones, when we sit in meditation we have to be very careful. All the satsangis, as I have often said, before you sit in meditation, make sure that you remember the Five Holy Names, because those are the Words, those are the Names given to you by your Master. If you are doing the Simran, then you will also remember the Master who has given you the Simran. The Form of the Master will appear in front of you by Himself if you will remember Him, if you will do the Simran given to you by Him.

So when you will do the Simran like that, remembering the Form of the Master, then all the worldly thoughts will go away.

That is why I always say that you should remove all the anxieties, all the worries, thoughts, and desires of this world when you sit in meditation. When you weed out all your thoughts and all the worldly things, when you throw out all these things using the broom of the Simran, then your within will become empty, so either your Simran will remain there or the Master who has given you the Simran will remain there.

When we do the Initiations, Pappu and Gurmel do not close their eyes and meditate when the people meditate, because they have this duty. Also during the morning meditations there are a couple of dear ones here who just keep guard. In the early days, even though I would tell people, "I promise you that I am not going to leave you sitting here, I will also sit with you." But in the early days, what would happen, some dear ones would open their eyes and get up, and they would walk a little bit and then they would again sit there. Or sometimes they would open their eyes to see if everyone was still sitting there or not.

I am very pleased to see that now the dear ones are getting into the habit of sitting in meditation. That is why I prefer not to miss any meditation sitting. If I have to miss a Satsang then it may be all right, but I don't like to miss the meditation sittings. That is why, when I come here to do the meditation, I am very pleased looking at the dear ones, to see how people are now sitting in the meditation. Because mind is such that if you make him do something, in the beginning he will not do it, but gradually, later on, the more you go on making him do something then he starts enjoying it and then you will become successful in it.

So I am very happy when I come and meditate with all of you, that you dear ones sit here with very much love. When I open my eyes, a couple of minutes before I make you leave off, I see my dear children sitting in meditation and that gives me immense pleasure, especially when I see on many dear ones a lot of glory and radiance. So that makes me very happy to see that my children are now meditating.

Often I have said that Sant Mat is based on Reality, it exists on the Truth, it is not a fairy tale. Whatever the Masters have said, whatever the Masters have conveyed to us, is one hundred percent true.

So with firm determination, with faith, with love, we should do our meditation. The Master also becomes very happy. Everyday one should make the effort of manifesting that Stream of the Shabd, that Current of the Shabd, to flow within us in the lifetime of the Master. The Master also becomes very happy when His disciples, when His dear ones, are able to manifest that Sound Current within them while He is still in the body. He becomes happy, "At least there are some dear ones who have become what I have wanted them to become."

57

Questions & Answers on Meditation

Sant Ajaib Singh Ji

excerts from various question and answer talks

When you feel in your heart that you want to see the Master; and you run into opposition, how do you know that you're doing the right thing? How do you know if you're doing the right thing, if you press to see Him? or if you choose not to? Yesterday, one person had said I could go with him to see Sant Ji, but then a bit later, I was told that I'd be doing the wrong thing if I did that, so I decided at the last minute not to go see Sant Ji. How do we know what is right?

A lover should always have the desire to see the Master for twenty-four hours a day. I don't call that a "desire to see the Master" if for a few days or a few minutes someone has that desire, and after that, it goes away without being fulfilled — then that was not desire.

Mahatma Chattardas Ji said, "Always, twenty-four hours a day, I have the desire to see my Master. Why am I not going to see Him? I should go, even crossing the river, to see Him. No matter what obstacles come in between, still I will go and see Him."

If we will remember Him twenty fours hours a day, and have the desire to see Him, at least for one moment in that twenty-four hours He will also remember us and He will also think about us. So that is the best time.

This is my personal experience, that you don't need to go to the Master and say, "I have the desire to see You, that's why I have come here." No matter how far away from Him you are sitting, if you have the desire, that Power will know. And maybe sometime that Power will come by Himself to give you His glance.

No matter if we are sitting in the dark night, in a dark room which is closed from all four sides, and if a storm is blowing — there is no way to come into the room — then also, if we have the yearning to see that Almighty Power, that Almighty Power can appear there and in that way He can quench our thirst.

But the problem is that our mind does not allow us to understand and believe in this thing. Our mind is always understanding the Master as the body.

---

from a talk given August 22, 1977, printed as "Only A Lover Surrenders Everything" in the December 1991 *Sant Bani Magazine*

* * *

If we work hard while we're here, could we perfect our Simran? While we're here at the ashram?

Yes. Yes, but it is different for different people. You know that some students are so bright that they learn the lesson in just one day, and some students are not so bright, and it takes a longer time for them to learn the same lesson. So it is different for different people; but you should understand why we have to do Simran. We do Simran only to change the thoughts of our mind. The thoughts or fantasies which we have in our mind, nobody has told us to have them; all those thoughts are coming from our mind, from within us, by themselves. We are not making any effort to bring them, but still they are coming. But we are very fortunate ones, because Master has given us Simran. This is the Simran on which They have meditated, and if we want, and if we work hard, we can perfect our Simran, we can change our thoughts, in just one day.

We people don't pay much attention to Simran. That's why we spend our whole life in doing it and still remain far away from perfection. We people do Simran for ten minutes and then give up for many minutes, and again we do, and again we give up. Sometimes we forget Simran for many hours, and sometimes we don't remember Simran even for many days. It is only because of this that we are not able to perfect our Simran. But if we paid attention to Simran, and if we did Simran constantly, then we could perfect it in no time.

Satsangis have no idea of the value which Simran has and the power which Simran has. And that is why they don't pay attention to Simran, and become careless.

If we are strong in doing our Simran, we can have many powers, just by doing it. Many supernatural powers come within us just by doing Simran, and if the one who has perfected his Simran wants, he can stop a moving train. Such power can be achieved by doing Simran.

There are many forces of mind. And when you do Simran and have control over your mind, then you will realize its value and you will not give it up. You will always want to do it.

In the cities you may have seen magicians — people who practice mesmerism and such things to impress others. They are able to do that only because they have some concentration of mind and they have some hold over their mind. You can also do all these things, you can also impress people if you do Simran; but in Sant Mat, on the Path of the Masters, it is not allowed to use such powers to impress people. But you can get all those powers by doing Simran.

In Sant Mat, as Kabir Sahib says, "The Saints are near God, but still They don't tell people that They are near God." In Sant Mat, if anyone has achieved anything, he will not impress people by what he has achieved. He will just keep quiet.

Many times I have told this story of when I was in the army. Once one retired English major came and he was a sort of magician. Before coming to our group he had performed many shows in front of other troops. People were very impressed; they said that he could even put life into a dead bird. So when he came there, he said, "Okay, I will show you a very great thing." He held a bird in his hand, and invited one person to come and cut off its head and someone did that. People saw the blood was dropping down on the earth and that the bird was dead. After some time, he joined the two different parts of the body of the bird, and he made that bird fly, and everybody was very impressed. Then he said, "Okay, bring some sawdust and I will turn that into sugar, and I will make tea and give it to you." There were many high officers there who wanted to see this trick also. So some sawdust was brought and he turned that into sugar and tea was made and the officers were given that tea to drink. When they took their first sip he asked them, "Is it sweet?" They replied, ''Yes, it's like regular tea." But then, when they took a second sip, they found that there was no sugar there — it was all sawdust. [*Laughter.*]

After showing many tricks he said, "I do all these things only because of my flute. (He had a flute with him that he played.) All my power is in this flute." He wanted to play that flute, but I also had some concentration of mind, and I used to play with people — I had a habit of harassing such people so . . . [*Laughter*] when he started playing his flute, I used my concentration and he was not able to. He was very surprised, because up until then nobody had done that. No matter how he tried, still he was not able to play the flute. And he was not able to do the rest of his show, either. [*Laughter*] He was worried, and he said to my commander, "Somebody in your troop has some power and he has stopped my flute. So I beg of him, to please release his power so that I can do my work." So that was released.

Then he said, "You should not understand that this is real magic; you should not think that I can really put life into a dead body. If I could, the people from England would never have allowed me to come here. The Queen or the King would have kept me in their service, because nobody wants to die. I can do it only because I have concentration of mind. Because my mind is concentrated, I can make your minds believe in me, and I can impress you." He meant to say that whatever he was doing was only because of the concentration of mind.

I had concentration because I was also doing meditation at that time. Of course, I did not have charged words; but still I was doing repetition, and I was doing it constantly. That's why I had concentration of mind. So if you people also do Simran — and you are fortunate, because you have charged words — and if you do it constantly you can also possess such powers and you can also show all this to people — but you are not allowed to do that once you achieve it. But there is no doubt that you can get all these powers when you do constant Simran. Simran has many powers in it, and if we practice it constantly, we can become the masters of it.

I would just like to have the power to make you appear.

[*Laughing.*] Simran is the only way by which you can do that. That's why, do Simran.

Regarding Simran, Baba Bishan Das used to say, "By doing Simran we can get many powers — we can read the hearts of people." He also used to perform many shows like this, many miracles like this, because the mahatmas who do not go higher than the second plane become pleased when they give boons to people; or when they curse people and it works out, they become very pleased. They are delighted when they can help people by reading their hearts or by helping them in any way. So Baba Bishan Das also used to do that, and he was able to do it only because of Simran.

---

from a talk given January 5, 1980, and printed as "Just By Doing Simran" in the March 1980 *Sant Bani Magazine*

* * *

Is repeating Simran the best way to get past pain while sitting?

[*Laughing*] I think that if we lovingly do the Simran, without understanding it as a burden, then we will never even remember if we are having pain. The soul gets the power of bearing the pain by itself if we are doing the Simran lovingly.

I was talking to Millie Prendergast last summer and she said you just go to the Eye Focus and then you repeat the names; that's how she described it. I was wondering, when you sit, are you supposed to go right to the Eye Focus or is that a process of doing the Simran and then you go to the Eye Focus?

We should take our attention right to the Eye Focus as soon as we close our eyes and sit for meditation. If we are able to do that then we will not find any difficulty in rising above. You know that when we are not doing our meditation at that time also our attention is at the Eye Focus. Whenever we have to think about anything or remember anything our attention is at the center of our forehead at the Eye Focus. So we should always keep our attention there. And if we want to progress in meditation, it is very important to keep our attention there and then do Simran.

The thing is that we are not giving so much attention to the Simran of the Satguru as we are giving to the simran of the world, that is the difference.

There is so much emphasis on Simran, but [it seems to me], at times I am just saying five foreign words that I can't relate to except that the Master has told me that this will bring me to different levels. How do we get to understand or have more of a feeling for the Simran?

Instead of thinking about understanding them, you should go on repeating them, which will bring the understanding to you by itself. When you go within then you will understand them. When you go within, everything will be like an open book. When you go within then you don't need to ask anything from anyone; there will be no doubts, no confusions. As long as we are outside, we don't know the importance of doing Simran, but when we have faith in the Simran and do a lot of Simran and go within, then we know the importance of Simran, and desire to do it more and more.

When we do bhajan should we stop doing Simran?

Yes. You can do only one work at a time.

You frequently mention to do meditation with full devotion, but frequently the mind is racing away like a wild team of horses, and you're sitting with pain all through your body so next time you want to sit for meditation the mind immediately picks up on "It's going to hurt." It's going to be fighting the whole time.

[*Laughing.*] Don't obey your mind. If you will do that only love will be left with you. The mind is our enemy and we should not obey our enemy. Mind will not let any opportunity go from his hands without utilizing it.

The Sadhu who has struggled with mind all his life long knows that this is the path of patience, and unless we have patience we cannot become successful. That is why it is very important for us to be patient, and with all our love and devotion keep on doing our meditations. If we do that with patience, we will definitely succeed.

When your mind tells you that you are having a lot of pain and you should not sit any longer, at that time, instead of obeying him and giving in to him, you should punish him by sitting for a longer time by suffering pain for a little bit more time so that he may know that if he will bring that feeling again you will make him sit for a longer time. . . .

Once I came from the army to meet my first Master, Baba Bishan Das — I have told you many stories about him because he was the Mahatma who made my life. When I came to see Baba Bishan Das my mind played a trick on me. He used to wake me up at one o'clock because he used to get up then to meditate. So whenever he got up he would wake me also. One day my mind made me think, "What is the use of coming here to the ashram of the Master if you still have to get up at one o'clock to meditate?" I was thinking of the ashram as a resort place for me because I was spending my holidays there. So when Baba Bishan Das woke me up at one o'clock I said, "Master, why do I have to get up when you are already up and you are sitting for meditation." At once Baba Bishan Das knew that this was a trick of the mind; I was being fooled by the mind. He said, "Well, if you don't want to meditate, don't, but at least get up and come here. I want to tell you something; come with me." I didn't know what Baba Bishan Das had in His mind — what He was going to do to me. Near the Dera there was a pond — this was in the month of December, and it was one o'clock in the morning — the water was very cold. He started talking with me and suddenly he took me near the pond. He held my hand and was just about to push me into the pond; I said, "Well, Master, if you want me to go there, I will, but let me take off my clothes." But He said, "No, because I know that if I give you that much time, your mind will fool you again, and you will run away." So He pushed me into the pond, and when I came out my condition was like that of a mouse which has been thrown into water; when it comes out it is shivering with the cold. That was the last day when I thought about sleeping later than one o'clock. After that I never in my whole life slept after one o'clock. That is why I always say, "It is not in my heritage to sleep in the early hours of the morning." What Baba Bishan Das did was the best thing for me; that was his way to teach me that we should never obey our mind. Mind is always with us and it is out enemy. If we will obey our enemy, then how are we going to conquer our enemy? If we obey our mind once, if we procrastinate or postpone our meditation once in obedience to our mind, then next day — he is still within us — he will play the same trick. And in that way, day by day, he will take us far away from the Master, and the time may come when we might even leave the Path, if we continuously obey our mind.

So in the morning the mind says, "Sleep now, tonight you

have plenty of time and you will meditate later on; sleep now." Later he will advise you to meditate tomorrow and in that way he will never let you meditate.

---

from a talk given October 28, 1980, printed as "Question and Answers in Rajasthan," in the November 1980 *Sant Bani Magazine*

* * *

We hear these commands or suggestions you make to still the mind and to concentrate only on Simran, and not to let the mind be taken by worldly thoughts. But even though I pass this command along to my mind, the mind doesn't seem to care very much about my orders. Either it doesn't receive the order in the first place, or it doesn't care to execute it. So how do I deal with this dilemma?

If you will continue passing on these messages to your mind, then definitely one day he will accept this and he will work on this. Because you can bring the mind under your control or you can make your mind do the things as you want, if you keep telling him to do this. As Swami Ji has said, "This mind is such a thing which comes under your orders gradually."

When we are closing our ears with our thumbs, I find that the effect varies depending on how much pressure is applied to the ears. You can more or less modulate the Sound by applying more or less pressure. Now what is the proper procedure here?

It is different for different people. Whatever suits you, you should do that. But let me tell you that you have to close your ears only in the beginning. After you do a lot of Simran and start rising above, and you start reaching the Eye Center, after that you will not need to close your ears. Because once you get to the Eye Center, you will hear the Sound coming there without closing your ears and your attention will always go up.

Now we need to close our ears because we have become extroverted, and we are in the habit of listening to sounds coming from the outside. That is why we feel as if the Sound is coming from outside, but that is not true. The Sound is coming from above our head at the Eye Center, and that is why, in order to cut off the sounds and distractions of the outer world, we need to close our ears. When you hear the higher Sounds, you will feel as if the Sound is Sounding in the area of thirty miles, and people far away from you can also hear that Sound, because the Sound is very loud. But at that time only you will hear that Sound. But what is our condition? We people do not pay as much attention to the Simran, and that is why when we sit for Bhajan, our attention is not concentrated — it is spread all over — so even if we hear the Sound Current, that Sound does not pull us up.

In the old days, Saints used to give Initiation in two parts. First, they used to give the Simran, and after the disciple had perfected the Simran, then They would connect the disciple with the Sound Current. But many times it happened that either the disciple left the body before he perfected his Simran, or the Master left the body before the disciple had perfected the Simran. In that case, liberation was not granted, because the Sound Current is the thing which gives us the liberation — climbing on the Shabd our soul goes back home. So Kabir Sahib and Guru Nanak introduced this new method of giving both Light and Sound, both Simran and Bhajan, at the same time. This was a special grace of these Masters to the souls. That is why nowadays we are given the Initiation into both Simran and Bhajan at the same time.

Satsangis do not know how important the Simran is, and why it is so important to do constant Simran, and what Simran does.

If we remain awake for twelve or fourteen hours, because we are in the world, we do the simran of the world. And when we go to sleep, then also we remember the world in the form of dreams. So while sleeping also we do the simran of the world.

That is why, neither awake nor asleep do we have any peace, because we are doing the simran of the world. If you do Simran for five or six hours, and then compare it with the amount of time you have done the simran of the world, you will find how much more you have devoted to the world. But what do we do? Some people do Simran for one hour, an hour-and-a-half, or two hours. The most fortunate ones do it only for three hours. And that also not in one stretch. That also is divided into many parts. And before sitting for Simran, they have their watch in front of them, and they keep the account of how much time is spent for doing Simran. But they never pay attention to the time they did the fantasies of the world.

I saw this at Sant Bani and at Shamaz and Nanaimo also, and I said this many times: that some people, those who were not in the habit of meditating even for one hour — when they were sitting with the other people in the meditation in front of me — they would sleep after a few minutes, and then when they would wake up, they would think that the other people had gone for breakfast, and they would be very much afraid, and worried also. So I told them, "Don't worry, I guarantee that you will not miss your breakfast." They were not in the habit of meditating in their homes.

Those who were meditating in their homes, for them it made no difference if I would give them a sitting ten minutes longer than one hour. And when I told them to get up, then also they would wake up peacefully. And whatever time they sat for meditation, they sat peacefully. This was only because they were meditating in their homes.

Every satsangi should put a lot of emphasis on doing the Simran. We should understand the glory of Simran; we should understand why it is important for us to do the Simran. We should work very hard on developing our constant Simran, because we have to forget the simran of the world and remember the Simran of the Master.

But isn't it right that doing Simran is not sufficient if it's not done with proper concentration? But how can we increase our concentration in doing Simran?

You see, when you will do the Simran, the concentration will come by itself. Because by doing Simran our mind and soul gets concentrated.

Since we're from the West, and Western society is based on materialism and lust and all of those things are shown to us every day, I feel that the Path is more difficult for Westerners to keep up the discipline. Since Master just came back from the West again and saw the lifestyle there, does He feel it's more difficult for Westerners, or is it the same for Westerners and Indians?

A similar question was put to me by some dear one in the West, and I told him the story of Sukhdev Muni, who went to King Janak for Initiation. When he asked for Initiation, King Janak gave him a cup of milk and told him to take that cup of milk around the city and come back, but if he dropped any milk he would not get Initiation. And moreover one man with an open sword would be following him, and if he spilled even one drop from that cup, he would be killed right on the spot. In order to distract the attention of Sukhdev Muni, King Janak had many dancers and many enjoyments going on in the city to attract him. But Sukhdev Muni, because he was afraid of death and he wanted Initiation very badly — he had waited a long time to get Initiation — paid no attention to all the dancers and all the things that were happening there. There were so many things which would have attracted the attention of anyone, but Sukhdev Muni was very steady, and he fulfilled the condition of King Janak, and he got Initiation. When King Janak asked him, "Did you see any dancers or anything in the city?" He replied, "How could I have seen them? The man with the open sword was behind me, and moreover if I looked at them, I would have dropped the milk and you would not have given me Initiation."

So no matter how much materialism there is, or how many distractions or lust or all these things there are in the West, those who have to improve their lives, those who have to do their meditation, for them it doesn't make any difference. They should make their minds like Sukhdev Muni's if they want to progress.

You people have got Initiation. You people come to the Satsang, and you should know that God has been very gracious on you. So you should improve your life.

---

from a talk given on October 31, 1980 and printed as "Only a Quiet Mind Can Meditate" in the May 1981 *Sant Bani Magazine*

* * *

I know that it is very important to have a very good attitude about meditating, to be in the right frame of mind, and You say continually not to feel it as a burden. What is the best way to get our mind to stop feeling it is a tremendous burden to meditate?

Dear One, you know that our mind is a very obstinate enemy and since he is an agent of the Negative Power it is his duty to stop the souls from doing the devotion of Almighty Lord. So that is why he is performing his duty well; he is obeying his Master. In the same way when we sit for meditation, when we are sitting to do the job of our Master, we should also perform our duty very well. As mind is doing his duty and he is trying his best to stop us from doing the meditation, in the same way, at the same time, we should also perform our duty very well. We should obey the commandments of the Master and not listen to the mind; we should only listen to the Master and do what He has told us to do.

Could one visualize the Master's Form while doing Simran?

If we will do the Simran lovingly and affectionately then without visualizing the Form of the Master, the Form of the Master Himself comes there and starts dwelling within us.

It is a natural practice; you know that if you remember anything you will start seeing or feeling that thing in your within, in your mind. In the same way when we will do the Simran given by the perfect Master, lovingly and affectionately, then by Himself His Form will start appearing within us. If we are making any efforts from our side, if we are trying to visualize the Form of the Master, then we will not be able to get any success in that, because we won't be able to visualize the complete Form of the Master. Sometimes we may be able to visualize only the eyes of the Master, sometimes the beard or turban, and in that way our meditation will be disturbed, we won't get any success at that. So it is better just to do the Simran lovingly because if we remember the Master lovingly He will start to appear within us by Himself.

---

from a talk given March 31, 1981 and printed as "Masters Always Shower Grace" in the November 1991 issue of *Sant Bani Magazine*

* * *

The mind is very strong here and also the mind is a very great marksman and it finds its mark all the time. I find that I am being besieged by temptations and attacked on all sides. By doing the Simran just the way I hear the Master do it before we do meditation and by thinking about the Master I find that I am able to dispel those temptations. But there are so many temptations that, although I have great faith in the Master, I am starting to have real doubts about myself. I wonder if these also will diminish as we leave here and are not in the Master's grace anymore or will these things leave scars — these thoughts, these battles, that we have had from the Negative Power?

Satguru never leaves the disciple not even for one moment. He is always accompanying the disciple like a shadow and not even for one moment does He go away from the disciple. The only difference is that always there is a veil drawn between the Master and the disciple. Until the disciple has complete love and faith in the Master, he cannot see the Master walking with him and doing things for him. When you leave here the Master will not leave you, He will be with you; if you will do your Bhajan and Simran wholeheartedly, and if you will remember this holy trip, then definitely you will get help.

In the Bani of the Masters it mentions bathing in the dust of the Feet of the Master. Should this be taken figuratively or literally?

In the Banis of the Saints and Masters They have said a lot about this dust, and They say that it is very important.

The dust in which we have to bathe is in the Tenth Door because all the nine openings, the nine doors, open outwardly; the Tenth Door is the door which opens inwardly, so after rising above these nine openings, when we enter the Tenth Door there we see the Feet of the Master. By saying that you should bathe in the dust of the Feet of the Saints it is meant that once you reach there you have to bathe, you have to surrender yourself; at the Feet of the Master. That is the Mansarovar, the Pool of Nectar in which you have to bathe. Both things are one and the same.

Tulsi Sahib has said, "Moment after moment, bring your attention to the Eye Center and keep your attention there. Purify the mirror of your body and mind, and beautify it with your attention." If your attention will be constantly towards the Master, only then will you be able to reach His Feet and bathe in the dust of the Feet of the Master. Only then will the Light be manifested within you.

We bow down to the dust of the feet of the Masters outwardly also, because if we do not get the dust of the feet of the Masters outwardly, we cannot get the inspiration of going within and bathing in the dust of Their Feet inwardly.

Guru Nanak Sahib has also said, "O Nanak, I ask only for

this bounty — please make me the dust of the feet of the Saints."

To be able to achieve and to bathe in the dust of the feet of the Masters is the reaction or the result of our very good karmas and it is a very big thing.

There are sixty-eight places of pilgrimage in India. Guru Ramdas has written, "All those places long for the dust of the feet of the Saints. They say, "In us the drunkards, the people who have done bad karmas come and bathe, thinking that they are removing the dirt of their sins and that they are putting all their sins and dirt in our water. But we long for the dust of the feet of the Masters or Saints, because by having a little bit of the dust of the feet of the Saints, all our dirt and impurities and sins will be removed."

Once I expressed my desire to Baba Bishan Das of going to Hardwar. I told Him that I very much wanted to go and bathe in that holy place, the holy waters of Hardwar. Baba Bishan Das told me, "Not this year. Next year I will take you, and I will also go with you." At that time I did not realize what Baba Bishan Das was going to show me, but whenever the Masters or the Saints say or do anything it always has some deep meaning behind it and I was not aware of that. So next year when He took me to Hardwar we arrived there late at night and as soon as we got there one woman came there and she requested Baba Bishan Das to let her wash His feet and let her drink that water. Baba Bishan Das replied, "No, I cannot let you do that, because I have not done so much meditation and I am not yet as perfect as you understand." Although she was very insistent and she wanted to do that very badly, Baba Bishan Das was very strong and He did not let her do that, and then that woman left. I had never seen that woman coming to Baba Bishan Das any time previously, so next morning I asked Him, "Who was that woman?" Baba Bishan Das told me, "She is that river Gunga where you have come to bathe. Since many sinners and bad people come and bathe in the waters of Gunga, she is polluted with all the impurities and sins of the people and she is also longing for the dust of the feet of the Saints so that she can get liberation."

In the history of Guru Angad Dev, before coming to Guru Nanak [when he was Bhai Lena], he was a devotee of one goddess and he was like a group leader of his area. He used to collect the people and he would take them to have the darshan of the idol of that goddess. Once it so happened that he came in contact with a disciple of Guru Nanak Dev who asked him a very simple question. That disciple of Guru Nanak asked him, "Have you ever met that goddess whose darshan you are seeking all the time you are going to visit her temples and all that?" Bhai Lena was very surprised. Until then nobody had asked him such a question, so he was worried because he had never met that goddess and he was very devoted to her. So he replied, "No, I have never met that goddess."

So that disciple of Guru Nanak told him, "Well, this time when you go to visit the temple of that goddess, on the way you should stop in the place called Katarpur." (That is where Guru Nanak used to live, and it was on his way to the place where the temple of the goddess was.) So the disciple told him, "You should go and see my Master, Guru Nanak, and then you will know whether what you are doing is correct or not." So when Bhai Lena, along with other devotees of the goddess, came to Katarpur and met Guru Nanak he was impressed. Then he told his friends, "I will not go with you tonight; you should continue your journey, and I will stay here." So when Bhai Lena remained with Guru Nanak, at three o'clock that night he saw that one woman was sweeping the floor of Guru Nanak's house. He was very surprised to see that woman there because it was so early in the morning and there was no point of cleaning the floor, but still she was doing that wholeheartedly. So Bhai Lena approached her and asked her who she was and what she was doing there. She replied, "I am that goddess whose devotee you are, and I am begging at the door of this great Saint, because I long for the human body so that I can do the devotion of Naam and go back to the plane where my soul was separated from Almighty God."

Hearing that Bhai Lena was very surprised and then he realized that the devotion which he had been doing was not correct and that he should be practicing the Path of Guru Nanak. He asked that goddess, "Up until now I have done a lot of devotion to you, but still you did not give me your darshan, but today I have seen you. What is the reason behind this? Why did you not give me your darshan earlier?" She replied, "I am always here begging at the door of Guru Nanak, so how can I go and give darshan to anybody else? When I myself am longing for liberation how can I give liberation to others?"

So when Bhai Lena saw this, only then did he get Initiation from Guru Nanak, and then he became the gurumukh disciple of Guru Nanak.

If we have faith in the Master outwardly, only then will we have the inner faith for Him. If we have love for the outer dust of the Master, only then will we long for the inner dust and will we be able to go within.

Only those who meditate have love for the Feet of the Master and only they have appreciation and respect for the dust of the Feet of the Masters.

---

from a talk given April 3, 1981 and printed as "To Bathe in the Dust of the Master's Feet" in the August 1991 *Sant Bani Magazine*

* * *

Regarding the problem of anger, which a lot of us seem to have, You say that the remedy for the disease of anger is meditation, but also that an angry person can't meditate. So how can we break the circle? I can't imagine me sitting down after a storm of anger, it would be more than impossible.

I like your question very much [*much laughter*] and I would like to tell you that suppose an army comes to attack your home, if at that time you try to teach your army the skills of fighting, it is not possible, you will definitely lose the battle. Or if you try to dig a well when you are thirsty, you will not be able to quench your thirst, because it will take some time for you to dig the well. That is why you should be prepared for it from the beginning, you have to work on it gradually.

When a person is about to drown in the ocean, if he thinks he should learn swimming at that time, he will not be able to, he will not be saved from drowning, he should learn swimming beforehand.

In Colombia I gave a Satsang on a *bani* of Tulsi Das in which I said: Once a potter was going to take some sand to the palace of a king and on the way he was telling his donkeys, "Let us go dear sister. Let us go dear mother." Someone asked him why he was calling those donkeys as mother, and sister?

He replied that he was an illiterate, and that is why he had not controlled his speech. He did not know what he would say, as he was used to saying the slang words and things like that. That is why he was afraid that if he did not practice before going to the palace of the king it was possible that over there also he might say something wrong which might upset the king and it was possible that he might be hanged by the king. So that is why he was practicing beforehand, he was trying to call all the donkeys "mother" and "sister" so that when he went to the palace he would not say any bad word.

Similarly the Bhajan and Simran practices which we have been given by the Master are for removing these diseases, and we should do the practice, we should work on them beforehand.

---

from a talk given February 26, 1984 and printed as "To Stop the Fire of Anger" in the March 1993 *Sant Bani Magazine*

* * *

This isn't a question, it's just a statement. I sat right in front of you today for the meditation, and I moved eight thousand times.

[*Laughing*] All Saints have said that for the Masters distance makes no difference. Whether you sit close to the Master or away from the Master, for Him it makes no difference. But it does make a difference for us, if we do not understand the meaning of meditation. Do you understand the value of meditating here? If you understand the importance, the significance, of meditation, only then you will not move so many times, because you are understanding the value of it. Right from the beginning you will take such a position in which you don't have to move so many times.

---

from a talk given February 29, 1984 and printed as "A Million Times a Day" in the May 1984 *Sant Bani Magazine*

* * *

Sant Ji, when I sit for meditation and close my eyes, my attention goes up to my forehead, but I can sense the direction that my eyes are pointing and I feel like I'm looking down. So I feel very conflicted about the attention. Can You explain what's happening and how I can get my attention to go up?

Often I advise the dear ones that they should read *Sant Bani Magazine* thoroughly and very attentively because most of such questions are answered in the magazine. So if you would read those magazines properly you would find the answer to your question.

Often I have said that when we sit for meditation our body should be still, our mind should be still, and *surat* and *nirat* should also be still. When our body is still it will help us to make our mind still; and when our body and mind will be still it will be very helpful in stilling our surat and nirat.

Surat is that faculty or power with which we hear, and *nirat* is that power or faculty with which we see. So that is why it is very important for us to keep our body, mind, surat, and nirat still when we sit for meditation. In this regard I have often given the example of how we were taught to use a gun. When I was in the army they used to teach us that in order to send the bullet straight to the target we need to keep our body and the gun and the target all in one line. If any of those things are not in line or if any of those things are moving, we won't be able to hit the target. In Sant Mat also the same principle applies: If you want to meditate properly your body should be still, your mind should be still, and your attention should not be very much upwards or downwards. It should be just a little above the eyes, between and behind the eyebrows, and you should be looking inwardly and not outwardly as you have said.

At the time of Initiation the dear ones are told, "You do not need to form any images or anything when you sit for meditation. You should just close your eyes and whatever you are seeing inside, it is your third eye which is seeing those things; and you do not need to find the third eye." When you close your outer eyes your third eye starts functioning. That is why I always advise dear ones that when they sit for meditation they should not exert any effort to look or see things, or form images by themselves. They should just keep their attention at the Eye Center and do the repetition of the Words. Why does it happen that dear ones do not know where they have to concentrate, and why do they sometimes look upwards or downwards or to the left or right? Because they have not collected their thoughts. Their thoughts are dispersed everywhere; that is why they spend all their time struggling over where to concentrate, and where to keep their attention.

Sant Ji, we're supposed to use the Simran to control our mind, but we also need to rely on our mind to remind us to do the Simran. It sort of seems like setting the crows to watch the corn. I don't quite understand.

It's not like that. At the time of Initiation, you are told that when the disciple is initiated, the Master sits within the disciple in the Form of the Shabd. So when you are doing the Simran you should seek the support of the Master and you should be remembering and longing for the support of the Master for doing Simran, instead of the mind.

Could you please tell us a story? [much laughter]

[*Sant Ji laughs.*] When we are talking about meditation, only the stories regarding meditation seem nice to talk about. And if, in the reply to any question, a story comes up naturally, only that looks good; otherwise it doesn't look nice to tell stories.

Sant Ji, when I listen for the inner Sound Current, I hear different sounds, and they vary in pitch, and I wonder: can I concentrate on a pitch? Do the higher pitches make any difference, or should I be happy just to have the Sound?

This is why I always advise the dear ones to read *Sant Bani Magazine* thoroughly, because all such questions are answered in that magazine. I have often said that when the water is coming down from the mountain, that water has one kind of sound, and when it is traveling on the stones it has another sound, when it flows over the sand it has a still different kind of sound, and when it finally merges into the ocean it has a different kind of sound.

But the water was the same; the sound varied only because the places where the water was traveling were different. In the same way, there is only one Sound coming from Sach Khand, but because it travels through five different planes, that is why Masters have said there are five different sounds. In fact, there is only one Sound coming from Sach Khand, but because it travels through the five different planes, that is why it sounds different. So in the beginning, whatever sound you hear, you should catch that sound and concentrate on it, whether it is low tone or high tone. Every day you should try to catch that sound and concentrate on it. You should not change the sound from day to day; you should catch one sound and concentrate on that, because all the sounds which you hear have the connection with that higher Sound which is coming from Sach Khand

These are the general questions which almost everyone has, and they have been answered many times. So that is why we should carefully read *Sant Bani Magazine*. If we have not read the earlier issues we should read those also, because that will be beneficial for you. I do not mean to say that you should not ask me any question. I don't mind replying to your questions, no matter if you ask me the same question again and again, but I want you to read the magazines and the holy books so that you will know what the Masters have written in those books and how those things can be helpful to you.

Sant Ji, sometimes when I get sick, I get the feeling that, even though I feel sick, the mind is doing it to keep me from meditating. And I wonder does that happen and is there some way to tell when that's happening and how to overcome it?

In fact, pain, happiness, wealth, poverty, good health, and bad health are due to our own karmas As far as the mind is concerned mind only presents excuses within us so that we will not sit for meditation. If we have real love and faith in the Master, if we are devoted to the Master, if we have self-confidence, no matter how sick we are, still we will not postpone our meditation. If we do not have that love for the Master, that self confidence within, then even if we are not very sick our mind will tell us, "You are very sick," and we will postpone our meditation because of that.

Sant Ji, You've told us in the past that sometimes the Master keeps us from having inner experiences because our ego wouldn't be able to handle it, so they are postponed on and on. Also You've told us that we should look to our outer life to see why we are not progressing, because we're failing in the discipline. Is there any way to know which it is?

Supreme Father Kirpal invented the diary for us only for this purpose: so that we may know where we stand and what good and bad karmas we are doing. Do you think that you won't be aware of whatever good or bad karma you have done? Whatever good or bad karma we do we always remain aware of it; it is not as if somebody else will come and do good or bad karma for us and we will get the benefit of it, or pay the reaction of it. All the karmas, whether they are good or bad, which we have done, will bear fruit; we will have to pay off their reaction.

Sufi Sant Farid Sahib said that the farmer is longing to have dates but in fact he is planting chilies. How can he get wool when he has not worked for it, and when he has sown cotton? I have often said that when we are doing any deed we know what the reaction of it will be, what result we will have. When we are sowing anything we know what will grow. Baba Bishan Das Ji used to say, "You are planting useless bushes and hoping that you will harvest a very good dish." While you are planting useless trees you are expecting to have sugar cane. How is that possible?

When we will do our meditation honestly and with good thoughts, then we will have no complaints like this. Because then we will be capable of seeing what our Master is doing for us. Those who want to see where they stand and want to see progress in their meditation, they also work hard in making their life pure, and they always keep their thoughts pure. Those who do their meditation wholeheartedly and honestly by keeping their life pure, with pure thoughts, they can not only see their own progress, but they can also see how Master is pulling their own soul up and how He is working even for others.

Often I tell the story (and the question of that dear one who wanted me to tell a story will be answered now) of one fakir whose name was Suthra. He was a very fearless fakir and had written many humorous parables. Once he asked someone how to make a house strong. That person replied that if you put many pillars in a house it can become strong. So he started putting in pillars and he filled the whole house with pillars until there was no room in the house for him to sit. Suddenly it started raining, and since he did not have any place in the house he was standing outside, shivering in the rain. Someone came by there and asked Suthra why he was not in the house. So he replied, "If there were any place inside the house, I would have put one more pillar in there." So on one side we ask how do we know that Master is protecting our progress, how can we be convinced? But on the other side we are not ready to give up lust, we don't want to give up anger, attachment and all the bad things. We have all sorts of bad deeds and bad habits, and still we argue and complain, "How can we be convinced that Master is protecting our meditation?" So our condition is like that fakir who has filled up his house with pillars and hasn't left any place for himself. We have filled up the place where our Master, our God is, with lust, anger and all the bad things of the world. We have all kinds of worldly desires and attachments, and we don't have any place for Him to come and reside. And still we have this question: "How do we know that Master is protecting our meditation?" Unless we have a place within where we can go and see what the Master is doing, how can we know that He is protecting our meditation?

Do you think that the Master, Who is within you and is always watching over you, does not care for you? He knows about your thoughts even before you think them. He knows every single action you do; He knows every single feeling and thought which you have. Even without your asking He knows everything that you want. Since He cares for you, He wants you to leave your body and go back to the Real Home. That is why He always works and cares for you. Sometimes when the disciple is doing bad karmas or bad deeds, the Negative Power makes Master feel embarrassed and says to Him, "Is he the person to whom You gave Initiation? Was he worthy of getting Initiation?" At that time Master has to keep silent, but still He says, "No, he is my dear son, but he is innocent, he does not know what he is doing. Gradually he will understand his mistakes and he will come back." The Master has a huge amount of patience with the disciple and always patiently waits for us to come back to the Real Path: because He knows that some day we will definitely come back. That is why the Master Who is sitting within us, cares for us and always protects our meditation. He has given us Initiation and He knows that when we become free of our karmas, when we will give up doing the bad karmas, our soul will go up to the Real Home very quickly like a bullet shot from a gun; we will go up, riding on the Shabd, to our Real Home. It is only our bad deeds and karmas that keep our soul in the body; otherwise there is no other thing which keeps our soul from going back to the Real Home.

About four years ago, one initiate of Master Kirpal Singh reported that his soul was getting pulled up within and that he was getting a beating from the Master. He used to sell vegetables and he would deceive people by adding water to the vegetables to increase the weight. So Master pulled his soul within; and he told the people that he was getting a beating from the Master within, and Master was telling him that he was doing a bad thing. After some time he came to 77 RB and asked for forgiveness. I told him, "The Lord Who is going to forgive you is within you; now if you take a vow that you will not add water to the vegetables, then you can be forgiven." Then he took the vow. He is still alive and he still does the same business, but now he has repented and he has taken a vow that he will be honest in his business. Generally Saints do not do things like this, but sometimes in order to show the people, in order to make people know that Master is aware of every single one of our actions, sometimes They perform such miracles.

So we should know about the good and bad deeds which we do during the day; when we sit for writing our diaries at the end of the day we should know how many good and bad deeds we did today — and why we did the bad deeds. We should know why we did not meditate for this much time today, why we were lazy. We should fill out the diary honestly so that we may know where we stand and what things are keeping us from progressing.

You people are Satsangis. You follow Sant Mat and you have a Master; therefore your life is insured. Your Master is determined that He will definitely take you back to Sach Khand. There is no doubt in this fact. But just imagine the condition of the other people in the West and all over the world: how the flood of pleasures and lust and all those bad things are harming them. People do not understand how serious this thing is. They just take it as a very ordinary thing and that is why they do not make their lives pure. They always stain their life. Often I have said, quoting Kabir's bani, "When we are married, it is all right for us to have the connection with our wife, but to have lust for someone else outside of married life is counted as adultery. And those who are involved in committing adultery can never be forgiven, and their soul can never become pure. They can never ride on the Shabd and go back to the Real Home."

Guru Nanak Sahib has said that the person who gives up his own wife and goes to another's wife is like a blind man who does not see the reality and goes after the unreal thing. We have made our life like that. We do not pay any attention to our companion and we go to other people. In that way we are wasting and losing our life.

In Sukhmani Sahib, [see *The Jewel of Happiness*] Guru Arjan Dev Ji has written that we should not look at other women. We should always remain in the company of the Master. He says that women should not look at other men with lust in their eyes. He has not written only for women; this applies for men also. Men should not look at other women with lust in their eyes, nor should the women look at other men with lust in their eyes.

Guru Arjan Dev Ji Maharaj says that the woman controlled by lust does not want to miss any opportunity to indulge in lust with another person. And in the end she is eaten up by lust, greed, and anger. Do you think that when a person commits adultery or is involved in bad deeds, his brain is not affected by that? His brain is also affected by that because there is a power within us who always curses the person who has done something bad, and even he himself thinks about it and knows that he is doing something bad; and he always repents for that and worries that if someone else finds out about his bad deed he will be embarrassed.

I had many opportunities to sit at the feet of Beloved Master Sawan Singh and I heard many of His talks, and still the words of great Master Sawan Singh are sounding in my ears. He often used to say in the Satsang, that if you cannot remain celibate, then you should get married. What is wrong in getting married? From outside we pretend that we are good meditators — we are celibate, we do not get married, so we are maintaining chastity. But from inside we are always thinking about women and we are always thinking about indulging in lust. Outside sitting with the other people we pretend that we are good meditators, but inside we are committing sins. Do you think that our Master is not aware of the sins we are committing inside? Master always knows everything we are doing. If you don't have thoughts of indulging with a woman even in your dreams, then you can shout from the rooftops that you have maintained chastity, and that Supreme Father Almighty God has been very gracious on you that you have controlled this element. Then it is all right if we don't get married. But if lust is bothering you even in your dreams, in your thoughts, then there is no harm in getting married. You should without any hesitation get married.

This will help you a lot in your spiritual upliftment. Many times in Satsang I have said, "Why do the Masters emphasize remaining loyal to your companion? Because it affects our spiritual progress." Those who do not maintain chastity in this physical world, I often say that when they go to the astral world they will meet astral men and women over there who are very radiant and very beautiful. So those who cannot control lust while in the body, just looking at the physical body of another person whether it is man or woman, those who get involved in lust — do you think that they will be able to maintain chastity when they come in contact with the radiant astral men and women?

So that is why we should always try to maintain chastity. Guru Arjan Dev Ji Maharaj says that just for the pleasure of one moment, one suffers for one *krore* days. (One krore days means thirty-three thousand years.) Just for getting the pleasure of one moment he has to suffer for that much time. Guru Arjan even says that lust is such a bad thing that it takes you in many different bodies and even into hell.

Saints have been householders as well as renunciates. Yesterday I said that there were many Saints who lived a householder's life and there were many Saints who were renunciates. And neither the householder Saints have said that renunciation is bad, nor have the renunciate Saints said that the householders are bad. They say that it does not matter whether you live a householder's life or the life of a renunciate: the thing that counts is your strength or maintenance. If They have been a renunciate They have been completely renunciate, and if They have been a householder, They have always maintained that religion of the household. Saints always say that if your mind does not bother you for lust and if you can do without getting married, there is no need to get married; but if your mind bothers you, then in Sant Mat there is no bar against getting married, you can easily get married.

I often say that you should just live a pure life for some time and start enjoying the purity of life. Start enjoying the maintenance of chastity. The time will come when you will not be willing to give up your chastity — no matter what you are offered, you will not be willing to give up your chastity.

The question which was asked was, "How do we know whether it is our Master Who is holding back our progress and not letting us see it, or if it is because of our shortcomings in our outer life that we are not progressing?" You know that when it rains or snows the wind which blows through that place where it has rained or snowed becomes cold and spreads coolness everywhere. In the same way, if you have maintained a pure life, if you are living a pure life, Master is no doubt aware of it, because He is sitting within you. So when you are living a pure life, not only you will be aware of your progress, but even the people who are living around you will know about your purity, and they will also say that you are a pure man or woman.

Once in the army there was a theft and many guns were

stolen. They said that it was because of the carelessness of the guards, and the commander and everyone was very upset because they did not know who had stolen them. They were going to punish many people including many innocent people. They did not know how to find out the truth of who had really stolen those things. In the army they often used to call me "Bhai Ji" or "Gyani Ji," and they knew that I was a very sincere, truth-speaking person. They respected me a lot. Our commander told everyone in our group in the army to come and touch the body of this man, "Gyani Ji" and say that they were sincere and didn't know anything about this theft. Out of fifteen hundred people, there were only four people who were involved in that theft. Only they were not able to touch my body and say that they were true and did not know anything about it. I did not tell them that I was pure, and I did not threaten them or do anything. It was only because of my purity that they could not dare to touch me and lie. The others who were sincere had no problem; they came and touched me and said, "I do not know anything about it." But the real thieves when they came near me started trembling.

So I mean to say that when you are living a pure life, when you are pure within, your purity is so great that it will be spread everywhere and even the bad people will not dare to lie in front of you. Do you think that when you live a pure life, your friends and neighbors will not be aware of that? They will definitely be aware of it, because purity spreads like a fragrance. Those who have their nose open always smell it and know about it. In the army it was a very unusual thing for a person not to eat meat and drink wine, and I was one of those people who did not. So people knew everywhere that I did not eat meat or drink wine. I have often said that while serving in the army I never visited any city; even for buying small things, I would tell my friends to go and buy them for me, because I was very religious minded. I would spend my time in the religious places and live a pure life. Only because of that purity I was known everywhere, and people even used to swear in my name.

I often say that the house which we live in, or the land where we live, at least that land or house should be proud of us, that such a good person lives here. Your Master is very pure and very holy. He is above the dirt and bad things of this world. So why don't you rise above the dirt and bad things of this world, and become as pure and holy as He is, so that He may manifest Himself in you and be proud of you, that His disciples are so pure and holy?

When Supreme Father Kirpal came to my ashram for the first time, I told Him, "Master, I don't know what question I should ask You, because my heart and brain are empty; since my childhood I have kept them empty." He smiled and became happy and said, "Only because your heart and brain are empty have I come so far. I have traveled five hundred kilometers only because your heart and brain are empty, and I have come to give you something." And because I was hungry for His grace and He had the grace, He showered His grace on me. I was burning like a fire and He had Naam with Him. He caused the rain of Naam to shower and He cooled down my heated heart.

---

from a talk given March 28, 1984 and printed as "The Master Cares for You" in the November 1985 issue of *Sant Bani Magazine*

* * *

Sant Ji, is the ability to do Simran at the Eye Center obtained by hard work, chastity, Master's grace, or some other quality?

Efforts and the grace of the Master work together. If we are working hard, then there is no doubt in the fact that Master will also shower His grace on us.

As far as chastity is concerned, it [not only] has many physical benefits, but it also has a benefit in Spirituality.

If a child is interested in going to school, if he is hard-working, if he respects the teacher, and if he puts all his attention and concentration on the studies, then the teacher also finds it very important to put all his attention towards that child. He puts a lot more attention on that child who is hard working and who respects the teacher, and he tries to give the best possible education to that child.

Master Sawan Singh Ji used to say, "If we make efforts and the Master doesn't shower His grace on us, then we cannot achieve anything." Our efforts alone, without the grace of the Master, will not lead us to success. But Master Sawan Singh also said, "The Master in whom God is manifested is not unjust." You know that if someone has people working on his farm or in his store, he is responsible for them, he is worried for them, he knows when he has to feed them, he knows when he has to pay them. So Master Sawan Singh Ji used to say, "When even the worldly master is responsible for his servants, do you think that the Master within whom God is manifested is unjust?" No, He is not unjust. He is responsible for us, He is worried for us, and if we are making efforts for Him, He will definitely shower His grace on us.

This is an incident of my childhood: once when I was about thirteen or fourteen years old, I was walking along the canal and an old man who was a lawyer by profession passed me on his bicycle. When he saw me, he stopped and said, "Dear Son, if you don't mind I would like to ask you a question."

I said, "It is all right, you can ask me anything, and I will try my best to reply to that."

He said that he had read in a book that whatever a person has in his heart, that shows on his face. If there is someone who can read the face he can easily know what the person has in his mind and, "As far as I can see on your face, you are a devotee, you are doing some kind of devotion of God."

I replied, "No, up until now I have not started doing any meditation, but it is true that I am looking for the [path of] devotion. I am searching for the practices, but I don't know yet how to do the devotion."

So I mean to say that if there is anyone who can read the faces, he will easily tell you what is in your heart. Those who are driven by lust, outwardly their faces may look bright and they may look very healthy, but if there is any experienced man he can easily look in their eyes and look at their faces and tell that they are suffering from the disease of lust.

Nowadays neither the men are taught about the importance of chastity, nor are women given the knowledge of how important it is to maintain chastity. Since the parents do not maintain chastity themselves, they are not a good example for their children, that is why even before the children reach their youth, as soon as they start producing the vital fluid in their bodies they start losing it by many unnatural ways. Since they have lost a lot of their vital fluid before their bodies are fully developed, they do not have good health and they are not physically fit, because they have lost a lot of vital energy from their body. When we lose the vital fluid in a great amount it affects our body, it affects our mind, it affects our thoughts also.

When the children are given the knowledge of lust and dirty things right from their childhood, how can they keep their thoughts pure? And when their thoughts are not pure, how can they keep their minds pure? If their mind is not pure, how can they get any strength of the soul to concentrate at the Eye Center? How can they collect their soul at the Eye Center and go beyond that? How can they bring that soul in contact with the Shabd?

You know that a piece of iron which is rusted will not be attracted by a magnet no matter how powerful the magnet is. In the same way the soul which is affected by lust and the other dirty things will not be pulled up by the Shabd, no matter that the Shabd is very powerful. Unless you remove the rust from the iron, and unless you remove the dirt from the soul the Shabd will not pull the soul up. This is only because of the lack of chastity. People do not understand the value of chastity; this is why they don't keep their thoughts and their minds pure. And if the mind and the thoughts are not pure, the soul will not become pure and it will not go up.

Nowadays many doctors advertise in the newspapers: "If you want to regain your lost youth, if you want to regain your lost vitality and vigor, come to us and we will give you the medication." But instead of regaining their lost youth and vitality people create even more heat in their body, because the medicines which those doctors give them in order to become healthy do not work. It causes more heat in their body and it inspires their minds to indulge in lust more than before.

When I came back from Delhi on the sixteenth of last month, I had to stop in the town of Sri Ganganagar because a dear one of Master Kirpal had left the body and I had to go and meet the family. Before I got to Sri Ganganagar a doctor from Delhi had made a lot of publicity. He advertised in the newspaper and distributed a lot of handbills and he was having something like a campaign there boasting that he could restore people's lost vitality and youth.

When I went to meet the family of that dear one who had left the body, that doctor also was there and whenever I looked at him, he would not look at me, he would close his eyes. I thought that maybe he was feeling sleepy, but that was not the case. He did not have enough courage to look into my eyes. He had come to see me because people had told him that a Saint was going to come and so he came to see me.

After awhile he told me that he would like to see me in private and that he wanted to talk about something with me.

I said, "Okay, you can do that." When he came in private to talk with me he told me about his disease — that even though he was sixty years of age and he was telling people he could help them in regaining their lost youth — the problem with him was that he lost his vital fluid whenever a woman was near him. Or many times if he could not find any woman he used unnatural ways to lose the vital fluid. He was very much affected by that disease, and he was tired of it and he wanted to get rid of it. So he asked me to shower some grace on him.

I told him, "What are you teaching the people? You are telling the people that you can help them in regaining their lost youth, but you yourself are not capable of doing that. Is your publicity not misleading the young people of the country?" He felt very embarrassed and he did not have anything to say.

Kabir Sahib says, "O Man and Woman, both of you listen to the teachings of Satguru. This poisonous fruit will affect both of you, don't even taste it."

Masters do not give the teachings only for the men. Maintenance of chastity is not only important for the men, but it is equally important for the women.

Those who have maintained their body right from their childhood, those who have preserved their vital fluid from their very beginning, naturally they have light within them. And for such people it is very easy to get the Light of Naam; it is just like bringing a flame in contact with gas or petrol, it explodes. Similarly, when such people who have kept themselves pure are given Initiation, they go right up.

Kabir Sahib says, "The unchaste person can never worship the Master, can never meditate. He is always affected by the doubts and fears; he is always worried because he is doing this bad deed. When will he get rid of this bad habit? He always goes on thinking about it and never does the meditation. He is controlled by the sense organs and he never gets the opportunity to meditate and go up."

---

from a talk given October 28, 1984, and printed as "The Nectar of Kirpal," in the April 1993 *Sant Bani Magazine*

* * *

I read a few different times about how You had meditated for seventeen years in a cave and then after You met Kirpal, for another five years, and I wonder, did You sleep at all or were You doing something else?

[*Much laughter*] This body needs food and also to keep it light it needs some rest, some sleep also. But the meditator's sleep, as well as his diet, reduces by itself.

It is because I have meditated in a special way, that is why I inspire all of you to meditate. Many people complain that they do not have enough time for the meditation. I tell them, "Look here, make a schedule of your day-to-day life in which you show at what time you have to get up, what time you have to go to your job, what time you have to eat, and what time you have to go to bed. In that schedule you should have a time for meditation also." [If you] follow that schedule wholeheartedly, then you will have no complaints that you do not have any time. Master graciously gave us the diary to keep, and by the help of the diary also we can maintain our daily meditation. If we follow the schedule which I have just mentioned, then we will have no difficulty in meditating and achieving our goal.

In the beginning it is very difficult to reduce the amount of sleep. In the beginning when one tries to reduce the amount of sleep, he feels heaviness in his eyes, he feels heaviness in his head, and it becomes very difficult for him to stay awake. But after he develops the habit of sleeping less then it becomes difficult for him to sleep more.

The appetite is the same. In the beginning it is difficult to reduce your diet, because you feel like eating too much, but later on, when you develop the habit of eating less, then you can never eat a lot of food, because then your stomach has become used to eating less food.

This is my personal experience that the pleasures which the men are running after, and which they do not want to give up — they give first importance to the pleasures — in the beginning it is difficult to give them up too. But when we give them up, a time comes when, from our within, we start hating those pleasures and then they never bother us, we never feel like enjoying those pleasures.

All the Saints, those Who got the blessings from Almighty God to bring the souls back home, meditated for many years in Their lifetime before They started doing Their job. They meditate for so many years, for so much time, because until They have perfected Themselves in meditation, They do not get permission from Almighty God to continue the mission.

If I had known that after my meditation and after perfecting myself in the meditation that I would be given such a big responsibility of taking care of the souls, of doing the Satsangs for the dear ones, of flying in the planes, of having the restless nights and days going here and there to meet the people and do all this work, I would never have meditated this way. Because I was initiated by the Master and once the Master gives you Initiation then you are sure that He will take you back to the Real Home, so what is the use of doing the meditation? If I had known that I would be given such a big responsibility I would never have meditated; I am telling you the truth. But I did the mediation for some other purpose. I thought that when I do the meditation and perfect myself in it, I will meet God and it will be fun. It will be a nice thing, after that I will not have to worry about anything once I have realized God.

But after I did the meditation, when He gave me the permission, when He gave me the orders, to continue His mission only I know what happened with me and how I felt. I felt in myself like a thief that is caught red-handed. He cannot run away, he cannot sit down there. He is confused, he does not know what he is; he cannot do anything, he just waits there for the judgment to come.

I felt the same way after meditating for so many years on the first Two Words. After perfecting myself for the first two planes, when Master Kirpal graciously gave me the Initiation, at the same time He told me, "Now you have to do this work. Be careful and don't let my teachings be destroyed in this world. You have to continue to spread my teachings in this world."

Only I know how I felt at that time, because I had not done the meditation to become the Master. When I was meditating on the first Two Words and when I perfected myself on the first two planes there was no question about being the Master and doing this job. One who has perfected himself on the first Two Words cannot get the permission to do this work, because he is still not perfect. Afterwards when Master Kirpal graciously gave me His Initiation and at the same time when He gave me the orders to do this work, I felt very sad and I wept but He didn't hear my weeping. I told Him, "Master, I did not do the meditation for this sake, I did the meditation because I was a devotee of Your Feet and I wanted to sit in Your lap. I wanted to be a honey bee of Your Feet and a lover of Your Feet; I feel the pleasure, I feel the happiness by doing that, and I do not want to do this work." But He did not listen to me because He wanted me to do all the work which He is making me do now.

So once again I am saying that if I had known in the beginning that He would make me do all these things, after making me meditate for so long, I would never have done the meditation in this way.

Those who do not meditate, only those people form the parties, and only those people are desirous of becoming the Master. They do not know that they will have to settle the accounts of the souls with the Negative Power and that they will have to take the karmas of the souls on their own body. Since they do not know what job they will have to do, they are anxious to become the Master; that is why they form parties and they criticize other people.

But those who meditate and who know the Reality are not desirous of becoming the Master; they are not anxious to do this work. They are not willing to become the Master, because they know what duty they will have to perform and how much burden they will have to take on their shoulders if they become the Master.

Guru Nanak's sons struggled very much and they even became upset with their father that He did not give them the guru- ship. But when Guru Nanak told Bhai Lena, who later on became Guru Angad, to do this work, he said, "Master, this load is too much for me; how will I carry it?"

When Master Sawan Singh gave this responsibility to Master Kirpal, He asked him to count and tell him how many people were initiated. He was told that so many people were initiated, hearing which Master Sawan Singh said, "Kirpal Singh, I have done half of your work, now you have to initiate the other half."

At that time Master Kirpal Singh wept in front of his Master and said, "Master, You be the one to do the other half; You do the rest of the work too." But Master Sawan Singh said, "No, you have to do that."

At that time Master Kirpal said, "Let me become the pipe and whatever Water You will send to me, I will just let it pass through me and give it to the people. Whatever grace You will give to me I will give it to the people."

Master Kirpal was not pleased, He was not happy, to do that work. Those meditators who meditate and go within do not become happy, because they know the load or the burden, and they are not anxious to become the Master and do this work. But when they are given the responsibility by their Master, when they are given this work, when they are given the orders by the Master, they cannot refuse their Master and they happily accept whatever comes in the Will of their Master.

You people have tasted so much of life. You have travelled so much, you have been so many places and you have enjoyed many pleasures of life. But you know how my life was — I never went to any city for sightseeing, I never went to eat any delicious foods, I never wore any beautiful clothes, I never went wandering and roaming here and there, and I never went out for picnics. You know that whenever I go to the foreign countries I am locked in an airplane, and over there in the ashrams I am locked in a room. I never go out to see places; I never go to meet people outside. People come to see me in my room. Even when I go to Delhi or Bombay, Pappu knows and whoever has had an opportunity to be with me in Bombay or Delhi, you know how much time I spend going into the city. I never go to visit any place in the city, I am always locked in a room where people come to see me. My life is much different than the life of most people. You can very well imagine what is the mission of my life on this earth and what is the mission of the worldly people's life on this earth.

People give first preference to meeting people and enjoying the pleasures of the world, whereas in my life there is no place for all those things. And even now, when I am doing this work, I never go for sightseeing or picnics or anything like that. I travel only for the sake of my job and that is all.

---

from a talk given October 31, 1984, and printed as "The Restless Nights and Days" in the May 1993 *Sant Bani Magazine*

* * *

Sant Ji, to meditate seems to require enormous endurance. How do the very old grandmothers and grandfathers in India meditate when they do not have that kind of endurance?

You see, there is not much difference whether an American person meditates or if an Indian person meditates; they all have the same kind of problems. It is universal whether it is here or there, and unless they have the endurance, the patience, to meditate, they cannot do it. If we do not have endurance we cannot become successful either in our meditation or in worldly work. It is not only for older people; for the young people it also applies. If they do not have the endurance to meditate they cannot become successful either.

I'll tell you one incident of the time of Master Kirpal. Once an elderly initiate came to see Him and he wanted to tell Master Kirpal, "Even the farmers forgive an old bullock, they don't take any work from that bullock but they feed him. In the same way when I have become old, I should be excused from meditation. I should not be told to meditate, I should be given this concession." He told me that he wanted to ask that from Master Kirpal and I should arrange his meeting. So I did. When he went to Master Kirpal he said, "All my worldly responsibilities have been taken care of; I have four sons and they own a very good grocery store and they are well settled, now I have nothing to do. But I have become old and even farmers don't allow the old bullocks to work. So like that, You should also excuse me from the meditation. You should not tell me to meditate because I have become old; You should take me without meditation." Supreme Father Master Kirpal laughed and said, "You are right that farmers don't make old bullocks work, but if all your responsibilities have been taken care of and you have nothing to do, then why don't you meditate all the twenty-four hours? From now onwards, you should meditate twenty-four hours; all day and night you should be meditating." He could not argue and he came back.

That old person used to have the habit of keeping a watch in front of him when he would sit for meditation, and since I knew that he had been told by Master Kirpal to meditate for twenty-four hours, I was surprised to see him using a watch — because when you are told to meditate always, then why do you need to have a watch? So once I said in front of all the people in the sangat, "Why does he use a watch when he has been told by Master that he should meditate for twenty-four hours?" And afterwards he gave up that habit.

So I mean to say that it makes no difference whether an old person is from India or from America — when you have taken care of all your responsibilities, when you have finished all your give and take in the world, when everything is all settled for you in the world and you have all that free time, then you should use that free time in doing meditation.

Maybe the older American people have the impression that Supreme Father Kirpal or Master Sawan Singh used to give a concession to the older Indian initiates and they were excused from the meditation, but that is not true. The old person whose story I told you was about a hundred years old at that time and he left the body after living a very long life. So Masters never excuse anybody from the meditation whether he is American, or Indian or African. Because you have to do the meditation; that is very important.

---

from a talk given January 2, 1985, and printed as "Faster than a Bullet" in the September 1985 *Sant Bani Magazine*

* * *

If our own will intervenes at the beginning of the meditation when we sit, when we make our mind quiet and concentrate, could You then tell us when does our own will stop and when does the grace of the Master start? Do we have to become completely empty or can we visualize the Form of the Master and still go within with our own will or the grace of the Master?

If you sit for meditation making your mind quiet and emptying yourself of worldly thoughts, then there is no question of your will intervening in your meditation; you have already made your mind empty.

If you sit with the desire that you want to go within, it is possible that the mind may make you lose this determination and attach you to some other desire of the world. Yesterday I described how our mind works like a competent lawyer. Sitting within us he goes on presenting excuses to us. Sometimes he tells us in a friendly way, sometimes he comes as an enemy and frightens us; he tries his best to make us give up doing our meditation. So when we sit for meditation it is very important for all the satsangis to remember the few things I often say before we sit for meditation: that you have to make your mind quiet, you have to make your mind empty of worldly thoughts, and you should not allow your mind to wander outside. You should sit there with your mind quiet, and concentrate.

I have often repeated what Master Sawan Singh Ji used to say, that the person at whose door a bullock or some animal is standing, is worried about that animal; he knows when he must bring it from the sunshine into the shade, and when he has to give it water or feed it. He is worried for it and he takes very good care of that animal, because he is responsible for it. In the same way, if you have some servant working in your home or in your store, you know when you have to pay him and what time he should be released, and so forth. And you will take care of every possibility, because you are responsible for him.

In the same way when we are working for our Master, when we are sitting at His door, He is responsible for us; as we do not keep our servant unpaid, do you think that He will keep us unpaid, if we work for Him? He is not unjust. He is full of justice, and He always takes very good care of all those who sit at His door and work for Him. Our job is to do the meditation, to keep our mind quiet and concentrated. When we sit at His door, when we do our work, then He performs His duty, He also does His work. Our job is to sit at the door, our job is to do the meditation; it is the job of the Master to pull our soul up. We don't have any way, any technique, by which we can pull our soul up by ourselves; it is the job of the Master. Our job is only to sit at the Eye Center and do the meditation as we have been instructed. It is the work of the Master to pull our soul up.

Swami Ji Maharaj says, "The Shabd will be opened with the grace of the Master, and the mighty Master pulls the soul up." Whenever our Shabd is opened, it is only with the grace of our Master, and He will pull our soul up. If we are doing our job, if we are taking even one step towards the Master, Master will come down fifty steps to take care of us and to pull our soul up. So we should also honestly and sincerely do our part: the part of the meditation which we have been given by our Master.

Master, I'm confused about when to sit for the Sound Current. I've heard that we're not to sit until the last ten minutes of meditation, and also it's been said, not until we've risen to see the Light within. Could You please answer this for me?

Usually I have said that we should spend at least one-fourth of the total time for meditation in sitting in the Sound. By doing that we get the habit of sitting for the Sound practice. And every day, by trying to listen to the Shabd, our mind also gets intoxicated by hearing the Shabd. If all the satsangis make Simran as the principle of their life, and if they go on doing the Simran even when they are not sitting for meditation, when they are doing other things of the world, or of their work — if they do the Simran at those times, they will not have to work hard for doing Simran when they sit for meditation. When you sit for meditation after doing so much Simran during the daytime, your attention goes straight into the Light and you will not have to work very hard, you do not have to give so much pain to your body, trying to do Simran and sitting for meditation.

---

from a talk given March 31, 1985 and printed as "The Reality of the Saints," in the October 1985 *Sant Bani Magazine*

* * *

Master, please will you tell us how to die while living?

Well, every day I try to make you people prepare for that. Every day in the morning and evening. But still I will try to explain some things to you. You know that our soul, after coming down from the Eye Center, has spread in all the cells of the body. It has not only spread in the body, it has also spread outside the body. It has gone into religions, communities, societies, in the family, in friends; it has spread all over.

Saints ask us, "Why are we born again and again into this world?" Because we do the simran, or remembrance, of the world and because of the simran of the world we are born into this world again and again. Whatever thoughts we have at the time of death, according to that we get our birth in the next lifetime. Most of the time we come back into the same family, into the same homes, and if not there then we might go somewhere in the neighborhood.

It is a personal experience of the Saints that *Simran cuts the simran and Contemplation cuts the contemplation.* The Simran given by the Master is the only thing which can cut down the simran or the remembrance of the worldly things and the Contemplation of the Form of the Master is the only thing which can make us forget the contemplation or the remembrance of the worldly things. Saints tell us that when we give up doing the simran of the world, when we do the Simran given by the Master, gradually the simran of the world goes away and then whom do we see? On whom do we contemplate? We contemplate on the Form of the Master who has given us Initiation and the forms of the world will also go away.

The simran of the world is also going on at the Eye Center. You know whenever you try to remember anything, whenever you try to visualize the form of anybody or try to remember anyone's face, at once your attention goes to the Eye Center. It is not like you are putting your attention at some other part lower than the Eye Center and thinking about some person. Always your attention is at the Eye Center whenever you are trying to remember something or some form. So at the Eye Center the rosary of the simran of the world is going on twenty-four hours a day.

So when sitting at this place, if you are doing the simran of the world, for instance, if you are remembering your father, your mother, your son, your daughter, your wife, your husband, what will happen? Since all those people are outside your body, your attention will go outside your body and you will become extroverted, and because we have been extroverted for many births, we have never thought of becoming introverted and that is why we find it difficult for our attention to go within.

When the Master gives us the Initiation what does He tell us? He tells us, "The Master is within you; God is within you." He gives us the Simran to do internally. He tells us that all the things are within us and we have to come to the Eye Center. So when we do the Simran given by the Master, since the Master is within our soul, and God is also within us, when we start stilling our attention at the Eye Center, when we start sitting there, then that beautiful Form of the Master is manifested over there and then not even for one moment will we take our attention away from that beautiful Form of the Master. The Master who has given us the Initiation is not different from Almighty God. The Formless Lord has taken up the Form of the Saint and He resides within us. So when the Master gives us the Simran and we do it honestly, in the beginning we find it difficult to bring our attention inward because we have become extroverted. But when we do it, when we still our attention at the Eye Center, Master is there, God is also there, and when we see His Inner Form even once, then we won't like to come outside.

In the Satsangs as well as at the time of Initiation we are told that by doing the Simran we can withdraw our attention from all the outer things and from our body and come to the Eye Center. In that process when our soul starts to withdraw from our body, first it is withdrawn from the outer world and when it comes to withdraw from the body we feel as if ants are biting our feet. When the soul goes upward then the body below becomes numb and finally when the soul comes to the Eye Center we feel as though the body below the Eye Center is not there; it is all numb and we lose the feeling of it, and then we feel that it is like a rented house, it does not belong to us.

In the process of death also the same thing happens. Those people who have made their Simran very strong, for them it is easy to withdraw from the body, it is very easy for them to bring their soul to the Eye Center. For them it is like pulling a hair out of butter. But some people who have not perfected their Simran and who only meditate occasionally, if their soul tries to leave the body they find it very difficult. They find it very painful, like the process of death, and sometimes people get so frightened that they don't like to sit for meditation again.

On the last Tour, at Sant Bani Ashram, one person who was getting Initiated was sitting on a chair doing the meditation. At once his soul left the body and it was very painful for him because it was the first time that he had meditated. He fainted and fell down off the chair. Earlier, I had told Russell Perkins and Pappu about such happenings, because sometimes when the soul is pulled up like this the person feels a lot of pain and even faints. But if that happens, we should not worry; if we give a massage to the back of the neck then the soul comes back into the body and the person does not feel any pain. And when that person fell down, they both gave him some massage and he came back into the body and he did not feel any pain.

All the Saints have said, "Those who want to do the meditation of Naam should make their heart like iron." One day everybody has to die; why not do that thing — which we have to do one day — while we are living? Why not die while we are living? Guru Nanak Sahib also says, "The place where we have to go after death, why not go there while we are still in the body?"

Since the soul is spread throughout all the cells of the body, when it is withdrawn from all those cells and goes upward, it is natural for us to feel pain; because in the process of the soul's withdrawal the lower chakras are broken. When they are broken it is natural for a person to feel the pain. But if we have the Simran given by the perfect Master, if we have the grace of the Master, then we do not find it difficult.

In the beginning when I had the Initiation into the first Two Words, many initiates of Baba Sawan Singh who had the full Initiation of Five Words would come to meditate with me. We were about ten or twelve people and they were very loving, devoted souls and they would come to meditate with me. And we always had one person standing up, while the others were meditating, to check the other people. If anyone was falling asleep in meditation or if he was trying to move, the person who was in charge at that time was told to slap the person on both sides. So I mean to say that only the brave courageous people can do meditation and only those who have real love and faith can become the real meditators.

No one was allowed to make tea, no one was allowed to sit in meditation after drinking tea, and no one was allowed to bring any kind of food to be distributed as parshad. Because it was a very strict period of meditation and we used to think, "He who brings parshad and he who distributes food to the other people wants to take away the meditation of others and that is not fair."

At that time I did not sit on any kind of cushion; I had only some sticks or hay underneath me, and I never even put a gunny sack under me; sometimes I sat on a flat wooden platform.

You could read, in the book written by Mr. Oberoi [*Support for the Shaken Sangat*], the stories of Sunder Das, who was an initiate of Master Sawan Singh. With him I used to have sittings of eight hours at a stretch. In that you would read about how we can die while living. Once when we were meditating we had a fire burning and a log fell out of the fire onto his leg; he did not know that his leg was burning, because he was so much absorbed in the meditation.

When he got up from that meditation, he told me, "The intoxication that I have received today in meditation, I have not gotten that any time before." Imagine to what plane he must have gone in that meditation. If he was in the body — you know that even if we get a little bit of pain, we move — but he was not in the body, that is why he did not even know that his leg was burning.

Mr. Oberoi did not write all those stories only from hearsay, he tried to find every possible person who had meditated with me, and after meeting them and confirming all the things with them, he wrote down the stories.

Usually when the western dear ones have the yearning and longing to do the devotion, they also have a feeling of hurry. They want to get results right away and in that they do not become successful. Master Sawan Singh Ji also used to say, "Western dear ones have this habit that when they have the yearning to do the devotion, they sit for meditation, but they want the results right then, and it does not work like that." We should do our devotion, our meditation, with love and faith, and patiently we should wait for the results.

---

from a question and answer talk given April 3, 1985 and printed as "Simran Cuts the Simran" in the January 1989 *Sant Bani Magazine*

* * *

Master, I would like to ask a question about darshan. I was wondering if this blessing comes from our longing or if it is from meditation or is it in our fate that He gives us His darshan?

The root of everything is meditation. When we do the meditation, we get the feelings for the Master. If you have good feelings for something, you get it's good results. If you have bad feeling for something, you get the bad results. Guru Nanak also said, "A person sees the image of God according to his own feelings." When we do the meditation we get good feelings for the Master, and when we have good feelings for the Master we get His darshan according to our feelings.

Master Kirpal Singh used to quote from the sacred book of the Muslims, the Koran, He used to say, "It is written there that Prophet Mohammad said, 'The *momin*, or the *gurumukh*, the beloved disciple of the Master, is like the image of God, whatever feeling you have, you will see that in the Master. Whatever feeling you have for God or for the Master you will see your image accordingly.' "

You know that Sant Satgurus always love everyone equally, for Them everyone is alike and They want to give equal things to everyone, but whatever our feelings are and whatever our vessel is, according to our feelings and the vessel we have prepared, we get the grace and we get the things from the Master.

Last night in the Satsang I said that once when Master Kirpal told me to explain the theory to some dear ones who were sitting there for Initiation, I told Him, "Master, why don't you show them Your Real Form, why don't You show them that You are God? Why don't You show them what You really are so that all the disputes of the temples and mosques will get cleared up? And in every home they would talk only about You and they would know that God is in this world in the Form of Kirpal." Because when I was seeing Him as God that is why I told Him that He should shower that grace on all the dear ones who were sitting there. Master Kirpal replied, "Don't make them tear my clothes."

At that time there were many other old initiates of Master Kirpal present there, they could have also told Master the same thing, "You are God, why don't you show all the people who are sitting here for the Initiation?" But they did not say anything like that. If they had also understood Master Kirpal as

God Almighty, if they had also understood His real glory they would have said so. But they did not do that because they didn't understand the reality of Master. They didn't understand Him as God, that is why they said things according to their own receptivity, according to their own feelings.

So everyone in this world sees the Master according to his own feeling, according to his own vessel. And according to the feelings we have for the Master, according to the receptivity we have to the grace of the Master, we get the blessings and darshan of the Master.

Once in an Initiation that Master Kirpal did, about fifty people were initiated. Everyone had good experiences except for one dear one who did not see the Light. So he told Master Kirpal that he did not see any Light. I was there and I got confused and I said, "Well God is Light and Light also belongs to God, and here God is giving the Initiation, and God is present here in front of you, what else do you want? Why are you looking for any other Light when the Form of Light, when the Form of God is standing in front of you?" But anyway Master Kirpal gave him another sitting and he was content with that.

Even now when I meet him he repents — why did he ask for the second sitting? Why did he ask for the Light when God Almighty was there in front of him, when the Form of Light, the Abode of Light, the Abode of All-Consciousness was in front of him, why did he ask for the Light.

I have often told Russell Perkins that in the beginning, when people used to tell me about not having the Light, and this and that, I would always get confused. I would say, "God Almighty came in the human form and if you had the real receptivity, you could have seen the Light emerging from every single cell of that human form of Almighty God who came in the form of Kirpal; but you did not see Him. What else do you want? Why are you looking for the other Light when that real manifestation of the Almighty One is in front of you? Why are you looking for the other Light and other experiences?"

I have caught hold of my Master, what He told me, I did that and I became successful. If we would also take the real refuge at the feet of the Master and if we would also do our meditation, if we would also follow and live up to the teachings of the Master with this feeling, we can get everything. Our purpose can be solved and we can get everything. We can progress and we can get everything that we are looking for. But the thing is you have to do what the Master is telling you to do. It is not good if Master tells you to rise above the mind and the organs of senses and if you do not do that. If you are going in the opposite direction, what can the Master do for you? When you have got the Master and He has given you the Naam and when He is telling you to do certain things, it is your job to do what He has told you and then you get everything. If you fall at His feet with sincerity, and if honestly you are doing what He has told you to do, then everything you need will get done by Him.

If we are like that prisoner who, when he is getting released from the jail, tells the jailer, "Don't clean my room, don't make any changes in my room, because I am coming back again." If we are like that prisoner, how can we progress on this Path? What that prisoner should have done was that he should have forgotten about his room or whatever he had in the jail, and after coming back into the world he should have improved his life and he should have forgotten everything of the past. So if we also become like that, if we also forget everything of the past, and since we have come to the Master we should become His, and we should sincerely and honestly do what the Master is telling us. Then we can also progress and we can get everything from the Master.

Sant Mat is the Path of improvement. If we improve our outer life after joining Sant Mat, then it becomes very easy for us to go within. The inner Path becomes very clear and easy for us if we have improved our outer life.

---

from a talk given January 14, 1986 and printed as "Sant Mat: the Path of Improvement" in the June 1993 *Sant Bani Magazine*

* * *

Master, I have a two-part question, on going within. What are the steps necessary for the disciple to actually go within? What things does he have to do and when he starts to go within, how does he know that he's starting to go within?

First of all the disciple needs to have love for the Master. And the second thing which he needs is to have faith in the Master. If he has both these things: love for the Master and faith in Him, then he gets the inspiration to work hard in meditation and go within himself.

Both these things work side by side — the grace of the Master and the efforts of the disciple. But if we are not making the efforts, if we have become the thieves of meditation, what can the Master do? Where can He shower the grace? The Master is not unjust; if we are making the efforts He will definitely shower His grace upon us.

Now, when we are sitting in this room, we can see everyone; we can see how they are. We can see everyone's face, we can see who has his head covered, who has his head uncovered, who has long hair, who is wearing glasses, and who is not wearing glasses. We can see everything very clearly.

So Dear Ones, when you go within, over there you will see things even more clearly than what you are seeing here outside, and you will even bear witness to those things. You will say, "O Lord, the things which we are seeing within, the things which You are doing for us, we cannot pay You back for that in any way."

Many of your brothers and sisters go to Rajasthan to do the meditation, some of them who work hard and go within tell us how much grace they get from the Master. They talk a little bit about what they have seen inside, and they express their gratitude for that.

The disciples who do not become lazy, those who give up laziness, they become successful in this. The Masters do not like to follow the same speed as that of the disciple, They want and They are determined that in Their lifetime, the disciples may go within and become successful. The Master wants that the stream of the Shabd should start coming within the disciple when He is living in the body, so that after He leaves the body, they should not wander away.

---

from a question and answer talk given January 12, 1987 and printed as "It is Never Too Late to Mend" in the November 1991 *Sant Bani Magazine*

* * *

Sant Ji, will You comment on what it is to rest in Simran, and how we might learn to make proper effort without straining, so that our Simran can continue more and more in our work and in our daily life?

In the beginning we have to do a little bit of struggle in order to rest in the Simran. But later on it becomes very easy. We have been having thoughts and doing the fantasies in all of our past lives. And even in this lifetime we have not paid much attention as far as doing the Simran is concerned, because we have kept our mind free. We have allowed our mind to wander outside in the world. That is why we do not have the habit of controlling our mind. But fortunately we have taken refuge at the feet of the Masters Who tell us, "The remembrance of the worldly things is what is bringing you into this world again and again. If you want to finish the cycle of coming into this world again and again you had better do the Simran of the Masters and forget the simran or the remembrance of the worldly things.

There is no one in this world who has fulfilled all his desires. You may find many people who have fulfilled nine desires out of ten and still one desire remains unfulfilled; or there are many who have fulfilled only a couple of desires and they have so many desires unfulfilled. So what happens is that when we are not able to fulfill all our desires, then at the time of our death, if we do not have the guidance of a perfect Master, we start thinking about those things which we have not yet obtained, those desires which we have not yet fulfilled. When we leave the body, according to those desires, we get another birth. And since the desires of our past lifetime have to be fulfilled, we are born in such circumstances where they can be fulfilled. Those past desires get fulfilled, but in fulfilling them we create new desires; and again some of our desires are fulfilled and some of them are not, so this cycle goes on and on.

Saints and Mahatmas know about our weakness and that is why They give us Their own Simran, so we can forget the desires of the world. They know that the crop which has been ruined by too much water can be restored only by watering it properly. They know that only the Simran of the Master can cut the simran of the world. They know that only the contemplation of the Master can cut the contemplation of the worldly things. You know that even though you may not make any effort to remember the image of any person, whenever you think of him, his form will appear in front of you. In the same way, if you do the Simran of the Master properly, and if you would remember His Form, then you can easily see His Form and do the Simran. And if you are able to cut the simran and the remembrance of the world you can easily make yourself rest in the Simran.

If you love your children, you just need to think about them and you will remember their beautiful faces. In the same way, suppose that your wife has gone somewhere outside. If you have love for her you will think about her and her face will appear in front of you. You will start remembering her form. In the same way, anything of this world that you love, if you remember it, the image of that thing will appear in your mind. This is because you have so much attachment to the worldly things that sometimes without even making any effort, they are remembered in your subconscious mind. They are always there, and you always remember them.

Masters tell us that you remember all these worldly things because you have love for them and are attached to them. If you would love your Master, then His remembrance would also come to you by itself and you would start seeing His beautiful face. They tell us that if you really love the Master, then do His Simran, remember Him, because His Simran will help you forget the simran of the world. Now it is very difficult for you to do the Simran given to you by the Master because you are involved in the simran of the world. But if you develop the habit of doing the Master's Simran, if you develop your love for Him, and if you remember His form all the time, then it will be very easy to do His Simran. As it is now impossible for you to give up the remembrance of the world, then it will become impossible for you to give up the Simran of the Master.

We do not know the Power of Simran. If we knew the Power of Simran, we would never want to give it up. We would always want to go on doing Simran. When we do the Simran we start gaining concentration. As we go on gaining the concentration, we can easily experience spiritual miracles within ourselves, which are often referred to as supernatural powers. But Saints always tell Their disciples, "You should not get involved in this; you should not use those powers, because your journey is further up." If we would do the Simran we would gain concentration and then we would never want to give it up.

Masters do not need our love, because They are already in the love of Their Master. But unless we have real and sincere love for the Masters, we cannot do the Simran given by Them. If we really love Them, if we really remember Them, we will do the Simran They give us, without understanding it as a burden. And that Simran will start happening within us by itself. Just as now the worldly simran is happening without making any effort, in the same way, if we really love the Master, then the Master's Simran will happen by itself. We will not have to make any effort, because when you love someone you obey Him, and you will definitely remember Him.

Now, because we are doing the simran of the world, it is making us dry. But when we will keep our tongue absorbed in the Simran of the Master, we will not be dry. In fact, we will always remain wet in the remembrance of the Master, and the grace of the Master will flow upon us.

We have to take the help of our mind only when we do some accounting job. Otherwise, no matter what work we are doing, we can easily do the Simran along with that work, while we are sitting, standing, or doing anything of the world we can still do the Simran very easily. Guru Nanak Sahib says, "The dear ones deal with the people in the world, but within they are always linked with their Beloved Master."

Such a dear one can make a jungle or wilderness in his own home. He can easily create seclusion in a crowded place. Guru Nanak Sahib says, "For him who has stilled his mind, anyplace is secluded."

---

from a talk given September 30, 1987 and printed as "If You Love Your Master" in the December 1987 *Sant Bani Magazine*

PRINCE

PART V

The Glory of the Company of Saints

Collect the wealth of God and fill up your store.
Nanak bows down to the perfect Master.

GURU ARJAN DEV

Whatever meditation we are doing from day to day is counted, and we are collecting a big store of meditation. All the remembrance of God which we have done — even one moment's remembrance — is counted in our devotion. Don't ever think that whatever time you are devoting is not being counted. Master knows about our devotion; He knows how much we have done. He is perfecting our path of meditation, and when the time comes, He hands it over to us.

SANT JI

58

To Keep the Sweetness

Sant Ajaib Singh Ji

a darshan session given at Sant Bani Ashram, Rajasthan, on April 6, 1981

How can we keep the sweetness that we feel, after we leave here, and all year, all the time?

One way is by remembering your holy trip which you took to this place. If you will remember that you have been here, then you will always get the inspiration of doing more meditation. When you remember that you have been here, then you will also think about why you came here and what you learned here. Here you are taught meditation, and the second thing you are taught is to make your life pure. And the other thing which is brought to your attention at this place is that Master Power is always within us, and from behind the curtain He always does things for the disciple. But we cannot manifest Him within ourselves until we have complete love for Him and faith in Him. Even though He is working for us all the time, we cannot manifest Him unless we have complete love and faith in Him. So here you are taught to have complete love and faith for the Master, and to surrender yourself at the feet of the Master.

We should never forget our trip and we should never lose what we have been given here. If we always remember what we learned and received here, then we will definitely get help in maintaining the gift which we have received during our stay here. I am very pleased that many dear ones, although when they come they report that their condition is not good and they are not doing well in their meditations, when they obey my instructions and meditate wholeheartedly, after a few days they start changing; and at the end of their stay they tell me about their experiences and how much they have improved their life just by coming here and doing the meditations here. So those who continue doing the meditations even after going back to their home, they maintain the grace of the Master and they maintain their experiences. But those who do not maintain the grace of the Master by doing their meditations continuously after going back to their home, they get affected by the world and worldly things very easily, they come under the control of their mind and the organs of senses, and they lose what they have been given here. And later when they come another time, then they repent and feel sorry for losing all they received in their last trip. So I hope that if you will always remember your trip here, and if you will continue doing your meditation wholeheartedly as you have been doing here, you will definitely be able to maintain the grace of the Master and you will not lose what you have been given here.

In this group also there are many dear ones who were not doing well in their meditations when they came here, but later on, after meditating for just a few days, they have changed so much that now they tell me about their higher experiences. And I hope that they will maintain it.

59

Where He Quenched the Thirst

Sant Ajaib Singh Ji

a talk given March 2, 1985, before visiting Sant Ji's underground meditation room, Village 16 PS, Rajasthan, India

You would have heard a lot about this place since most of you have already been to have the darshan of this place and a lot has been published in the magazine also. You all know very well why this place was made and what was done in this place.

The first thing which we need to think upon is whether we sincerely do our meditation and mold our lives according to the instructions of the Master. If we follow His commandments and if we follow Him completely, then Master does not hide anything from us. He enters within such a soul the same way as the rock candy is dissolved in milk. The color or the appearance of the milk does not change, only the taste of the milk has changed. In the same way those souls who live according to the instructions of the Master, Master sits within them bringing all the prosperities and all His confidence.

What do we do? For a few days we become like a toy in the hands of our mind, we do whatever mind is telling us. Later when that wave of mind goes away and the Satguru's Shabd inspires us from within to come towards Him and do the devotion, then we start following the Path of the Masters instead of the mind, and we start living according to the instructions of the Master. Sometimes we pass the test and sometimes we fail. Sometimes we have love for the Master; sometimes we waver in our love for Him and that is why we do not become successful. Kabir Sahib says, "If we could maintain the yearning and the love which we had for the Master on the very first day of our meeting with Him, then what to speak of one's own liberation, such a person could liberate millions of other souls."

Satsangis should live as an example in the world, in the family, in the society, in the community. The family should know that he is a satsangi, he is an initiate of the perfect Master. He is very good, he is very pure and he has all the qualities which a good initiate should have and whatever he speaks, he lives up to that. So a satsangi should live like that, as an example to the world.

If a satsangi lives as an example, his home can become a heaven on earth, because the fragrance of Naam will come out from within him and those who smell that fragrance will also be affected by it. They will also try to get that wealth of Naam which is manifested in that satsangi, and they will also become prosperous.

The teacher pays more attention to the student who awaits the teacher and, in the same way, if some disciple is following the Path of the Masters with all his strength and if he is obeying the commandments of the Master then the Sant Satguru also gives all His attention towards that disciple.

I have often said that I have not spent or lived my life as a bookish life; I have not been a mental wrestler. I have never argued and read the books. I understand myself as the most fortunate one because I was able to do what my Master told me to do. He gave me the order and I did exactly what He told me to do. So I feel myself as the most fortunate one because with His grace I was able to accept the commandment of the Master and live up to it.

Kabir Sahib has said, "He who is thirsty will drink the water with appreciation and respect and he will also appreciate the one who is giving him the water." In the same way, if we will also obey the commandments of the Master, if we will also understand every word of the Master as His commandment, and if we will try to live up to it, Master will also become very pleased and we will appreciate Him and He will be ready to give us His everything.

Since you people have done the meditation for the past ten days, this place has been opened up for you, so that you can go and have its darshan. This is according to the orders of Supreme Father Kirpal because He has graciously given this permission that only those who have spent ten days in meditation here, those who try to concentrate their attention, only they should be allowed to visit this place. Not everybody is allowed to visit here; not just anyone who wants to see it can do so. We tell them, "No, it is not like that; only those people who spend at least ten days in meditation are allowed to visit this place."

Even when I was living in 77RB, this place was kept closed and its purity was maintained. The dear ones who lived here never allowed anybody to come and visit it. They would clean this place and burn the incense the same way as the people maintain the purity of the temples and they burn incense there. In the same way, they maintained the purity of this place and didn't allow anyone to come and visit this place. It was the order of Master Kirpal that not everybody should be allowed to come and visit this place, because this is the place where He has put His blessed feet. This is the place where He quenched the thirst of one thirsty soul by making him drink the Nectar of Shabd. This is the very place where He had cooled down the heated heart of a yearning soul.

Swami Ji Maharaj has said, "The place where the Sadhu or the Master puts His feet, that place becomes pious, becomes holy, and it is more holy than the sixty-eight places of pilgrimage."

So I hope that you will take so much inspiration from this place that even after going back to your homes, along with attending to the responsibilities of your families, and along with doing all your worldly duties, you will be able to keep your thoughts pure and holy and you will be able to do your meditation.

60

To Sit at the Master's Feet

Sant Ajaib Singh Ji

a talk given during a visit to Sant Ji's underground meditation room on October 5, 1985

Many dear ones have already had the darshan of this place many times. Most of you know the importance of this place, and why this place was made, because a lot has been published about this place in *Sant Bani Magazine*. So I will not speak more about it at this time, but I would definitely like to tell you this one thing — that was the most pleasant time when, within the soul of this poor one, the yearning to realize God was created, and the love for God was created. Only because of that yearning and love for Almighty God, Beloved Kirpal came and quenched the thirst of this poor soul, because God Kirpal had the competence of connecting the souls with Almighty Lord.

This is the benefit of having the living Master. The living Master connects your soul with Almighty Lord and He gives to you according to your receptivity. The giver does not have any difficulty because He has come into this world to give. The question lies with the receivers. It depends upon how much receptivity we have. It depends upon our yearning. So I say that it was the most pleasant time in my life when the yearning to do the devotion of God was created within this soul, and when God Kirpal Himself came to this place to quench my soul's thirst and to satisfy my yearning.

I have often said that my worldly parents, those who brought me up in the worldly way, had a lot of wealth. God had given them all the worldly conveniences and comforts. But right from the beginning, right from my childhood, I did not find any interest in that worldly wealth or all the things they had. I always used to understand all those worldly things as not less than hell. And always I had this yearning within me to meet some Perfect Being. Because I was born in a Sikh family I used to read the bani of Guru Nanak, and when I read the stories of the disciples and the Masters, then this yearning would come within me, and I would wish that I could also meet a Master like Guru Nanak. Many times I would wonder about the luck of those disciples who were fortunate enough to sit at the feet of the great Masters like Guru Nanak and the other Sikh Gurus. I always used to wish that maybe sometime in my life the day would come when I would be able to sit at the feet of such a Perfect Being. I prayed for Him all my life long. I cried for Him; I made so many pleas; and when the appropriate time came, my pleas, my prayers, my requests were heard and they were answered.

God Kirpal Himself came to me and He quenched the thirst of this poor soul. He Himself came to this blessed place and He put His blessed feet on this place. And this is according to His instructions: we do not open this place for anyone who wants to see it, because He has told me only to open this place and allow people to have the darshan of this place to those who come here and meditate for at least ten days. Similar instructions were given to Master Kirpal, that is why He would never open the door of the room where Master Sawan Singh had stayed in Master Kirpal's home in His own village. He always maintained the sanctity of that place — only for some special retreat program or things like that, would He open the door for people to have the darshan of that room. So He instructed me to do the same over here. So that is why I don't allow anyone who just wants to see this place, no matter how dear they are to me, since it is the instructions and order of my Master, I don't open this room for anyone unless they have meditated for ten days here.

So I hope that when you visit this place you will take inspiration from it. What inspiration do you have to take from this place? You have to take the inspiration of how a soul, when given the opportunity, was able to struggle with the mind. You know that the struggle with the mind is what we call meditation, and those who struggle with their mind also get the grace of the Master. So you should take the inspiration from here of how one soul became successful in struggling with the mind and was able to realize God.

61

According to His Instructions

Sant Ajaib Singh Ji

a talk given at Sant Ji's underground meditation room, on March 1, 1986

You always read something about this place in *Sant Bani Magazine*. I have always said that a soul was longing and thirsty in this desert, and Lord Kirpal, Who was the ocean of nectar and grace, came to this desert and quenched the thirst of this suffering soul by making her drink that graceful nectar. He made this soul drink so much nectar, and by closing her eyes to the outside world, He opened her eyes from within. And in His love and intoxication, He intoxicated her. How can I thank that ocean of nectar, of grace, for all He has done for me? Outwardly we can only use words to thank Him, but we can thank Him in the true sense by going within. Only by going within can we thank Him and express our gratitude in the real sense.

Only that thing bears fruit in Sant Mat which is done according to the instructions of the Master. And only those things which are done with the orders and obedience of the Master become successful.

This place was not made to fulfill my own desire. In fact, right from childhood I had the habit of staying alone and being indifferent to people. I would always make some underground place and go and sit there. But this place was not made because of that habit or desire of mine. This place was made with the instructions and orders of great Master Kirpal. Many times He came here and put His blessed feet — His blessed feet for which many people yearn — upon this place. Even the gods and goddesses yearn for those blessed feet. People yearn and have tried so many things to manifest those blessed feet within them, but they have not been successful. He came here with those blessed feet many times. He manifests Himself only within those blessed souls who mold their lives according to His instructions.

Graciously Master Sawan Singh also made a kind of underground room for Mastana Ji of Baluchistan. When He made that cave for him, at that time He asked Mastana Ji, "Mastana, should I make you the owner of Baluchistan?" (Baluchistan was the place from where Mastana Ji came.) Mastana said, "What do I have to do with becoming the owner of Baluchistan? I have only You and need only You. I don't need to become the owner or king of any place."

Mastana Ji was given some instructions when Sawan made the cave for him. He told him that He would make him the owner of Bagghar, which is the name of the area in which we are now living. In this area there are many farmers, and it is called the area of farmers. And when Sawan Singh told Mastana Ji that He would make him the emperor of Bagghar, the people who were there could not believe what Master Sawan Singh was saying. People did not understand what He was saying and did not believe that what He was saying would come true. They started saying, "How can Sawan Singh make Mastana Ji the emperor of that area of Rajasthan?" But Saints have their own ways of working. So when Sawan Singh made that cave for Mastana Ji and said that he should go underground and do the meditation, He also told him that he should not come out even to attend Master Sawan Singh's funeral, and all those people who do not believe in what He was saying would repent later when the time comes. So when Mastana Ji went underground and did the meditation, he did not even come out for the cremation of Master Sawan Singh.

Afterwards, when the words of Master Sawan Singh came true, when Mastana Ji became the king of this area, everyone knows that He went on distributing riches and money to people day and night. Everyone was surprised and wondered where He was getting that money to give to the people. The government of India tried many times to search His premises, but they could not find anything except pebbles and stones. But He kept on giving the grace and blessings of Master Sawan Singh to the people.

Mastana Ji had a lot of love and respect for Master Kirpal Singh. He often said that Master Sawan is God and Kirpal is the Son of God. He also would say, "Master Sawan Singh has showered grace on me. Whatever I am is because of the grace and blessings of Master Sawan Singh. Those who want to see the fruits of meditation should go to see Master Kirpal Singh." He called Master Kirpal the great meditator.

Mastana Ji showered grace on this poor soul also. I went to see Him because I wanted to confirm what Master Sawan had told me when I went to see Master Sawan Singh with Baba Bishan Das. Master Sawan Singh had told me that the Power who would give me Initiation would come to me by Himself. So I wanted to know from Mastana Ji whether He was the One Who would come and give me the Initiation. When I asked Him, He said, "No, I am not the one; He is a very powerful one — so powerful that if two cannons are firing, He could put His hands up to both the cannons and stop them from firing. He is very powerful and He will come to give you Naam Initiation by Himself." So because of the best wishes and blessings of those great Masters, when Master Kirpal Himself came here to shower His grace on me, I understood that it was very fortunate for me.

I thank Master Kirpal for all the grace He showered upon me, because of which I was able to do all that my Master told me to do. We cannot do anything unless it is the grace of the Master. Master Kirpal came to see me and He Himself showered grace on this poor suffering soul.

In my childhood when I would read about the great Masters and Their disciples, the yearning would come in me — would I meet a Master Who showers such grace upon His disciples? I used to wonder what kind of people came in contact with a perfect Master. I also read about those disciples who got Initiation from a perfect Master and then later on went away from the Master. I wondered, "How could those people do that when they had a perfect Master? How could they not believe in their Master and not believe in the commandments of their Master?" At that time I had in my mind that if, by grace, I came across a perfect Master and got Initiation from Him, I would do what He told me to do. So I am very grateful to my Master who came and gave me the Initiation. Because of His grace I was able to do the meditation which He ordered me to do.

When Master Kirpal gave me the orders to go underground, at that time He told me some other things which I have also told earlier. He said that Americans will come. And the fragrance will come out of my body. At that time the other people who were there wondered how that was going to happen. They said: "How is it possible that the fragrance will come out from a human body, because fragrance usually comes out from a flower? How can it come out from this man?" But when the words of great Master Kirpal came true, they all wondered how this was happening. But I know that I am very fortunate to have His blessings showered upon me and that He cast His blessed feet on this place. I am very grateful that I was able to do all that He told me to do.

We know that when someone criticizes a dear soul, he will tolerate the criticism when it is of him. But when it comes as criticism of his Master, he will never tolerate it. When Sawan Singh was doing His work, a group of people opposed Him a lot. They even published a book against Him saying that Master Sawan Singh had bought property and He was running the langar with the money of His sangat. So when those people wrote that, Mastana Ji could not bear that. And only to show them the truth He started giving out money. He used to say, "You people say that Master Sawan Singh has bought property and is feeding the langar with the money of the sangat. I am not even calling myself the dog of Master Sawan Singh because dogs are better than me. I am just a lowly being of His. You people don't know what Sawan Singh is and how He works. I will show you what He is and how He works." To respond to that criticism against Master Sawan Singh, Mastana Ji gave out money and people could not find out where He got it. There was no estimate of how much He gave. He did that only to prove what Master Sawan was. He used to tell them, "You people do not know what power Master Sawan Singh brought into this world. You have only seen Him outwardly and do not know how He works."

He used to talk to the sangat also about Master Sawan Singh. I had had many opportunities to sit at the feet of Master Sawan Singh, and when I would go to Mastana Ji, since his Sangat had not seen Master Sawan Singh. He would always ask me to stand up and tell about Master Sawan Singh. So I would describe Master Sawan Singh as I had seen Him — how beautiful and radiant He was. When He talked, even the birds and animals would stand still, and they would also melt like wax. Both the sun and moon were under His control. Whenever He wanted, the clouds would go and cover the sun or moon. So I would describe Sawan as I had seen Him. Many times Mastana would ask me to describe Him. He used to say, "You people do not know how great Master Sawan Singh was." He always said, "When a person who cannot even call himself the dog of Master Sawan Singh can give out so many riches, just imagine what kind of power Master Sawan Singh has."

I hope that all of you will go to the underground room with the prayer that you will also do your Bhajan and Simran, that your meditations will purify your life, and that that Ocean of Love will shower all His grace on you and fulfill your desires.

I have often said that not everyone is allowed to go into this underground room. Only those who have come here for eight or ten days are allowed to go in. This is in accordance with the instructions of Master Kirpal. He used to say that no one should sleep here or do anything here; only God should be remembered here. No one should have any bad thought while visiting this place.

62
The Heart-to-Heart Way
Sant Ajaib Singh Ji

two talks from the October 1986 group visit, during which Sant Ji was too ill to be with the disciples for several days

at the Underground Room, October 5, 1986

Regarding this underground room, I have said a lot, and a lot has been published in the magazine, which you would have read. Today I am not going to speak much about it, because, as you know, I am not supposed to talk much because of my health. But I hope that you will always remember and get inspiration from what happened to this poor soul in this place. In fact, it was Almighty God Kirpal Himself who made him go inside this underground room. At that time this poor soul had given up the support of the whole world and had relied on the support of the Almighty Lord. He Himself made me go inside; He Himself put His loving, gracious hand on my eyes, and closed my eyes from outside. And He Himself opened my eyes within. Whenever He wanted, He came to see me. Whenever He thought appropriate, He came and gave me His darshan.

Master is not unjust. He is the person who is truly just. If anyone is sitting in remembrance of Him, if anyone is lovingly devoted to Him, He definitely comes and quenches the thirst of that disciple. When He gives the Initiation He gives the initiate the right to enter Sach Khand. But He also puts one condition for the initiates, and that is, as Master used to say, that if you cannot do the meditation, if you cannot do any other thing, at least have love for the Master. Never understand the Master as a human being, because you should know that He has assumed the human body only to come into this world to free us. We are the people who are suffering and who are captive in this prison of the world. He has taken the human form only to make us free from this prison. I hope that you will also take the same inspiration from this place, so that you may also be able to obey the commandment of the Master, maintain true love for the Master, and may make a heart-to-heart way with the Master.

a farewell talk, in the upper room, October 6, 1986

Once again I thank you all, because you people did that work which the Saints always expect and hope from their disciples. You people were very patient, and you did a lot of Bhajan and Simran. Many dear ones told me about their very high experiences, which I cannot describe. I appreciate all this and I am thankful to you for doing your meditations.

This world is full of suffering, it is the world of the Negative Power. Saints come into this world only to ease the burden and sufferings of the dear ones. They are sent into this world by Almighty God only for this purpose. Whatever pain or suffering comes in the Will of the Master, They always accept it. They accept the sweet Will of the Master. Kabir Sahib has said, "If there were no Saints in this world, it would have burned down, because it is full of suffering." Now you can maintain this patience and meditation when you go back to your home only by doing your meditations, because you know what discipline means, and you can maintain that discipline only by doing your Bhajan and Simran regularly.

Outwardly you know the condition of the world. At this moment it is very important for all the satsangis to have a lot of love, as much as possible, and they should do meditation as much as possible, because that is what is needed at this moment in this world which is full of suffering. Because the satsangis, only the satsangis, have the real meditation and the real Path by which they can connect themselves with Almighty God. It is possible that looking at your love, looking at your devotion, God Almighty may forgive many other souls.

I wish you all the best for your return journey, and I am very thankful to our Masters Baba Sawan Singh and Hazur Maharaj Kirpal Singh Ji for graciously giving us this opportunity of sitting in Their remembrance for ten days.

63
The Long, Long Journey
Sant Ajaib Singh Ji

a talk given November 5, 1986, at the Underground Room, Sant Bani Ashram, Rajasthan

In each group I inspire all of you to remember a couple of things which I always tell you. Those things are that you should make the mind quiet and you should not pay any attention to the outer disturbances while you are meditating. You should not let your mind wander outside when you are meditating, and you should always keep your attention at the Eye Center. If you will remember these things which I say to every group, they will definitely help you in Spirituality, but they can also be very helpful to you in your worldly life.

Whenever Param Sants, the perfect Masters, have come into this world, no matter to which religion or community They belonged, They have always told us that there are two Beings which do not forget anything and do not make any mistakes: one is God Almighty, and the other is the Beloved devotee of God, the Saint who is sent into this world by God Almighty.

Whatever They explain to Their disciples, They are not explaining anything from bookish knowledge or from hearsay. They explain to Their disciples only what They have gone through and what They have experienced in Their life and what They have meditated upon.

Bulleh Shah said that God has come in the form of man. And when the inner door was opened to Ajaib, He also said that God has come after becoming a man. All the Saints have said this. Guru Nanak Sahib also says, "Don't understand the Master as a human being."

I had the very good fortune of sitting at the feet of Baba Sawan Singh Ji — I got many opportunities for that. The love which Baba Sawan Singh had for his Master, Baba Jaimal Singh, was so deep and so great that it cannot be described. It cannot be talked about, it cannot be written in any book. It was very deep, and whenever that Ocean of Love would come in Master Sawan Singh, when it would come in its full force, then it would break all the barriers and Master Sawan Singh would see Baba Jaimal Singh everywhere,

Baba Jaimal Singh always told Baba Sawan Singh that when the disciple gets the Naam Initiation from the Master, after that, not even in the state of dream, not even in the state of forgetfulness, should he think that the Master is a human being; he should always understand Master as the One who has come into this prison to release us, the prisoners.

Master Kirpal Singh Ji used to like bhajans very much. He used to enjoy hearing bhajans. Whenever I would get the opportunity, I would sing bhajans to Him with a lot of yearning. When a yearning soul sings a bhajan to the Master, it is so deep and so full of yearning that the Ocean of Love which is in that yearning soul comes in its full force and it breaks all the barriers. So when that kind of love would come up in the bhajans, Master Kirpal would also shed tears, He would remember His times with His Master, Baba Sawan Singh.

Many people encourage me to make an ashram which is on the road; and many people have even said, "If you cannot do it, we can make an ashram for you in the city. You do not need to come there — we'll make the ashram for You." Many people complain that the trip here is very difficult, and I should move to a place which is in the city or near the city where it is convenient for them to come. That journey which the people think is long and difficult, Master Kirpal, the God of my soul, took so many times, even when He was sick. Now you know that before you people come, we prepare for your coming. And you know that once you get to the ashram you get all the facilities, all the conveniences there, and we even spend three or four days before you come in preparing the road and things like that so that you may not have any difficulties. But when Beloved Kirpal, the God of my soul, came here, we did not have any facilities and conveniences waiting for Him here. The journey which our Beloved Master took without complaining, we should not hesitate in taking that journey. Master Kirpal Singh knew only this much, "I have made someone sit in my remembrance and he will not go anywhere else"; He would come, do His work, and go back.

I will explain to you the *Tisra Til* or Eye Center more clearly. I have often said that Tisra Til or Eye Center is the place where the mind and soul are seated. It is the place from where our journey begins. You people should sleep well in the night, get up early in the morning at three o'clock, with an empty stomach, and sit for meditation, for two hours or two-and-a-half hours continuously; do Simran while remaining at the Eye Center or Tisra Til. By doing Simran continuously, remaining at the Eye Center, reach the first plane, which is also called *Jot Niranjan*; the mahatmas called it Ishwar or God. Muslims call it Allah. This is the place where Arjuna was shown the real form of the creator by Lord Krishna, This is the headquarters of the astral plane, and this is the place from where all the other arrangements are being done.

Even if we are able to hear the Shabd or the Sound Current at present, still that Sound Current is not that effective; it does not pull our soul up, because we have not reached the Eye Center. If we had reached Tisra Til, or the Eye Center, then our soul would be pulled up by the Shabd Itself, because Shabd which is coming from Sach Khand is resounding at the Eye Center, and the soul who has reached the Eye Center goes to the other planes catching the Shabd. So when we have reached the Eye Center, after that when we hear the Shabd, that Shabd takes us to the other planes, to the further higher planes, and by catching hold of the Sound Current or the Shabd, we reach the peak of Trikuti, which is the causal plane.

Then the Shabd of the third plane starts coming by Itself and pulls the soul up into the higher planes. No doubt there is only one Shabd — only one Shabd or Sound is coming from Sach Khand — but because it is coming through different planes, that is why it is said that the Shabd is different; in fact there is only one Shabd.

So when the soul is pulled up by the Shabd of the third plane, then all the chains and all the entanglements and attachments of the mind and the organs of senses are broken. All the forces and powers of mind and the negative powers which were pulling the soul down, they all remain down below, and the soul, after becoming free from all these things, goes on to the higher planes. The soul shakes off all the three vestures physical, astral and causal — and when she goes to the fourth plane, only then she gets the awareness of her Real Home.

So when the soul reaches the third plane, since all the chains and powers which were pulling the soul down remain down below, when the soul becomes free from all those forces, then she prepares herself to go to the fourth plane, to the higher planes. When the soul reaches the fourth plane, which is also called by the name *Bhanwar Gupha* and which is often called the door to Sach Khand, then the soul gets unlimited amounts of intoxication. Then she comes to realize that she also has the same qualities as God Almighty and she is not different from God. The difference was only because she was separated from Him.

When the soul reaches Sach Khand, then she comes to realize herself, and only then the real faith in God Almighty or the Master comes within her. After that, no matter what happens, she does not lose faith in the Master. And after that, whatever pain or happiness comes, whatever comes in the Will of God, such a soul accepts that as the Will of God. When such a thing happens, only then the soul realizes that she is a drop of the water, and God Almighty is like a vast ocean. She was called a drop only because she was separated from Him. Now, when she has mingled in the ocean, she is also the ocean. The soul understands herself as a soul only as long as she is separated from Almighty God.

Sant Satgurus come from that plane and They are the incarnations of Sat Purush. Only those souls can go and mingle in Sat Purush who reach that plane. When a soul reaches this plane and becomes one with Sat Purush, only then within her, the sympathy and grace is created for the other souls who are suffering in this world. The Master soul thinks that the other souls who are suffering in this world should also come back to the Real Home where there is no pain, where there is no suffering, because that plane is worth seeing. It cannot be described in words. In that plane there are no tricks of the mind, there is no pain, there is no suffering. It is the plane of complete peace and happiness.

So when the soul reaches Sach Khand and becomes one with Sat Purush, then she gets the grace, then she feels pity for the other souls who are suffering in this world, so she comes back into this world assuming the body which is full of dirt and filth and which is full of sufferings, only for the sake of the other souls.

The fortunate souls — those who accept the instructions of that soul who has come from Sach Khand — they go back to the Real Home and they also enjoy the same kind of happiness and peace which that Master soul is enjoying.

Guru Nanak says, "He who has recognized Sat Purush is Satguru, and by obeying Him you can get liberation." So if you do the meditation after understanding it, then it is not so difficult. You can do your worldly work all day long, sleep during the night — we just have to get up early in the morning and spend two or two-and-half hours in meditation. And if you do that properly and perfectly, then you can also progress and become successful in this Path.

64

The Fragrance of Naam

Sant Ajaib Singh Ji

at the Underground Room, December 6, 1986

You would have heard and read a lot about this place. Any place becomes important and worth venerating if some beloved of God, some dear child of God, has taken the support of His Master there, and taking that support, has obeyed His commandments and done the work for which we get the human birth at least once after going through the cycle of eighty-four lakhs births and deaths. The place where a dear one has done the devotion of God and obeyed His commandments becomes important. The devotion of God is the only thing which we can do in this birth and not in any other.

Guru Nanak says, "That beloved of God is a fortunate one who gets attached to the feet of the Master, who falls in love with the Master."

It was a very pleasant time when my Master made me sit in this room. This place was made according to His orders, and He Himself made me sit in this room. He Himself closed my eyes from outside and told me, "You should not come to see me. Whenever I feel it is appropriate, I will come to see you myself." Even before I received Initiation from Him, it was He who came to me by Himself.

For twenty-five years in His life He went on saying, "It is up to the people to want to receive the grace of the Master." What is the fault of the One Who has come to give? [His grace] depends upon our receptivity, it depends upon how clean our vessel is, it depends upon how we look at the Master. But when this poor soul had the darshan of the Emperor of Spirituality, in his soul he knew that the person Who was going to give him something had come.

Since childhood I had always had this yearning: "May I meet an Emperor who would be a treasurer of Naam and made by God Himself." I was not yearning for any emperor of this world.

Ever since childhood I loved Gurbani or the writings of the Sikh Gurus, and I loved to read the banis of all the Saints or beloveds of God.

Regarding the kings of this world, Kabir Sahib says, "If someone is a king and has a lot of material things, and if a poor person goes to him, the king will turn his back on him because he will be afraid that the poor person will ask for something. But if a king goes to a poor person's house, the poor person will welcome him with all he has." We become kings and poor ones according to the karmas of our past lives in this world. But Kabir Sahib says, "The reality is that he who does not have the Naam within his heart is the poor one." He who has Naam is the real Emperor.

The day before yesterday I wrote a bhajan which says, "Getting the alms from Sawan Shah, He fills up our empty bags." It means that Kirpal got the alms of Naam from Sawan the Emperor. He did not ask for any worldly thing and He did not get any worldly thing, because Sawan was the Emperor of Naam. He did not just get a little bit of Naam from Him, He got so much Naam from Him that He filled up the bags of everyone. But we people are such that our bags are so full of material things, where is the place for Naam?

Those who asked for worldly things got them from Him. Those who asked for His darshan got His darshan. Often I have said that since my childhood I always had the yearning and the desire to see Him. I did not ask for any worldly thing, I only asked for His darshan, and He gave me His darshan. Even after receiving Him, I did not say that I should not get sick, that I should get all the happiness and riches of the world. I did not ask for anything of the worldly nature, but He gave me everything I needed. Often I have said, "If we ask for the Master and the Master comes and manifests within us, He comes with all the prosperities of the world. Whatever we need, He gives us those things. Because when we have surrendered ourself to the Master, it is up to the Master to give us what He wants to. He knows what is best for us, so whatever He gives, we should be content with that.

I hope that from this place you will get the inspiration and you will feel yourselves fortunate, because you have been chosen by the Master to do His devotion. You should know that Master has taken on the task of improving the condition of the world. You should become such an example for others that the fragrance of Naam should come out from within you. If one satsangi would improve the condition of a hundred other people, just imagine how many people would get improved in your country.

Dear Ones, I have seen in India that there was a time when nobody smoked, nobody drank wine — they didn't even use to drink tea. But after independence, the companies who were manufacturing these things went into every village, and in the beginning they gave tobacco, wine, and tea free of charge, so that the people would get into the habit of using those things. Gradually they involved them in those habits. And you know now how much all those things have spread, how everyone is using them. So when one person can spread bad things to such an extent, just imagine if all of you would bring out the fragrance of Naam from within yourselves by doing the meditation. [You would] affect the people in your neighborhood and [show] them that since you have improved your life by doing this devotion, they can also do it. If the bad people can spread their bad things, why can't the good people spread their goodness?

65
The Price of Happiness

Sant Ajaib Singh Ji

at the Underground Room, January 3, 1987

I am very pleased that Russell Perkins publishes whatever I say here about this underground room, in *Sant Bani Magazine*; he works very hard and publishes all the talks that I give here. So you should read *Sant Bani Magazine* with love and attention. If you are not doing that, you should do it; because there are many questions and answers, and many other talks, which Russell publishes time and time again. There is no question which is not answered, so if you read the magazine thoroughly you will get the answers to all your questions.

Even if you are not in the group, if you read the talks in *Sant Bani* you will be inspired and get the right direction for doing Bhajan and Simran. One of the dear ones here asked me in his interview a question about this underground room. I did not reply to that question, but I realized that that dear one had not read *Sant Bani Magazine*, because his question had been answered there. Many people still think, "Just by making an underground room and sitting in it we can control our mind." But that is not true — just by making an underground room and sitting in it we cannot control the mind — we have to work hard in controlling our mind. There were many reasons for making this underground room and sitting here. Only the Sant Satgurus under Whose direction and with Whose orders this underground room was made know why it was made.

The old initiates know how Master Kirpal held many conferences and invited many people to attend them; they know that many renowned leaders attended. The old initiates know how the people who went there to attend the conferences, instead of getting inspiration for meditation and doing meditation there, got the desire to have their picture taken with those dignitaries or with Master Kirpal — nobody wanted to sit underground and do meditation. I am the very fortunate one that I was selected by Him. He chose me for doing this work, and He told me that I should sit in this room and meditate; He told me that I should not come to attend any conferences, and whenever He would feel it was appropriate, He would come and see me. And this is true, whenever He wanted, He came and saw me.

Up to a certain extent, Hazur's purpose in having the conferences was successful. Because as He Himself told me at this place, in India there are so many religions and communities and people fight with each other; one community fights with another community. So that is why Master Kirpal invited and collected the leaders of all the different religions in India; He hoped that by presenting the truth of Naam within them, and by sewing them in the same thread of Naam, they would stop fighting with each other and would accept the truth.

My Gurudev, in front of a large gathering of the sangat in Ganganagar, said, "I wish, and I have suggested this to the government, that all the monasteries and so-called religious places should be sold, and with the money they get from selling those places, they should do things for the public welfare. I will be the first one to sell my place to contribute in that work." But He also said that the government did not wish to accept that suggestion.

Master Sawan Singh Ji used to say, "If your mind wanders and makes the connections with the outer world, even after making an underground room and sitting there, you should understand yourself as the greatest householder in this world. And if your mind is not wandering, if your mind has concentrated, even though you are living in the world, still you are one of the greatest *sanyasis*."

So first of all we should give up all our support and seek the support of the Master; we should turn our back on the name and fame and praises of the world. And we should work hard, because we know that even in the world, we cannot achieve anything unless we work hard for it.

A mother cannot give birth to a child unless she works hard for it. If we want to dig out gold from a mine we have to work hard for it. And if you want to get pearls from the ocean, you have to dive deep under the water. Even to achieve the worldly love, we have to work very hard. You know how many sacrifices and different tricks a man plays to achieve even the love of a worldly nature.

Saints tell us that the price of happiness is pain. If someone says that he has achieved worldly success or worldly comforts without working hard for it, it only means that he is putting one more burden on himself, because one has to work very hard in the world even to achieve worldly comforts and conveniences. The Path of Spirituality or meditation is even more complicated, because in this Path in order to achieve some success in meditation we have to struggle with our mind. We have to deal with the obstinate enemy who is our mind. And if we want to take even one step in the Path of Spirituality we have to fight with it. He will not surrender to us easily, so we have to work very hard in struggling with our mind.

Dear Ones, this is not a matter of just talking. Our hearts are very weak and we have become the thieves of our practices. We want to achieve success just by talking, but we cannot do it. We need to work hard for it.

It is a good idea to make an underground room, there is nothing wrong in that; but a hundred times more important is to sit inside and do the meditation.

Often I have said that during the Second World War, I was not very old, I was still in my teens. At that time people accepted imprisonment for twenty years or more rather than to fight in the army, because they knew that death was certain for them; they knew that they had to embrace death if they went into the army. But I happily gave my name to join the army;

I did not have any difficulty going into the army at that time. But also I have said that when I went into the underground room then I realized how it was very easy for me to join the army, and how it was very difficult to sit in the underground room. Because the mind comes and stands in front of you like a lion, and he tries his best to prevent you from going within.

Those who struggle with the mind, only they realize this. I am not the only one who says this. Master Sawan Singh Ji used to say, "If you make your mind stand in front of a cannon, he will easily do that; but if you make him sit in meditation he will not do it."

You know that Supreme Father Kirpal worked hard in meditation, became practically successful, and He gave us the keys so that we could become practically successful in meditation. Did He not have comfortable beds to sleep on during the night? Did He not have a quilt to cover Himself and be comfortable in the night? Why did He spend His nights standing in the waters of the River Ravi up to His neck? He did that only to become successful in meditation.

First of all we need to develop outer faith; once we have developed faith in the Master outwardly, if we have developed it so much that no one breaks that faith, then it becomes very easy for us to go within. When we go within and concentrate, then we see everything. Within us there are stars, suns, moons and the Form of the Master. If we have developed faith in the Master and go within with full faith in Him and concentrate, we see all these things. When we lose our concentration, and drop our attention down from the Eye Center, then we do not see any stars, suns, moons, nor the Form of the Master.

I am very pleased that for the past eight or nine days you did your meditations. In the Satsangs that you attended every day, I talked a lot about purity. We should maintain purity in our lives. We should not continue becoming the slaves of our mind in all our births. Sometime, in some birth, at least in this birth, we should obey the orders of our Master and refuse the mind. We should not obey him anymore, and we should maintain purity. If we maintain purity outwardly, then it will become easier for us to make our mind pure, and the purer the mind, the purer the soul. And when the soul becomes pure then it will not find it difficult to concentrate.

There is one more thing that I would like to tell you. It has nothing to do with the Satsangs, but it has a lot to do with your body. You know that nowadays the wave of drugs is flowing, and everywhere people are involved in the use of drugs. The people who sell drugs say that if you use them you will be able to achieve concentration of your mind, get relaxation, and things like that. In the temptations of those words, people start using drugs, which is very destructive for their mind and for their body also. By using drugs, you will not get any relaxation or concentration of the mind, you will spoil your body and damage your brain and your consciousness. It can do much other harm to you. You have the Naam with you; you have the Simran with you. There is no medicine other than the medicine of Naam which can bring relaxation to your mind, or help you achieve concentration of your mind. You should do Simran because you have Simran, and it is the only thing which can help you achieve concentration.

I hope that you will understand the importance of this trip. Master Sawan and Master Kirpal have graciously given us this opportunity of coming here and you should understand its importance. I hope that you will do your meditation and take inspiration from this place.

The purpose of my calling you here is just so that you may develop the habit of doing meditation every day.

66

Use The Time You Have Now

Sant Ajaib Singh Ji

a talk given in February 1987, to a group visiting Sant Ji's underground meditation room

I am very pleased that God gave us this opportunity of sitting in His remembrance for this period of ten days. Only because of His grace were we able to spend time in His remembrance. But spending this time in His remembrance can be worthwhile only if we maintain this, only if we continue being in His remembrance, and only if we continue doing the meditation. Then this time that we have spent in His remembrance can become worthwhile and successful. If we do not continue doing the meditation, if we do not remain in His sweet remembrance after we leave here, then the meditation we have done for the past ten days cannot become successful. The meaning of becoming successful in the meditation and in His remembrance is that we should rise above the mind and the sense organs. God Almighty, our Master, has given us the responsibility of withdrawing to the Eye Center, and we can become successful in that only if we rise above the mind and sense organs.

Dear Ones, those who come here in these groups and who continue doing the meditation after going back from the group, when they get the opportunity to return to the ashram again, they tell me about their progress in meditation. I become very happy to know that they continued doing the meditation after they left this ashram and that because they continued meditating they have progressed a lot. They tell me about their high experiences, which gives me a lot of pleasure; I become very pleased with them. But those dear ones who do not meditate after going back from the groups, when they come back here again, they complain that they cannot still their mind, their mind wanders a lot, or they have pain in the back, they have pain in the knees and things like that. They spend all their time over here just complaining about those things.

So Dear Ones, you see that those who continue doing their meditation get a lot of progress, they improve a lot in their meditation. Whereas those who do not continue doing the meditation have all sorts of complaints and they do not progress. You know that we can become competent in any work only if we do it regularly and wholeheartedly. Even in worldly work, if we do something for two days and then stop, we do not become as successful in that as if we were doing it regularly.

I did not start doing the devotion just by looking at other people doing the devotion. I did not learn to do the devotion by looking at others; it was something from my own within which I started in my childhood.

This is why I call myself as the most fortunate one because right from my childhood my thoughts were very pure and I was devoted to Almighty God. So what Master Kirpal used to say, "There is food for the hungry and water for the thirsty," that is exactly correct. And He also said that it is not as difficult to realize God as it is to become a human being. He also used to say that God is in search of man, if someone makes himself a real human then God Himself will come and find him. That is why I understand myself as the most fortunate one that, with His grace, my thoughts were very pure in my childhood. That is why that gracious Almighty Lord Kirpal came to me Himself and He awakened my sleeping soul.

You know that if someone is in love with someone outwardly, if he has the physical love, even in that outer or worldly love, the lover does not feel hungry, he does not feel thirsty; he gives up everything of this world just because of that love. In the same way, those who have this divine love, those who are in love with their Master, with Almighty God, they also do not pay any attention to their hunger and thirst, they pay no attention to the public shame or anything like that, because right from the beginning, right from childhood, they have the real yearning, they have the real love for God Almighty. Even though they have not seen the Almighty God, but still, within themselves, they always feel as if they have lost something. They always remain sad; they are waiting for Him. If someone asks someone like that, "Why are you sad? Have you lost anything?" He would say, "Well, I don't know." He always feels that he has lost someone or something. Outwardly he may say, "I am all right." But deep within he feels that sadness because of not seeing his Beloved God Almighty. All the Saints have had this sadness. Guru Nanak also had this sadness, and because of it people used to say that He had lost His senses, "He does not have that power of intellect — " "He does not have the power of thinking — " or "Some ghost has taken him over." In the lives of many Saints such things have happened when They have gone through this period of deep sadness. People have always talked about things like this, but the dear ones, the Saints Who have felt this sadness, only They know what They are looking for.

Such dear ones, right from their childhood, always get the messages of love in their soul. If they are born in a rich family they throw away that richness and do their devotion. If they are born in a poor family they do not crave to become rich and they do not go on collecting the material wealth of the world. Their effort, their desire, is only to find that thing which they have lost, and they always crave for the Beloved. They always wish that they had met the Almighty Lord, right from their childhood; within them, they have this desire.

The true lover does not have any complaint if he goes through any painful moment, or any difficult moment; he does not wonder why this moment came, or "Why do I have to go through all this suffering?" because he knows that the One Whom he loves, knows only to shower grace on him and that He knows the best. The real lover only knows how to love.

You know about the love of the moth for the light. The moth loves looking at the light and the moth is so much in love with the light that the moth goes there and it burns itself in the flame of that light, but it does not complain, "Why do you burn me when I am in love with you? when I live only by looking at you?" He always maintains his tradition of love, that is why whenever he sees the light burning he goes there because of that love and he burns himself in that.

Majnu and Laila were in love with each other. Laila was a princess and Majnu was from a very poor family, but their love was not like the love which the Majnus and Lailas of this present time have. Their love was pure, free from all the worldly pleasures and indulgences. In the Muslim scripture it is written that those who cannot maintain purity in the worldly love, they can never become successful in the Divine Love. Master Kirpal also used to say, "Worldly love is like the bridge to cross over to get to the divine love. The bridge is not the place to live, it is meant only for crossing the river." In the same way, if we can become perfect in the worldly love, it is only meant for getting to the real or Divine Love.

Majnu used to wander in the forest with the fakirs because in the love of Laila he also had become a fakir. Once it so happened that Laila wanted to have the darshan of Majnu, she wanted to see what Majnu looked like, how he was at that time. So she performed something like a *yajna* to which she invited all the fakirs and the holy men. Because she wanted to see Majnu, that is why she arranged that.

Now when she did that, everyone went to attend that feast. The fakirs with whom Majnu used to wander told Majnu, "Let us go there, because Laila has invited us and they will be serving good food there. Why don't you come with us to eat the good food?" Majnu had become a fakir because of the love of Laila, but he thought, "I should not go there unless I learn whether she remembers me or not. I should do something so that I may be convinced whether she remembers me or not." So he didn't go to attend that feast; when one of his friends asked him to go with him, he said, "Well, I am not going, but you take my cup." So he gave him his cup and told him that after he ate the food, he should tell the servers to give him some food for Majnu. He said, "You should make sure you say that this cup belongs to me, that it belongs to Majnu."

When everyone went there to attend the feast, the people sat in lines and as the servers served the food to them Laila would come out to see if Majnu had come, because she had done that only to see Majnu, but Majnu didn't come there. When the fakir who was carrying Majnu's cup finished eating, he asked for some food for Majnu. He said, "This cup belongs to Majnu." Laila was also standing there, she heard that, and she was upset, so instead of putting any food in that cup, Laila kicked that cup with her foot and she broke it.

That fakir went back and Majnu asked, "Dear One, did you bring any food for me?" He said, "Well, what can I tell you? I didn't bring any food, because Laila kicked your cup and broke it." He said, "Well, you should have said that it belongs to me." He said, "I did say it, and only when I said, 'This cup belongs to Majnu,' that's when she kicked and broke your cup." At that time Majnu started dancing in joy and said, "I am very pleased that at least she remembers me."

So Dear Ones, I do not want to say a lot about myself; I do not want to go on talking about myself. But since we are talking about this, I would like to say about myself also — this is a true thing — that my love with Beloved Master Kirpal was exactly the same as the love of Laila and Majnu. When Beloved Lord Kirpal came in the human form and when He came to see me, at that time I accepted Him as God Almighty, I welcomed Him, I respected Him, and I believed Him to be Almighty God. I was so happy because I realized, "At least He remembers me." Because I used to understand my love with Him as the love of Majnu with Laila.

I went to many different communities and religions, at a time in India when people believed in different castes and religions and they used to consider these things very much. So I went to all the different groups, because I was thirsty and I was looking for God Almighty. I did not criticize anyone, I did not comment on anyone's practice or their path; I went there with all my faith and love for them. When my beloved Master came to see me, when I was thirsty, He came in the human form, He gave me the Water [of Life] to drink and I drank that Water with all faith, love, and respect for Him. I did not ask Him whether this Water belonged to the Hindus, Muslims, or to the Christians, or to the Sikhs. I did not even ask Him from which religion did He come, or what was His name, what was His caste, what was His religion? I did not even care to ask Him from where He had come.

Since I was thirsty and He had the Water for me, I drank that Water which satisfied my thirst. Dear Ones, when He came here, I did not even ask Him whether He was a renunciate or a householder. I did not ask any question from my beloved Gurudev. You know that I was thirsty for Him right from my childhood, and He had the Water for me, so He came. No one had told me any critical words about Him and no one had even praised Him to me; I did not know anything about Him.

You can very well imagine: how did He know about me? How did He know that somebody had been sitting in His remembrance since childhood? He sent me a message that I should stay at home because He would be coming to see me, and He Himself came to see me. So you can see that He knew that someone was sitting in His remembrance.

He made me leave that place right away and He told me to come and sit here. He Himself made this place; with His orders this underground room was made. We have not made any changes in this part of the building except for the place where I am sitting now. Because we used to have a bathroom inside, that is why we had to raise the level of this room, otherwise everything else is the same. It was all His grace that He made me sit here in meditation and this place was made according to His wishes.

I don't know why He wished for this place. He told me I

should not come out, I should not go to see Him, whenever He wanted He would come to see me. And He also told me that I should not wait for Him, whenever I would remember Him He would come here to give me darshan. Outwardly, there is no way I can thank Him; one can really thank Him only after going within.

The Story of Love cannot be described in the words of the mouth; one can understand the Story of Love only by mixing himself in the Love.

Those who have sowed the onions all their life long, how can they know the fragrance of apple blossoms? In the same way, those who have always used heavy, rough blankets, how can they appreciate and know the value of fine wool and silk?

We worldly people have put the worldly pleasures on our head, we give importance to the sensual pleasures. The Mahatmas give us the Elixir, give us the Nectar of Naam, only when we divert our attention, our mind, from the worldly pleasures.

Dear Ones, when the dear one goes within and manifests the Form of the Master within, the Form of the Master is brighter inside, and there whatever question the disciple asks, the Master answers that. Sometimes there are even the moments of humor inside, when the disciple says, "Look what I am, and what You are."

After going there one realizes, "How dirty I was, how impure I was, and my Master is pure, He is a Holy Being, He is a Holy One and He had pity on me; He had mercy on me and He brought me in."

All the Saints Who have gone inside, Who have gone within, have called Themselves as the "guilty one," or as the "inferior one," and They have always called their Master as the "Pure One."

Ajaib also confessed the same thing in front of His Master Kirpal; He said, "The life of Ajaib is full of the bad qualities, You take me across."

When He showered grace upon me, He came here. And when they took me out from the meditation in this underground room, at that moment I remembered the times when I used to go from door to door searching for God Almighty. I used to call my search, "going from door to door." Because when I was searching for God Almighty, I had gone to so many different communities and religions only in search for Him. So I said this couplet in front of Him, I said, "I have gone from door to door praising people in the name of God, and telling them to come and put the alms in my cup."

You know that the people who go begging from door to door always go on rousing the people in the name of God. They shout aloud so that people may wake up and come out and give them the things that they are begging for. So I said, "My Dear Beloved Master, I went from door to door begging for the alms and I roused people in the name of God so that they would give me the alms. And when I roused You, when I came to Your door, You gave me the alms, You gave me the donation. And those who will give the donation to me, their desires will be fulfilled." This was a part of the couplet.

When I said this to Master Kirpal He laughed and said, "What desires of mine can you fulfill, if I give you the things?" I told Him, "O Father, that is true, there is nothing I can do for You, Your desires are already fulfilled. But I am requesting You only to put the alms in my cup, because You are All in All, and You can do everything. But I want to say that Master can get a true disciple only if He is the most fortunate one, just as the disciple gets the perfect Master only if he is the most fortunate one. In the same way a Master also gets a disciple if He has good fortune."

The reason for saying all these things to you is that you should not wait for the future time; you should not think that as time passes we will come close to Him. In this Path, time is not a factor. You should use the time you have now. And also we should not say that we will meditate only if the Master will shower grace on us. Dear Ones, you have to become receptive to the grace; He is always showering His grace on you. You have to receive the grace.

That is why Master Sawan Singh Ji used to say, "The man at whose door the animals are tied, he knows when he has to give them water, when he has to feed them, when he has to bring them from the shade to the sun, etc. So in the same way, if we remain devoted to the Master, if we go on doing the Path of the Master, then He is also aware of us and He also showers grace on us."

So that is why I say that we should not waste any time; we should appreciate the time, we should make our lives pure and do the meditation.

67
The Distribution of Grace
Sant Ajaib Singh Ji

at the Underground Room, April 4, 1987

Often I have asked, "What inspiration can we take from this place?" We should not make our coming to Rajasthan as a ritual or ceremony, that we come to Rajasthan every year or every other year, then go back, and then we again come here and on and on. We do not have to make our trip to Rajasthan a ceremony or ritual. This trip which you people take is for a practical purpose. You should know what was done here and you should try to imitate that poor soul who received the love of the Master, who was so small that when he sat underground no one knew about him in the world. He had the yearning for God Almighty ever since his childhood and he sat in His remembrance. He worked very hard, and first he received the love and grace of the Master himself, and then, when he went outside in the world, he did not remain hidden from the world because he had done the meditation. When he went out in the world he went far and near and he gave that love to those seeking souls who were desiring [God's] love and grace; he gave the grace of Almighty God to all the souls who were desiring it.

Master Sawan Singh Ji said, "Most of the western people are in a hurry to get experiences and obtain results from the work they do; but they do not pay attention to, or control their thoughts. They do not have any control of themselves and they do not understand the importance of improving themselves."

Master Sawan Singh said this in response to a letter from a

dear one who had just gotten Initiation. Not even a week had passed since his Initiation, but as soon as he got back to his country he wrote a letter to the Master telling Him that he had not progressed.

All the Saints have said this — even I say this: "Dear Ones, this is not the work of days or months or years. If we become successful in this struggle, which we are doing every day, even after spending our whole lifetime, still I would say that it is a very cheap bargain." Because all the Saints have said that this is true: that if anyone goes on continuing his efforts, if one goes on struggling — then a hard-working person always becomes successful.

It is my personal experience that whatever your mind desires, you can achieve that. The condition is that your mind should go on doing it. If one remains devoted to any work he is doing with full faith and determination, he will definitely become successful.

What lacking do we have? We meditate for four days and then we give up for a week. Again we meditate for a couple of days and then for months we give it up. Since we do not do our meditation constantly, we wander.

The life of the satsangi should be full of fragrance. He should not let lust come even in his thoughts. The Master will come within you, the thoughts of the Master will come within you, only if you will become pure and have removed all thoughts of lust. If we understand our body as the body of the Master, if we understand that our body belongs to the Master, then we will not do any bad habits with this body.

Sant Satgurus have distributed Their grace with Their open hearts to all Their disciples. It is the fervent desire of the Sant Satguru that somehow, by one means or another, the disciple should work hard and make the effort so that he may become successful. So if we make our efforts and work hard in this, it is possible that They may shower Their grace upon us even more.

At Sant Bani Ashram [in May 1977], I gave a talk based on Swami Ji Maharaj's hymn on how Kal, the Negative Power, deludes us and how he even takes away the meditation which we have done.* If the Satguru showers grace on us in order to protect us from the tricks of Kal, if the disciple is strong in his efforts, and if the Master is also strong, then He definitely saves us. But still, what does Kal do to create difficulties within us? What he does is this: Sitting within the dear ones he takes their minds apart — outwardly we may not realize it, but inwardly he takes our minds apart from each other. We are all brothers and sisters in the Master Saint, in Spirituality, and it is our responsibility and duty to love and respect everyone. But the trick of Kal is such that without our realizing it, he will take our minds apart and he will create hatred within us for each other.

If we do our Bhajan and Simran we are awakened ourselves from within: Master gives us guidance from within. He tells us, "Now the mind is going to attack you, do more Bhajan and Simran."

So all of you dear ones should maintain love for each other and you should do your meditation. And you should keep attending the Satsangs, because only by going to the Satsang can we know about our faults and lackings.

*See Part I, Chapter 17, "The Enemy Within."

68
Concentration of Mind

Sant Ajaib Singh Ji

a talk given October 31, 1987, at the Underground Room

You might have read and heard a lot about this place in *Sant Bani Magazine*. The greatness or the importance of this place is something we have to understand, because Sant Mat is the Path of doing, of practicing; and it is not the path of reading or talking. Saints do not condemn reading, but They tell us, that when we read, we should look within and see whether we live up to what we read or not. It is so much better to practice ourselves than to teach others.

Master Sawan Singh Ji used to say that the minds of the Western dear ones are such that they always expect results in a hurry. He said this because one of His western disciples had just gotten Initiation from Him and he didn't let even one month pass, a week after he got the Initiation, he wrote a letter to the Master saying that he was getting nowhere. He used to say that our minds have been in the habit of doing the outward things and bad things from birth after birth. And the work of bringing our mind into our control is not the work of a few days or a month or even a few years. It depends upon the effort of the dear ones, and also it depends upon what kind of life we are living. It also depends upon the way we are earning our livelihood and also our devotion and faith.

Satguru never forgets anything, He never makes any mistakes. After giving us the Initiation He never forgets that He has initiated us. In fact, God Almighty Himself has come into the world in the Form of the Satguru. And while giving us the Initiation He never makes a mistake and He always remembers us. He always gives us those things which we need. When do we lose faith in Him? When do we stop devoting ourselves to Him? Only when we start craving for more things than we need, and create more desires than we should; when those desires are not fulfilled, then we start losing faith in the Master.

No mother becomes happy looking at the suffering of her child. Many times for the betterment of her child, she has to give him some bitter medicine from the doctor. Many times to restore the health of her child she must take him to the doctor who does surgery to remove a boil or pain that he has. She does all that only because she wants her child not to suffer any more. She does not have any enmity toward the child, and the doctor also does not have any enmity toward the child. Whatever they do for the child is for his own good. In the same way whatever Master does for us is for our own good. We should not lose faith in the Master, and with all our efforts we should continue doing our meditation.

The Radiant Form of the Master, the Shabd, the moon, the stars, and all those things are within us. Whenever we collect our scattered thoughts with the help of the Simran, and bring our attention to the Eye Center and go within, we can see all those things there. But when we do not concentrate at the Eye Center, when we let our attention fall down, then we don't see anything. We don't see stars, moons, or anything, even though they all are within us.

Many times we lose our concentration for many days and we are not able to concentrate. And when we do not see all these things in meditation we feel as if the grace of the Master has been withdrawn, but Dear Ones, that is not the case. The Master never withdraws His grace from His disciples. It is only because of losing our concentration that we feel His grace is not there. And many times it so happens, that since we have lost the concentration, then we feel that the grace is not there, and we even make up our minds to leave the Path. But gradually we feel deeply hurt in our heart and once again, when we start doing the meditation and gain the concentration, we start seeing all these things.

In *Anurag Sagar* [*The Ocean of Love*] we would have read about the Pandavas. They lived in exile for twelve years. In those days, whenever any king in India had to marry his daughter, he would give an open invitation to all the kings, soldiers, and warriors. And he used to have an open ceremony which was called *seramba*. But in that ceremony the king had the condition that only someone who could shoot an arrow into the eye of a moving fish, not looking at the fish but looking at the reflection of that fish in the water, will be able to marry the king's daughter. Now it was not an easy thing to do. You cannot even look at the fish; the fish is moving. You have to look in the water, at the reflection or the image of that fish, and you have to shoot the eye. And only some person who has a lot of concentration of mind can do this job.

So in that ceremony Arjuna was the only one. He was one of the Pandavas; he was the only one who could do that and in that way he married Draupadi. At that time Arjuna and his brother Pandavas were living in exile in the form of renunciates. So when Draupadi got married to one of those renunciates, all her friends taunted her, saying, "You should have married some warrior or some king, but you have married this renunciate." Draupadi, who knew the inner secrets, said, "Whatever you say is all right, but the job which he has done can be done only by someone who has a lot of concentration of mind. And I can say that the day will come when he will become the winner of the whole world." And that thing happened when the war of Mahabharata was fought. Then Arjuna was the one who became the winner of the whole world. In the same way, in Sant Mat also, the concentration of mind counts very much. If we are more concentrated at the Eye Center we will come closer to God. We will be able to see more Light and hear more Sound.

I was a very fortunate one that whatever orders my Master

gave me, I was able to carry them out. I didn't make this place as per my wishes, it was made according to the orders of my Beloved Master. It was all His grace that this place was made. And when He put His hands on me and told me to close my eyes in respect to the world and go inside and do the meditation, I had only one request for Him. I said, "Master, now my honor is in Your hands; protect my honor." As I said earlier, Masters never forget anything. So after He put me in meditation here, many times He used to come to see me Himself, because He had told me that He would come to see me Himself whenever He wanted. And even when He was physically sick, He used to come here and give me His darshan.

69

To Glorify the Master's Name

Sant Ajaib Singh Ji

a talk given January 2, 1988, at Sant Ji's underground meditation room

Showering a lot of Their grace, Gods Sawan and Kirpal gave us this opportunity to do Their meditation for this period of ten days. And in this period of ten days I have always put a lot of emphasis on maintaining purity in our lives, because if we maintain purity it is very helpful for us in the Path of Spirituality. If we maintain purity, that also helps a lot in our physical life and in our worldly life.

Only those who do not live a life of indulgence in sensual pleasures can keep their minds quiet. If we spread our attachment with the worldly pleasures, our mind becomes restless, we go far away from the Eye Center, and we cannot come closer to the Shabd.

Dear Ones, you should always remember the incident when Beloved Kirpal said in front of many people, regarding me, "The fragrance will come out from his body, and will even cross the oceans and attract people to him." So you know that those who have lived a pure life, who have done the Lord's devotion according to their Master's instructions, their fragrance attracts other people. And looking at their way of life, at their devotion, other people also get attracted to the Path. They think, "We should also become fragrant like them and we should also do the devotion of God." So if you are living a pure life then you can attract people.

Master Sawan Singh Ji used to say that Saints do not fly

Themselves; it is Their disciples who make Them fly. It means that Saints do not go on spreading Their glory Themselves, it is through Their disciples that the glory of the Masters is spread. He also used to say that if a dog is bad, the master is blamed, and if the dog is good, the master always gets the praise. That is why satsangis should live such a life which will bring more praise and glory to the name of the Master, and when you live such a pure life He will be able to shower more riches of Naam on you.

First of all a satsangi should make the habit of keeping his attention at the Eye Center all the time. Whether he is talking, walking or doing any other thing, he should always be aware of the Eye Center; he should always keep his attention there. When a satsangi develops the habit of keeping his soul, his attention, at the Eye Center by doing the meditation, he can easily go to the astral plane. *Jot Niranjan* is the owner of that plane.

When the soul reaches the astral plane, the chains which tie the soul and pull her down in the body get broken one by one; then the soul becomes free to ascend to the higher regions. After reaching the astral plane the soul proceeds to the causal plane. In the astral plane the mind is not as strong and effective as he was in the physical plane, and in the causal plane the mind is not as strong as he is in the astral plane. When the soul reaches the causal plane then all the tricks of the mind, which pull us back into this world, are defeated. They are all destroyed and the soul reaches the place where the mind has no affect.

You know that time and tide wait for no man, so you should be very grateful that you have been given this very wonderful, this very blessed opportunity. You have the human birth, the Master, and the Initiation; *you have gotten One Who is willing to guide you, and Who is guiding you.* So we should always take advantage of this time, and not waste this opportunity which we have been given.

Don't think when you are doing anything wrong that nobody

is looking at you. Your Master is sitting within you and He is aware of every single thing you are doing, whether it is good or bad. So whenever you are doing anything wrong, any faults, any sins, He is watching you from the other side of the curtain. But He always keeps quiet; He just watches and does not make any comment at that time. The Negative Power doesn't let any opportunity go without using it, so when He sees that an initiate of the Master is doing anything wrong, at once He taunts the Master by saying, "Look at this one you have initiated. Look at what he is doing." The Master feels embarrassed but does not get upset. He is very patient, He is very gracious, He is very loving; and He says, "I will take care of him." Gradually He goes on improving us; He explains things in one way or another; and finally he improves our condition. If a five-year-old boy is guarding an orchard, we will not feel comfortable stealing any fruit over there. We know that God Almighty, our Master, is sitting within us and yet we do not even have as much fear of our Master as we do of that five-year-old boy. Even though we know He is watching everything, still we do all kinds of bad deeds. That is why satsangis should always develop the habit of living a pure life.

Saints and Mahatmas do not come into this world to break us off from our society or community. In fact They tell us that we should always do such things of which our family and community would be proud. If you do anything wrong, what will people think about your family? They will say that your family is also bad. Saints and Mahatmas always tell us, "If you do good things, then people will praise your community. They will say, 'He belongs to such a society that has devotion for God and they have come to the Path of the Masters.' " Saints and Masters do not come to make us cowards; in fact, They teach us how to live a good life. They also tell us how we have to live a life of Spirituality, how to do devotion in addition to the worldly things.

You have heard and read a lot about how, with the instructions and orders of Lord Kirpal, this poor soul who is sitting in front of you was made to sit in this place, and how he was made to do the things which Master Kirpal Himself told him to do. All these things were done with the grace and mercy of the Master. He showered such grace and mercy on this poor soul which could not be described even if we wrote millions of books.

We realize the goodness of a tree only when we eat its fruit. In the same way, only those who have obeyed the commandments of the Master know how much one enjoys the fruit of obeying the commandments of the Master. All those who are initiated by Master Kirpal will be liberated, because He has taken responsibility for them. But those who have obeyed the commandments of the Master while living — those who have gone within and seen Him while they are living — they are the brave ones. Even though He will liberate everybody, only they are the brave ones who do the work which He told them to do in their lifetime.

70

Take the Inspiration

Sant Ajaib Singh Ji

a talk given October 1, 1988, at the Underground Room

I am thankful to my Supreme Father, my Master, Beloved Kirpal who showered His gracious sight on this poor one.

The message of the Masters has always been: "Come along, walk with us, and see the Reality with your own eyes." They also tell us: "Dive into the ocean of love, and take out the pearl of love yourself." Dear Ones, we know that not even in the world can we achieve anything without suffering difficulties for it. We cannot become successful in anything of this world without working hard for it. If we want to search for the pearls, minerals, or any other valuable things from the depths of the ocean, then we will definitely have to dive deep into the ocean.

When the Masters come into this world They tell us, "Come walk along with me, come with me." Only a few people believe Them, and there are always very few people who want to go with Them. After coming into this world, when They find only a few people willing to follow Them, what do They do? They tell us things about this world, this plane on which we are living. They give us such arguments which we can easily understand, and by using worldly examples they convince us. With their astral intellect Saints and Mahatmas touch our hearts, They give us understanding, and make us realize what we are here for. They themselves put us on the Path and then our search for Almighty God begins.

The Path on which the Masters put us is not an artificial

path; it is the Natural Path created by God Almighty Himself. We can neither increase its length nor decrease its length. We cannot make any alterations in it. It is as old as man is; it is as old as God Almighty Himself is.

We know that teachers have their own responsibilities and the students also have their own responsibilities. The students are given only those responsibilities which they can fulfill, which they can attend to very easily. Regarding the responsibilities of the teacher, you should know that the teacher never runs away from his responsibility. He is always present there to attend to his responsibility. If the students, instead of attending to their responsibilities themselves, tell the teacher, "You attend the classes for us, you read the books for us, and after that give the degree to us and make us pass the examination." Just imagine such students — can they have any hope of becoming successful in their lives?

The duty or responsibility which the disciple has been given is that he has to make himself pure and clean without any passions of this world. Because the image of the pure thoughts has a very good reflection on the mirror of our soul. If our mind becomes pure, our soul will also become pure; and if our soul is pure, then she will easily go back to her Real Home.

On the banks of many ponds and lakes there are trees, but often the image of those trees is not very clear on the water. The reason is that either the water is dirty or the water is moving because of waves in that pond or lake. But when the water is clear and still, we can easily see the reflection of the trees and other things around the pond or lake. In the same way, God Almighty is within us; but why can't we see Him? Because our mind is dirty, and our mind is not still. When we purify our mind, when we make our mind still, then we can easily see the Form of the Master, the Form of God Almighty within us. Not only can we see Him but we can also talk to Him very easily when our mind is quiet.

For twenty-five years my Beloved Master always gave out this message — He went to every corner of this world and He gave out this message — He told people, "You should become true men, because God is always looking for a man. It is not difficult to find God, but it is difficult to become a man." So He always used to say that you should become a man so that God may come and find you. He always used to say that God Almighty is looking for the true man.

You know that there was a time when there was nothing in this place where I am sitting. All the greenery which you see around here now was not here; very recently all these changes have happened. Previously we did not have any water here, there were no good roads here, and nobody wanted to visit this place. According to what He said, "God Almighty is always looking for a man," so it was all His grace that He Himself came to this place and only with His grace He made this poor one sit in His remembrance. I hope that after coming to this place you will also take the same inspiration which He gave me. After going back to your homes I hope you will do your meditations as much as possible, and you will make your lives very high, very pure and very clean.

71

A New Year: Like A New Birth

Sant Ajaib Singh Ji

a meditation talk given January 1, 1990, at Sant Bani Ashram, Village 16 PS, Rajasthan, India

In the name of Hazur Sawan and Kirpal, I wish a very happy New Year to all of you. I hope that this New Year will bring all the happiness for you and you will be able to meditate, to do more Bhajan and Simran.

On this day today, people belonging to different religions in India go to the nearby rivers, ponds or canals at three in the morning to bathe, and they consider it as a very holy thing. We are very fortunate ones that we have been given this opportunity of connecting to our inner self and, as the tradition is going on, we have been given this knowledge that the real place of pilgrimage is within us. So just as they remember God in their own languages, we have been given this opportunity to go within and bathe in the holy place inside. We should also do the meditation and go within, because the real place of pilgrimage where we are supposed to bathe is Daswan Dwar.

When we withdraw from the physical, astral and causal covers and take our soul to Daswan Dwar, only then can we do this holy bathing. Guru Sahib also says the same thing: "Only he is the Saint, only he is a disciple, who goes to Daswan Dwar and bathes in that holy water over there." He says that one who is called as the disciple of the Master gets up early in the morning and goes to that pond of nectar which is within us. Every day he gets up in the morning and goes to that place; all day long he goes on remembering the words of the Master. So we are very fortunate that we have been given this opportunity of doing His devotion, and just as the people belonging to different religious communities remember God Almighty on this day and go to the holy waters for bathing, in the same way we should also go within and bathe in the holy place there.

We cannot reach the place that the Mahatmas have talked about by reading or by doing any kind of outer rites and rituals; no matter how much we do we cannot reach that place. We can get there only by doing the meditation. Kabir Sahib also says, "At that place the crows become swans or *hansas*. No outer water has the power to change the crows to hansas; it is only the water of the within." So when we go within we are the manmukh ones, we are the dirty ones, and we are like the crows. You know that the food of the crow is the dirt, and the food of the hansa is the pearls. So in that way we are the dirty ones, we are like the crows, and when we go within and bathe in that holy water in Daswan Dwar, only then do we change from crows to swans. Then our food also changes; then we become the Saints, we become the holy men, and then our food becomes that of doing the meditation of the Naam.

So those who go within and those who are changed from crows to hansas, they do the meditation of Naam and they make other people do the meditation of Naam.

Rishis and Munis have worked very hard. After withdrawing from their physical body they have gone to Brahm, and to the higher planes, and whatever they have seen or experienced on their way, they have written that down in the holy scriptures. Whatever they wrote about the inside, we find those things outside also. Kabir Sahib says that in your within, in Trikuti, there are three rivers. Ganga, Jamna, and Sarasvati are three rivers which come together at one place outside, and in the within also, in Trikuti, there are three rivers which come together. This is the place which the Mahatmas have written about, going where we can get rid of our crow-like habits and we can become like the swans; we can become the Gurumukhs from the manmukhs.

When Guru Amar Das Ji Maharaj went within and He saw the real Amritsar, or Pool of Nectar, He said, "The real Amritsar, or Pool of Nectar, is within you and your mind can become satisfied only after drinking the water from there." The foundation of the outer Amritsar was started by Guru Ramdas, the fourth Guru, and it was completed by Guru Arjan Dev, but Guru Amar Das meant the inner pool of nectar or the inner Amritsar.*

When they were laying the foundation stone of Amritsar, Guru Ramdas Ji Maharaj told the person who was going to make it, "You have to make it like the Lotus of Daswan Dwar so that the dear ones will get the inspiration to go within and bathe in the real Amritsar, the real Lotus of Daswan Dwar. In that way, by doing their meditation, they would remove the dirt of their karmas from life after life." Only to inspire them to go within, He wanted to make Amritsar in the same design as that of the Lotus of Daswan Dwar, but the person whom He was telling to make it did not know, had not seen, the Lotus of Daswan Dwar. He said, "I cannot do that because I have not seen it." So Guru Ramdas Ji Maharaj gave him special attention and He took his soul up and showed him the Lotus of Daswan Dwar in the within, and afterwards when his attention was brought down by Guru Ramdas, He asked him, "Now, will you be able to build it?" He said, "Yes, I will make it, but please let me remain there. I want to remain there." So Guru Ramdas said, "No, first you make it outside and only then I will bring you back there." So that is why that Amritsar, that pool, was made in the same design as the Lotus of Daswan Dwar.

Dear Ones, we people read the writings of the Mahatmas in the morning, the evenings and even during the day, but we are not prepared to do what They have written. They say, "If you do these things you will also accomplish your work, you will

* Guru Amar Das, who was Ramdas' Guru, wrote about the inner Amritsar before the outer city of Amritsar was even started.

get this benefit"; but we are not prepared to do anything like that.

Maharaj Sawan Singh Ji used to say, "Doing only the outer reading is like singing songs of other peoples' weddings and not getting married yourself." By reading the writings of the other Mahatmas, about whatever They have done in Their meditation, we cannot get any liberation. It is just reading about Their experiences, reading about Their lives, and not doing the things which They have done in Their lives. What is the use of always singing the song of other peoples' weddings if you yourself are not preparing yourself for marriage? If we always go on reading that such and such a Mahatma has done this or that kind of meditation practice, or He had that kind of experience — how is that going to help us? If we always go on relying on those past Masters Who have done a lot of meditation and if we do not do it ourselves — then what is the use of reading Their books? As we read Their books, as we read in Their writings that They did so much sacrifice and so much meditation, at the same time we should also be preparing, we should also make every effort, to live our life according to the teachings and instructions of those Mahatmas.

On New Years Day we always wish our dear relatives and friends all the best for that new year; we wish them Happy New Year. And if they are far away, we write them letters, cards and things like that. When the Saints and Mahatmas come into this world, They also give us this message of the New Year. They also say, "This is like a new birth for you, and in this new birth, in this new year of your life, you should do the work which you did not do earlier."

Giving the message of the New Year in His own way, Guru Arjan Dev Ji Maharaj is telling His disciples, "Now the first month of the year" — according to the Indian calendar *Maav* is the first month of the new year — "now that the month of *Maav* has come, you should go and bathe in the holy waters. You should go and bathe in the dust of the Feet of the Holy Master, and you should live your life according to His teachings. Obey

Him so that the ego, the pride of your mind, may vanish and you may come closer to the Reality."

Guru Arjan Dev Ji Maharaj says, "All these passions: lust, anger, greed, attachment, and egoism, which are making you dance like a monkey, they all will become calm and quiet if you will do the meditation of Naam. And if you will do the devotion of Naam, you will be content in this world, because those who understand God Almighty as their very own, the whole world understands them as their very own."

Swami Ji Maharaj says that by doing the Bhajan and Simran we are not doing any favor to anyone, in fact we are having mercy on our own soul. He says, "Have mercy on your own soul and save it from the cycle of eighty-four lakhs births and deaths." Those who have mercy on their own souls, only they can be merciful to others.

Master Kirpal Singh Ji gave us a very good form of the diary in order to keep an account of our progress. He told us how we have to keep the account and in which categories — how many times we helped people, how many times we did the seva, and how many times we failed in different areas. So on this New Year's Day I would like to tell you that you should fill up that diary form with sincerity, keeping your Master in front of you. Do not spare your mind; fill the diary up sincerely. Start from the first day of the month and you will see how much you have progressed or how much you have deteriorated. You will see what you were thinking at the beginning of the month and what happened towards the end of the month.

So you should keep a complete account of all your deeds, your thoughts, and you should also keep an account of your progress in meditation. You should keep this account for the whole of the year, and then towards the end of the year you should make a balance sheet of your account, to see whether you have progressed in this year or not. If you progressed — what were the factors which were helping you make progress? And if you have not progressed — what were the things which were keeping you from progressing? So you should keep an account of all your deeds and in that way you should make your life successful.

Often I have said that God Almighty has showered so much grace upon us. He has given us this human birth; He has made us the leader of the creation. And further our beloved Master has showered so much grace upon us. He has given us this gift, this present of Naam. Now it becomes our responsibility to do the meditation of the Shabd Naam and make this human birth worthwhile and successful.

72

Awaken the Light and Sound Within

Sant Ajaib Singh Ji

a talk given at the Underground Room, Sant Bani Ashram, Village 16 PS, Rajasthan, January 6, 1990

God Almighty has created this human body in a very beautiful, very unique way. Whatever we see outside with our outer eyes, those things are within our body also, but they are present in their astral form. Mahatma Pipa says that whatever you see in the Pind, the same things are in the Brahmand, or in your body also. But we cannot get to know or see those things just by our own efforts. Mahatma Pipa says that the Supreme Essence of God Almighty can be realized only if the perfect Master makes us realize those things. All those things are within us, but without the help and guidance of the perfect Master we cannot find all those things within us. Since they are present within us in their astral form, first we have to go in the astral form, and then we have to go in the causal form, and from there we have to go further up. But we cannot do this unless we have the guidance of the perfect Master.

We know that the Great Artist, Almighty God, creates the baby's body within the womb of the mother. At that time, not even the mother within whom all this is happening is aware of that. She does not know at what time God Almighty came and created the body. Only He knows, and only He makes all the arrangements to feed and take care of that baby. Only God knows whether that soul should be brought in the body of a boy baby or a girl baby, and whether he should be born with a beautiful or deformed face — only He knows everything.

Guru Ramdas Ji Maharaj says that until now nobody has taught up to the level of the Science of the Saints. Even though this is the Age of Science, and the scientists have worked very hard and they have invented many things — you know that this human body is made up of five elements, and up until now nobody has made a body of four elements or six elements. All the elements in our body are all opposite to each other. Those five elements: ether, air, fire, water, and earth are present within our body, and if one of those elements is decreased, people get sick, or if one of them is increased, even then the body does not stay in good shape. And how do all those opposing elemental forces stay together in one place in the body? It is only because of the support of the Shabd Naam, only because of the Power of that Naam, that the elements, even though they are opposite in nature, still exist together within the body.

What do we look for if we lose our way in the pitch-dark night? We will always listen for some kind of noise or sound, and we will try to follow that sound, because we think that it may be coming from a nearby city or habitation. And very easily, following that sound, we can get to our destination, to the city or place where it is coming from. So what was the thing which helped us to get out of that darkness of night and come to the nearby city? It was the sound which was coming from that place. And if we had some source of light also, that would make things even better for us. Because if there are bushes on the way, or the ground is not level, if we had some light, a torch or flashlight, using that light we could easily find our way without getting into trouble, and we could get to our destination. So what were the things which helped us get to our destination? They were the light and sound. So the same things are within us. That Great Artist has manifested the Light and put that Sound within our body so that we can find our way back to our Real Home.

Regarding that Sound and that Light, Guru Nanak Sahib says, "Within you there is the Light, and the constant Bani or the constant Voice of God is ringing." All the Mahatmas have said this, that within you there is the Light and Sound of God. The Muslim Saints have called it the *Bang-i-Asmani* or *Kalma* which is coming from the heavens above, and the Hindu Mahatmas call it the Ram Naam or *devi dhuni*, or Akash Bani, the Sound coming from the skies. So all the Masters have said that within you God has kept this Light and Sound, with the help of which you can get back to your Real Home very easily.

Dear Ones, those who are the doctors, and others who are serving the people: teachers, engineers, philosophers, and other great people who are living their lives very comfortably — they did not become doctors or whatever they became just by their own efforts. They went to somebody to learn from them, and somebody was there to teach them, and only then they became what they are now. Everyone has the power of intellect, of knowledge, within them, but there must be somebody to awaken that power, to sharpen that power. Everyone has that intellect, that knowledge in them, but only those who go to the schools and colleges, those who go to their teachers and learn from them, only they become perfect. In the other people also, that power of knowledge is present, but it comes and goes sleeping because they do not go to the schools and colleges.

We also know that those doctors, judges, or other great people were not made to drink anything by their teachers or their guides. How did that change come in them? The change was brought into them only because they went in the company of their teachers, and they worked hard. In the same way, the Saints do not make us change our religion or faith, and they do not make us drink anything. All those things are within us, and they have been kept within us by that Great Artist, by Almighty God. But we have to go in the company of the Saints and Masters, and by spending time in Their company, and working according to Their guidance, we have to awaken those things which are already within us. Only by going in Their company can we realize what God Almighty has kept within us. God Almighty has kept everything in our within, and only the Saints and Masters can make us realize those things.

Regarding the underground room which you are going to see just now, I have said a lot. And you know that this place was not made as per my wishes, it was made according to the orders of Beloved Lord Kirpal. And it was only He Who made me sit there, closing my eyes toward the world, and it was only His grace that made it possible for me to sit there and do the meditation. Even now, some dear ones who visit this place say that their Shabd had stopped for many years, and when they came to the underground room that Shabd was opened once again and they got the grace.

I hope that you will understand the meaning of the repetition of the Five Sacred Names that I did every day before we sat for meditation. The meaning of repeating the Names was that I want you, whenever you sit for meditation in your homes, to remember those Five Sacred Names. You should do this so that whenever you sit for the meditation your mind won't make you forget those Names.

73

That Precious Jewel of Naam

Sant Ajaib Singh Ji

This was the final talk given to the Westerners in Bombay, January 14, 1993.

I thank Beloved Gurudev God Kirpal Who gave us the precious Naam. First of all I would like to thank Him Who gave us this opportunity to do His devotion. First of all He gave us this precious Naam and then He gave us the opportunity to do the meditation. Guru Ramdas Ji Maharaj also says, "We get the perfect Naam from the perfect Masters and if we do the meditation of Naam He gives us this jewel of Naam."

I have always said that the devotion of God Almighty is the only thing which is precious and which will go with us. It is the only thing which gives us real peace and happiness. It is the only thing which removes lust, anger, greed, attachment and egoism. We cannot get this precious wealth of devotion of God Almighty with our efforts. Until we go to the perfect Masters we cannot obtain this precious wealth. Even though the Saints, the Masters are not greater than God Almighty, They are not equals to God Almighty, but still They are the Beloved Children of God Almighty and you know that a beloved child can always make his father do whatever he wants to.

So Dear Ones, I was very happy to meditate with all of you. Many dear ones have told me about their very good experiences. Many dear ones who came here dry, told me about themselves and I told them that they should take advantage of this holy trip and do the meditation. I was very glad that obeying me they did the meditation and God Kirpal satisfied their hunger and He quenched their thirst.

What glory can I describe of Him? I can only say this in His glory, in His praise, "I am a thief, moment after moment, I am your thief of everything and I am full of sins. Please shower grace on me and forgive my sins."

He came into this world to teach us love, He came into this world to teach us humility, because He was the Ocean of Love, He was the abode of humility. Whatever love I received sitting at His feet I am distributing only that love in this world.

Everyday I have been doing the Satsangs on the *banis* of Sehjo Bai. Whatever She received sitting at the feet of Her Master, Mahatma Charan Das and whatever She told Him, She has written that in the Bani. She told us lovingly that God Almighty and the Master both are one and the same thing. In fact, Master is the One Who makes us meet with God Almighty. God was always present within us and even though He was present within us, still we came in this world so many times. We do not know how many times we came in this world and how many wives we had, and how many children we had, and how many parents we had. All this went on happening even though God almighty was always present within us. God almighty, even though He is always there, does not stop any thief from stealing; He does not stop anyone from doing the bad deeds. It was the Master Who, when He came, lighted this lamp of knowledge within us and He showed us that hidden God Who was always within us. Just as there is color in the leaf, and there is fire in stone, in the same way, our Beloved Master — lighting the lamp of knowledge within us, lighting the lamp of Naam within us — showed us that the Reality, God Almighty is within us.

I have given this message to everyone, that this was a very precious opportunity which God Kirpal has given to us — to sit in His Remembrance. And we should remember it even after going back to our homes so that we may continue getting the encouragement, the inspiration to do the meditation. Also, to everyone, I insisted upon keeping the diary. It is a saying in

America, that we can know the quality of the tree only after eating the fruit of that tree. In the same way, we can know about the devotion only after doing it. Sant Mat is not a fairy tale, it is based on the Truth and it is the ultimate Truth. All the Saints and Mahatmas Who have come into this world, They put us on that Path of Truth, and They make us practice that Path of Truth.

Guru Ramdas Ji Maharaj said, "By doing the seva of the Master, the Master takes out the jewel of Naam and gives it to you." So what is the seva which we have to do? Each day's meditation, and keeping ourselves clean and pure, is the seva which we have to do daily. And if we will do that seva, if we will serve the Master, then He will give us that precious jewel of Naam. As the Shabd Form of the Master sits within you to encourage you to do the meditation, in the same way, the Negative Power is also present within you; and he always plays the tricks on you. He always makes the efforts so that you may not be able to do your Bhajan and Simran. If he does not become successful sitting within you, what he does is — when you start doing the meditation — then sitting within some other dear ones, he makes them praise you. In that way, when people who are influenced by the Negative Power, when they praise that dear one who is doing the meditation, then that poor dear one stops doing the meditation and he easily falls down.

Suppose we are wearing a nice shirt, or a nice coat or trousers; we are looking good. If someone comes to us and says, "You look very good, you are wearing good clothes." Then we should say, "Yes, this is all the craft or skill of the tailor who has stitched these clothes." But our mind, who is sitting within us, does not make us realize that it is the tailor's work which made these clothes good and made us look good in them. Instead of giving all the credit to the tailor, we think that these clothes look good only because we are wearing them. But this is not wisdom.

In the same way, if someone tells us that we are a very good meditator, or we are a very good disciple, we should not get puffed up in pride. We should not have this ego — we should give the credit to our Master, because it is only because of the presence of the Shabd within us, it is only because of the grace of the Master, that people see that we are good or think that we are better than them. So we should not accept any credit for ourselves; we should always pass on that credit to the Master.

Look at our Beloved Master; He was the All-Owner, the Almighty One, but still He remained hidden; and if anybody would praise Him He would say, "This is all the grace of my Beloved Master, Baba Sawan Singh." Those of us who have been blessed with the opportunity to sit at His feet and drink the nectar from sitting at His feet know how much humility our Beloved Master had. If anybody would praise Him, He would always pass that credit to the Master and He would always appreciate the things of His Beloved Master. If anyone would ever tell Him, "This was a thing which was touched by Your Master," He would appreciate that very much and put that thing on His head.

You have read about His humility in the bhajan which He Himself wrote, He says, "O Lord, even your shoes are better than me, because they have the privilege to be attached to Your feet whereas I am away from You." Kabir Sahib lovingly says, "I offer my skin to make the shoes for him who does the devotion of God, who remembers God Almighty, even in the state of sleep — if he utters the name of God, I am ready to sacrifice myself, I am offering the skin of my body to make the shoes for that person."

The meaning of saying all these things is that we have to remember this holy trip and we have to do whatever Beloved Master told us to do. We should always remember His precious words — He said, "We should give up hundreds of works to attend the Satsang and thousands of works to sit in meditation." He also used to say, "We should not feed our body until we have fed our soul." We know that our body becomes weak if we do not eat; but we never pay any attention to the weakness of our soul. Just as food is good for our health, for our body, in the same way, the food for our soul is the meditation of Shabd Naam.

The Masters love the Sangat more than They love Their own selves. Guru Gobind Singh said, "O Lord, may my family live happily and may they all remain attached to Your feet, in Your Will." The family of the Saints, the family of the Masters, is the Sangat.

In the end, I would like to wish all of you a very happy and safe return journey. I wish you all the best for that. And I hope that after going back to your homes you will continue doing your Satsangs and you will also do your meditations.

74

To Have His Company

Sant Ajaib Singh Ji

a greeting talk given at Le Moulin de Sant Ji, Silly-Tillard, France, on June 10, 1994

I am very thankful to my beloved Lords, Almighty Kirpal and Sawan, Who have given us this opportunity to sing Their praises. As we all know, people knowing so many different languages have gathered here. And if we will translate the Satsang into all the languages which people understand over here, it will not create a loving atmosphere for the Satsang. Dear ones who have been to Bombay know that people of eight different languages get together there, but the Satsang is done in only one language: Punjabi. [*Much laughter during the five translations that follow as Sant Ji tries to continue and the translations go on and on.*] And still, the hunger of the dear souls is satisfied by the Giver.

After the Satsang is over, the group leaders take their own groups, and they translate to make their dear ones understand in their own language. So here, the Satsang will be done in two languages; we will translate it into English only. And afterwards the group leaders can take their groups and translate for them into their own language.

Those who have been to India in the groups will remember that many times this thing happens: when we ask people if they have any questions, they say, "No, just let us sit here quietly and have your darshan; we do not have any questions for you."

Kabir Sahib has said that the thing which is worth watching is the forehead and the eyes of the Master, because the glory of the Truth — the Light of the Truth — always accompanies the Master. Those who are able to still their mind and attention, they understand everything and they get the real bliss. The darshan of the Sadhu should be done looking into His eyes and forehead, because the glory of the Truth always accompanies Him.

Guru Nanak Sahib has said that one sees the image of Almighty God according to the feelings and emotions he has. If we look at the Master with happiness, if we look at Him with sadness, with whatever feelings we look at the Master, we see Him like that. The body of the Master is like a mirror. You know that if we look at a mirror with a smile on our face we see ourselves smiling; if we look at the mirror with tears in our eyes, we see ourselves crying. It is not the fault of the mirror that we are smiling or crying, it is our own fault. In the same way, with whatever feelings we look at the Master, we see Him accordingly.

After several bhajans were sung, Sant Ji continued:

I bow down at the Feet of Guru Dev Almighty Lords Sawan and Kirpal, Who have given us this opportunity to sing Their praises. It is all Their grace that They have made us devoted to Their Holy Feet. It is only because of Their grace that we, the forgetful minds, are doing Their devotion.

We can meet with God Almighty only by doing the meditation and the spiritual practices taught to us by the Saints and Mahatmas. All the Saints and Mahatmas have given out the same message: God is within us; and, up until now, whosoever has met with God has done so by going in the within. In the future also, anyone who wishes to realize Him will do so by going in the within.

Guru Nanak Sahib has also said that those who are searching for God Almighty outside of their body are wasting their time, just like those workers who work all day long but get no pay in return. Sant Satgurus tell us that we very quickly and easily get the effect of the company we keep. If we keep the company of thieves and burglars, we get the habit of stealing and robbing.

In the same way, if we go in the company of drunkards and meat-eaters, we also become like them; we become the drunkards and the meat-eaters. In the same way, if we go in the company of those who gamble, then we also become a gambler.

By doing the devotion of God Almighty, Saints and Mahatmas, the beloveds of God, become the Form of the devotion; and from every single cell of Their bodies that color of the divine devotion comes out. So those dear ones who go in the company of such Saints and Mahatmas, they themselves get the color of the Naam. They get the color of Naam without making any effort, just by spending their time in the company of the Saints and Mahatmas.

Such company is only of such a Saint and Mahatma Who is a Perfect One, going in Whose company, our forgetful mind understands the Reality. And, by going in the company of such a Saint and Mahatma, our mind is still. So we need to give up the bad company; and we need to go in the company of the beloveds of God.

Kabir Sahib said that even the dog of a devotee of the Lord is better than the mother of a sinner or a worldly person; because the devotee's dog at least hears the name of the Lord, whereas the mother of a sinner or the worldly person always drags you or leads you to the sin. If there is any animal who lives in the ashram of any Sadhu or Mahatma, even though he cannot speak, at least he can hear. So whatever it hears over there, it gets the effect of that.

Guru Ram Das Ji Maharaj says, "Why didn't that mother who gave birth to a worldly person remain childless, if a holy person within whom the desire and yearning to do the devotion of Lord was not created?" It would have been better for the mother not to give birth. It would have been better for her to remain childless, rather than give birth to one within whose heart the name of Lord does not reside. Such a person, in whose heart the Name of God does not reside, remains hollow [empty] and he suffers a great deal.

Baba Bishan Das used to tell a story about the influence of

the company we keep. He used to say that, once there was a nest in which there were two parrots. And one day, it so happened, that a very big storm came and as a result they got separated. One of them landed in a village which was full of thieves and robbers, and the other one happened to go and stay in the ashram of some Sadhu who was nearby.

The one who landed in the village of the thieves and burglars learned nothing but the tricks and thoughts of the thieves and the robbers. Whereas the other parrot, because of the company of the Sadhu, learned the good things.

Once a king who was out in the jungle hunting encountered a tiger. The king was so terrified that he ran away from the jungle. He went to the village of the thieves to seek some protection, some help. As soon as that parrot saw the king, he started saying, "Here comes the king, he has a crown which is studded with diamonds. Kill him, catch hold of him, don't let him go."

The king was able to understand the language of parrots, so at once he took out his sword to kill the parrot. But then he thought that it was better for him to escape from that village, because he realized that he had come to the wrong place.

The king ran away from that village. When he came near that ashram of the Sadhu, the other parrot looked at the king and said, "Welcome dear, welcome; this is your home. Come inside; sit down quietly and have some rest." So the king was very surprised that just a minute ago he had seen a parrot who was telling the people that they should catch hold of him and kill him and take all the wealth he had. And here was another parrot who was so kind and gentle that he was welcoming him and saying, "This is your home, and come and rest here."

He asked that parrot, "You and the other parrot both look alike, but what is the reason that he became my enemy and he wanted me to be robbed. And here you are, you are so kind and generous that you are welcoming me to your home."

So the bird told the king the story. He said, "We both were given birth by the same mother. We both lived in the same nest.

But because of that storm we were separated. He went into the company of the thieves and the burglars. That is why he learned all the tricks and language of the thieves and the burglars, and he became like them. I was a very fortunate one that I got the company of this Sadhu. Because of that, I see everyone as a soul, as a child of the same father. So that is why I am good and I am welcoming you here."

The meaning of this story is that one develops according to the company he keeps. Even though both the parrots were given birth by the same mother, they both lived in the same nest, they both ate the same kind of food, but because of the company they kept, they became totally different.

Hirnakash was the king of Multan, which is now in Pakistan. Hirnakash forgot the existence of God Almighty, even though he was given the Light by God Almighty. But his own son Praladh, who was born of him, used to say, "God is under the water, God is on the earth, God is in the sky. Everywhere, the Lord Almighty exists." So why so much difference? Only because of the company they kept.

One who believes in the words of the Master, and who obeys the words of the Master and becomes the mouthpiece of the Master is called a *gurumukh.* Whereas one who obeys the dictates of the mind, who acts according to the dictates of the mind, and who creates all the trouble because of the mind, he is called the *manmukh.*

75

In the Company of the Saints

Guru Arjan Dev

This is Ashtapadi number seven of the Sukhmani Sahib*; the remainder of this hymn, and the book of commentaries on it by Sant Ji, is published as* The Jewel of Happiness.

The Par Brahm is Inaccessible and Unfathomable;
Whosoever repeats His Name gets liberation.
Nanak requests: Listen O friend!
To this wonderful story of the Saints.
By going in the company of the Saints, the face becomes bright;
By going in the company of the Saints, one loses all impurities.
By going in the company of the Saints, the pride vanishes;
By going in the company of the Saints, the knowledge of God is manifested.
By going in the company of the Saints, God is seen nearby;
By going in the company of the Saints, everything is solved.
By going is the company of the Saints, one gets the jewel of Naam;
By going in the company of the Saints, only one effort is left.
Which soul can describe the glory of the Saints?

Nanak says, the Glory of the Saints is merged in the Glory of God.
By going in the company of the Saints, one gets the Unseen God.
By going in the company of the Saints, man ever flourishes.
By going in the company of the Saints, the five come under control.
By going in the company of the Saints, one tastes the Nectar.
By going in the company of the Saints, one becomes the dust of everyone's feet;
By going in the company of the Saints, one's speech becomes likeable.
By going in the company of the Saints, one does not run anywhere;
By going in the company of the Saints, the mind gets a stable position.
By going in the company of the Saints, one becomes different from Maya;
Nanak says, By going in the company of the Saints, God is pleased.
By going in the company of the Saints, all enemies become friends;
By going in the company of the Saints, one becomes very pure.
By going in the company of the Saints, one does not feel enmity with anyone.
By going in the company of the Saints, one does not go away from the good path.
By going in the company of the Saints, no one is seen as bad;

By going in the company of the Saints, one gets Supreme joy.
By going in the company of the Saints, one does not get the fever (of ego);
By going in the company of the Saints, one leaves egoism.
He Himself knows the greatness of Saints;
Nanak says, There is close friendship between God and Saints.
One should not run away from the company of the Saints;
One always gets happiness in the company of the Saints.
One finds the unseen things in the company of the Saints;
One bears the unbearable in the company of the Saints;
By going in the company of the Saints, one dwells in the highest place;
By going in the company of the Saints, one reaches the palace.
By going in the company of the Saints, one recognizes all religions;
In the company of the Saints there is only Par Brahm.
In the company of the Saints, one gets the treasure of Naam;
Nanak says, I sacrifice myself on the Saints.
By going in the company of the Saints, the whole family is liberated;
By going in the company of the Saints, friends and family relations get liberation.
By going in the company of the Saints, one gets that wealth
Which can be distributed to everyone without coming to an end.
By going in the company of the Saints, even Dharam Raj does seva;

By going in the company of the Saints, even the gods and angels sing His praises.
By going in the company of the Saints, the sins disappear;
By going in the company of the Saints, one sings the praise of the Nectar.
By going in the company of the Saints, one goes everywhere;
Nanak says, By going in the company of the Saints, the human birth becomes successful.
In the company of the Saints, one does not have to work hard;
By meeting and seeing Him, one becomes happy.
By going in the company of the Saints, the evil Negative Power gets defeated;
By going in the company of the Saints, hell is avoided.
By going in the company of the Saints, one lives in ease and peace in this world as well as in the other world;
By going in the company of the Saints, one gets united with the God from Whom he is separated.
Whatever one desires, he gets;
The company of the Saints does not go useless.
The Par Brahm lives in the heart of the Saints;
Nanak says, One gets liberation by hearing the Words of the Saints.
Make me hear the Naam of the Lord in the company of the Saints;
In the company of the Saints, I may sing the praise of the Lord.
In the company of the Saints, He cannot be forgotten;
In the company of the Saints, one will definitely be liberated.
In the company of the Saints, God looks very sweet.

In the company of the Saints, He is seen in every heart.
By going in the company of the Saints, one becomes obedient.
In the company of the Saints is our liberation.
By going in the company of the Saints, all diseases are healed;
Nanak says, One meets the Saints if it is preordained.
Not even the Vedas know the greatness of the Saints;
Whatever they have heard, they describe that.
The Glory of the Saints is above the three qualities.
The Glory of the Saints pervades everywhere.
There is no end to the glory of the Saints;
The Glory of the Saints is always limitless.
The Glory of the Saints is the highest of the high;
The Glory of the Saints is the greatest of the great;
The Glory of the Saints is known by Them alone.
Nanak says, Brothers, there is no difference between the Saints and God.

Other Titles Available from Sant Bani Ashram

by Sant Kirpal Singh Ji

The Way of the Saints
Baba Jaimal Singh
The Jap Ji
The Light of Kirpal
How to Develop Receptivity
God Power, Christ Power, Guru Power

by Sant Ajaib Singh Ji

Streams in the Desert
The Ocean of Love
The Jewel of Happiness
The Two Ways
In the Palace of Love
Sing the Praises of the Satguru
The Reality of Drugs and Alcohol

by other authors

The Impact of a Saint, by Russell Perkins
The Stranger of Galilee, by Russell Perkins
I Never Say Goodbye, by Kira S. Redeen
Support for the Shaken Sangat, by A.S. Oberoi
Servants of God: Lives of the Sikh Gurus, by Jon Engle
Cooking With Light: Favorite Vegetarian Recipes
Sometimes Heaven Chuckles, by Jack Dokus

also available

The Message of Love: An Introduction to Sant Mat
Sant Ajaib Singh: A Brief Life Sketch
Songs of the Masters
The Self-Introspection Diary
Third World Tour of Kirpal Singh